THE GIRL I
LEFT BEHIND

Stephanie Bain

To Beth,
I hope you enjoy the book.
God bless!

ISBN: 978-1-937260-33-0

Leaves text divider : Created by SilviaNatalia - Freepik.com

Sleepytown Press

www.sleepytownpress.com

Dedication

This book is dedicated to my favorite Storyteller.

Table of Contents

"Repent! Repent! Repent!"

--Old Joe to Elias Kelson on the day
Jonas Corbin was laid to rest

Chapter 1

Drake

April, 1861

ALEXANDRA dug her fingers deeper into Shadow's mane, praying she had enough strength to hold out until the end. If she didn't, she would fall to her death, trampled by the mob of men and horseflesh that was chasing her, tumbling across Monty's Field like round shots fired from a Napoleon 12-pounder. With faith in her horse, Alexandra didn't flinch as the charcoal gelding charged toward the high, split-rail fence at the end of the field.

The jump would have been disastrous for Alexandra had she not disguised herself in men's clothing. The billowing hoop skirt she usually wore would have caught on the post and wrenched her out of the saddle.

Once she was safely on the other side of the fence, Alexandra readjusted her hat, hoping no loose strands of hair had escaped. Glancing over her shoulder, she smiled, estimating her lead to be two lengths. She was no longer Alexandra Corbin, the dead sheriff's daughter. She was the girl who was gonna win the Jackson County Horserace.

* * *

"Why should we fight if it is all going to the Devil anyway?"

Elias Kelson looked up from the racing bill in his hand and turned to Garrett Rainier who was standing next to him on the front porch of his stone, Gothic Revival mansion. "Because, we all must play our part, Rainier," Elias drawled in response to the young man's question. "I'm sure your progenitor never misses a chance to remind you of yours."

Elias smiled when Garrett huffed at the word "progenitor." He often found it amusing, if not necessary, to remind his fellow elites that while he did not possess a piece of paper signed by the chief administrator of a prestigious university, in his case such stamps of approval would be…superfluous. Ten lifetimes at the best universities in the world couldn't educate a man on the things Elias had learned on his own over the course of four decades. Whatever Garrett Rainier thought he knew about the Devil, Elias knew two things: the South was hell-bent on going to war, and win or lose, it would be the Devil to pay.

Plucking a wad of U.S. dollars from his pocket, Elias waved the money at Garrett's father, Hanson, who was standing on the opposite side of the twelve-foot column against which Elias was leaning. "If you recall, Hanson, I advised you to put your money on the charcoal gelding."

With a stately tilt of his long, sharp nose, Hanson scoffed, "Anyone can see that mongrel beast does not have stamina. Besides, a man ought to bet on his own stock."

Elias chuckled as he returned the money to his pocket and tugged at the sky blue cravat that was cutting into his neck. "Oh, I never bet on my own stock. I find it more profitable when they lose, hence my lack of concern that both our horses are trailing by two lengths."

The porch rattled beneath Elias' feet as the horses thundered past the mass of onlookers who had gathered in his front yard for the annual Jackson County Horserace. At the commencement of the final lap, Hanson's blood bay was neck and neck with Elias' sorrel. The charcoal gelding was still in the lead.

Elias was just about to offer Garrett a cigar when he saw the blood bay stumble. The jockey tried to bring his head up, but it was too late. The bay went down and took Elias' sorrel with him.

The sorrel's jockey, a middle-aged black man whom Elias regarded as one of his better property investments to date, landed on his feet and sprang out of the way as the rest of the horses flew past him. The blood bay raised his head, but made no effort to get up.

The Rainiers' jockey wasn't moving at all. "Well, I suppose I ought to send someone to see about my jockey," Hanson grumbled as he scowled at the ball of emerald green racing silks lying in the middle of the road.

"Why, Hanson," Elias chirped, "you're among equals here. There's no need to pretend you care about the common man."

When the Rainiers' jockey finally stirred and crawled away from the injured horses, Elias waved his hand, and a large black man emerged from the smithy across the yard and trotted off to help the lad. It was neither the first nor the greatest disaster to occur during the Jackson County Horserace over the years. Elias hated to lose his sorrel, but that was a small matter. He had a dozen horses of equal speed and twice as much sense.

As for the people themselves, the initial shock would quickly subside, freeing them to carry on with the day's festivities as if no judgment would ever befall them. Elias considered sharing the correspondence he had received earlier that morning from one of his business associates in Charleston, but he chose to let the people consume their pies and cakes in peace. The official news would come soon enough.

Elias laughed. In the midst of it all, the self-composed rider of the charcoal gelding was spurring her horse through the last stretch of the race as if she was oblivious to the calamity closing in on her. The world was coming to an end, and all Alexandra Corbin cared about was winning that damned horserace.

* * *

As the horses settled into the final lap, Alexandra nearly lost her seat when a meaty hand with banged up knuckles and filthy nails clamped down on her arm. Prichard Benefield glared at her from atop his lop-eared champagne beast that was straining to match Shadow's speed.

If not for the danger of the situation, Alexandra might have laughed at her assailant. His large, menacing frame was stuffed into a hodgepodge of gentlemen's hand-me-downs and an undersized planter's hat, giving him the appearance of a trained baboon or a performing bear from the circus.

Taking the reins in her teeth, Alexandra extended her free hand and whacked Prichard in the face with her riding crop. He didn't let go, and she didn't stop hitting him. Finally, Prichard's mount grew tired of the jostling and darted to the outside. With Prichard still clutching her arm, Alexandra almost came out of the saddle, but the rider who had come up on the opposite side reached over and pulled her upright.

Alexandra barely had time to send her twin brother, Cass, an appreciative glance before he spurred his chestnut stallion into the final stretch of the race. Furious that Prichard's interference had cost her the lead, Alexandra kicked Shadow a little harder than she intended. He snorted in protest and veered to the side, costing Alexandra more time.

Dismayed but not defeated, she waited for Shadow to settle down before she made her move. She urged her horse forward until she was on her brother's heels. Instead of overtaking him, Alexandra held back and let him cut the way through the pack.

When Cass broke out in the lead, Alexandra swung to the inside and closed the gap. She kept stride with her brother until he tapped her knuckles with his crop.

"Back off," Cass warned.

"No!"

"You can't win."

"Yes, I can."

"No, they'll find you out if you win."

"I don't care."

Evidently unwilling to continue the argument, Cass bumped his mount into Shadow, causing the inexperienced gelding to lurch out of the way. When Cass' stallion lengthened his stride, Alexandra knew the race was lost, but she pressed on.

Cass and his sister crossed the finish line with Cass winning by a length. Alexandra gritted her teeth. She would have to be satisfied with second place. This year.

As the spectators gathered around Cass, Alexandra dismounted and handed Shadow's reins to Matthew, the spry, aging black man, who was waiting for her on the other side of the stable yard, away from the crowd. With a conspiratorial gleam in his eye, Matthew grunted, "Miss Alexandra, what you mean comin' in second place when I trained ol' Shadow here to outrun de Debil?" He rubbed Shadow's ears as he gave Alexandra a sideways glance. "I reckon Mr. Jonas be proud of this 'un."

Alexandra wasn't sure whether Matthew was referring to her or to the horse, but seeing as how he had consented to training them both only after she had threatened to tell on him for stealing sugar from the kitchen, she suspected he most likely meant the horse. It was Matthew who had given her that first riding lesson when she was eight. That he had done so at her father's request gave Alexandra hope that if Jonas Corbin had been alive to see his daughter take part in the most important race of the year, he would have been proud of her, despite her appearance. Her mother, on the other hand, would not. No matter how well Alexandra had ridden in the race, no matter how significant the trophy might have been, Laura Catherine Corbin would never forgive any daughter of hers who was caught dead wearing pants.

Alexandra kissed Shadow on the nose and stole away to change out of her man clothes before someone recognized her. Leaving the stables, Alexandra pulled her hat down, keeping her face turned away from the townspeople who were milling around the stretch of outbuildings that separated the stables from the cotton barn where she had hidden her female clothing.

She had just passed the smithy, when she spotted Prichard Benefield standing on the other side of the smokehouse. Curse his hide. If he hadn't slowed her down she would have beaten them all. After reviewing her arsenal of ugly words, she marched right up to him and stuck her finger in his face. "You cost me the race, you skunk-faced, swellheaded jackanapes."

Prichard seized her by the collar and dragged her to the back of the smokehouse. "You gonna pick a fight with me? The way I see it, *you* cost *me* the race," he snarled as he shoved her against the building and brandished his fist near her chin. "Now, you're gonna pay for it."

Alexandra caught herself before she reacted as any woman with a drop of Scots-Irish blood would react to such an affront. Trusting the shadow of her hat to conceal her face, she cleared her throat and replied in as deep and assertive a voice as she could manage. "You're the one who tried to knock me off my horse."

"You listen to me, boy. I was s'posed to win that race. I made arrangements, and I don't like it when folks interfere with my arrangements. That's how folks wind up dead 'round here."

"Well, I'm not gonna be one of them. Now, let me go!" Alexandra demanded, turning her head away from the stench of his rotten onion breath.

"I'll let you go when you give me what I want, and what I want is my winnin's."

"I don't have any money, and if I did, I still wouldn't give it to you," she snapped.

Prichard grabbed her shirtfront and pinned her against the building with both hands planted on her chest. Whatever foul thing he was about to say, he didn't say it. With a furrowed brow, he patted Alexandra's chest. His squinty eyes popped open. "What the devil...?"

When Alexandra dug her heel into his instep, Prichard drew in a sharp breath and hopped back. She twisted away from him, but he caught her collar and snatched her hat, freeing a mess of honey-colored hair.

Prichard's yellow teeth flashed through his thick, black beard. "Well, I'll be damned. You're that Corbin girl." His fingers crept up her neck. "I have been known on occasion to accept other kinds of payment, but you ain't my kind of woman, so maybe I'll pay your brother a visit and get what I want outta him instead."

Cass' voice came from behind Prichard's hulking frame. "What's this I hear about you paying me a visit, Prichard?"

Alexandra peered over Prichard's shoulder to see Cass standing no more than six feet away. Emboldened by her brother's presence, Alexandra elbowed Prichard in the gut. When he doubled over, she punched him in the nose. He shook his head like a bear stung by a bee. He reared back, but before he drove his fist into Alexandra's face, Cass attacked him from behind. When Prichard spun around to face Cass, Alexandra jumped on Prichard's back. Both men went down. Caught up in the struggle, Alexandra didn't realize that her extra weight wasn't helping the situation.

"Alexandra, get off!" Cass yelled from underneath the pile.

Prichard rose to his feet and slung Alexandra off his back. He was about to take a swing at Cass when Elias Kelson suddenly appeared and whacked Prichard on the back of the head with the silver handle of his riding crop.

Dizzy from the blow, Prichard stumbled and sank to the ground with his back against the wall of the smokehouse. With Prichard subdued, Elias directed his attention to Alexandra, eyeing her closely as he reached into his pocket and pulled out the racing bill. He read through the list of names until he found the one he was looking for. "Hmm. I've never heard of *Drake* Corbin before today. A long-lost cousin, perhaps?"

Cass started to speak, but Elias cut him off as he slid the racing bill back into his pocket. "Now, Cass, you know your sister's aberrations are safe with me." His eyes glittered with amusement as he retrieved Alexandra's hat and dropped it on her head. "Why, the Kelsons and the Corbins are like family."

Cass raised his chin and tightened his grip on Alexandra's arm. "As we are *not* family, Mr. Kelson, I trust you'll excuse us. Good day, sir."

* * *

As Cass led his sister away, Elias leveled his riding crop at Prichard's face. "When I give instructions, I expect them to be followed exactly as they were given."

Prichard sat up against the side of the smokehouse, making no effort to stand as he squinted up at Elias. "If you don't like how I handled the rider of the charcoal geldin' durin' the race, maybe you shoulda told me from the start she was a girl and I'd have done somethin' diff'rent."

"Which is why I didn't tell you she was a girl," Elias growled. "That shouldn't have mattered, anyway. I told you to scare her out of the race, and I made it clear you were to do it without laying a hand on her. She could've broken her neck."

"What do you care? You sweet on her?"

"That is none of your concern."

"Suits me fine, but next time you want somethin' done 'bout the Corbin girl, you do it yourself. I don't want no part in it." Folding his arms across his chest, Prichard sneered, "Now, the way I see it, I'da have won that race if it hadn't been for you tryin' to fix it. So, somebody owes me my winnin's. I don't care who. Just long as somebody keeps on fillin' my pockets. Otherwise, I might start to feelin' like I'm not 'ppreciated. You know how I get when I don't feel 'ppreciated."

Elias scowled as he waved a handful of Confederate banknotes in

Prichard's face. "I'm astounded as to how a God-fearing woman like Viola Benefield could have raised such a scoundrel."

"Fortunate for you she did," Prichard huffed as he crammed the bills in his pocket. "And if you stick that ridin' crop in my face again, I'm gonna take your arm off."

Elias leaned close to Prichard's face. "If that's the worst you can do, it won't be enough."

* * *

Cass yanked his handkerchief out of his pocket and dragged it across his face. Though Cass' handsome features and sandy blond hair were slightly tarnished by streaks of mud, Alexandra could see his frustration in the set of his shoulders and the expression in his deepset hazel eyes.

"Alexandra, what were you thinking?" he scolded as he dragged her along, away from the smokehouse and past the corncrib toward the back of the cotton barn.

"I told you I was gonna ride."

"I was talking about the fight."

"Ha! If you can call it that," she huffed, a little too arrogantly for a girl of nineteen who had narrowly escaped a fight she couldn't have won. She had just gotten the words out of her mouth when she suddenly dropped behind a rain barrel and covered her face with her hat.

Bewildered, Cass asked her what she was doing.

"Sshh!" She smacked his leg and pointed.

Cass stiffened as the cause of Alexandra's abrupt change in attitude approached.

"Congratulations on your victory, Cass."

Though the smooth timbre of Garrett Rainier's voice and his placid features usually masked any emotion he didn't want to communicate, Alexandra had known him long enough to pick up on the quirks that meant he was irritated. He cleared his throat just before he asked, "Where is your sister? She said she would be here today, but I have yet to see her."

Alexandra barely resisted peeking out from behind the barrel to gaze at the most sought-after young bachelor in Jackson County. Besides his good looks, Garrett Rainier was well-bred, well-mannered, and well-thought of by every female of his acquaintance. Hugging her knees tightly against her pounding chest, Alexandra begged God to send him away.

Whether by God's initiative or his own, Cass replied, "Rainier, I thought if anyone could keep track of Alexandra's whereabouts, it would be you. Are you her beau, or aren't you?"

Garrett chewed his lips, but otherwise gave no further indication of his frustration. "When you see her, tell her I am sorry I missed her."

As Garrett strode away, Alexandra relaxed her hold on her hat. Though he was not her beau, officially, she still would have been mortified if he had seen her looking such a mess.

"You know you're gonna have to choose between Garrett and 'Drake,' " Cass remarked as he helped her to her feet, his frustration giving way to brotherly concern. "You can't keep them both, not forever."

Alexandra sighed as she brushed a glob of dirt off Cass' coat. She knew she would have to choose, and when the time came, she would most certainly choose Garrett. Until then, she saw no reason to stop wearing pants and riding horses. Dismissing her brother with a teasing punch in the arm, she scampered into the cotton barn and retrieved the bag she had hidden before the race. She yanked out her crumpled skirt and a tight-fitting blouse with bell sleeves and hauled her petticoat and four-bone hoop skirt out from under a mountain of loose cotton.

Several minutes later, cloaked in nearly twelve pounds of cotton, buttons, and bone, Alexandra emerged from the barn and made her way through the crowd toward the food tables where she hoped to find Garrett. She was surprised at the number of people who had turned out for the race. Some folks had judged it unseemly to indulge in such entertainments when the country was on the verge of war until they heard Reverend Land's most recent sermon on Paul's letter to the Corinthians encouraging them to "run the race so as to receive the prize." Whether Reverend Land intended his congregants to interpret this as a divine sanction for horseracing was a subject of debate eventually settled by the reverend's presence at the race and the well-known fact that he hailed from the Commonwealth of Kentucky.

Perhaps it was national turmoil that made this race seem more important than all the races that had come before it. It was the one thing that had brought the local Unionists and secessionists together since the previous December when Alabama left the Union and cast her lot with the Confederacy. Now, here they all were, enjoying the festivities and keeping the peace, albeit at separate tables.

Alexandra frowned when Elias' son, Luke, got up from one of the "Unionist" tables and blocked her path.

"If you're looking for Garrett Rainier, he gave up and went home," he announced as his gaze skittered across Alexandra's body. Luke was a year older than Alexandra, but his dark, curly hair and the long lashes that fringed his big green eyes made him look much younger. According to the women in Marlbridge who were old enough to remember Elias' wife, Luke was the spitting image of Susannah Banks Kelson. The only resemblance Alexandra saw to Elias was his arrogant smirk.

Hiding her disappointment at missing Garrett, Alexandra ignored Luke and continued on her way to the dessert table. Her heart sank when she reached her destination. Crumbs and gobs of icing peppered the tablecloth stained with cherry pie spatter.

"I'm afraid the ravenous masses have left you nothing but scraps. Fortunately for you, I have a solution." Luke waved his hand. Immediately, a slave boy hurried over with a tray full of cookies.

Alexandra paused, caught in the middle of a struggle between her stomach and her pride. Her stomach won. She snatched two cookies and marched off to find Cass.

Before she had taken two steps, a shout arose from the crowd. Leonidas Beaumont, the only prominent citizen of Marlbridge who had not attended the race, reined in his lathered mount. He had scarcely completed a full sentence before the crowd's curiosity transformed into that peculiar blend of dread and excitement with which Southerners were expected to greet such news. As Alexandra strained to hear Beaumont over the crowd noise, two words overshadowed the rest: "Fort Sumter" and "war."

Chapter 2

A Fight's Comin'

April 11, 1862

DESPITE the best efforts of his foes, Cana Ramsey had lived to be a couple years shy of thirty. Whether he would live to see his next birthday was much less certain than it had been before he and his company of eighty-nine cavalrymen boarded the train bound for Chattanooga.

As he leaned on the railing of the last car and looked down at the track of the Memphis and Charleston running along beneath him, he finally let his mind contemplate the bloodlettin' he'd witnessed a few days ago at Shiloh church. What the farmers, shopkeepers, teachers, preachers, blacksmiths, and wainwrights on both sides had achieved in terms of battlefield formations did not exactly match up to the textbooks, but still, it had been one hell of a fight. The Confederates in their mismatched uniforms may have been less martial in appearance than the Federals, but they had made up for it in ferocity. It had taken two full days for them to lose the battle, their commanding general, and a fourth of their army.

In spite of Ramsey's love for a good fight, something about the battle at Shiloh church had deeply affected him in a way previous battles had not. It wasn't the carnage of the battle itself that had bothered him. Nor was it the stench of the blood and bowels of slain men that turned his stomach. It was the sight of all those dead horses. The images of dying men he could easily put out of his mind. He could choose to assume that they, like him, had committed enough sins in their lifetimes to warrant an early death. As far as he knew, laying down their lives on the battlefield may have been the only chance for redemption they had left, but he hated that the destruction of man bled over to the rest of creation.

In his lifetime, there had been only one death that Ramsey couldn't shake. On the night Jonas Corbin died, Ramsey had sworn an oath to never set foot in Marlbridge again. Even now, as the train carried him closer to his birthplace than he'd been in the past twelve years, he had every intention of keeping his vow, but the need for some form of atonement no matter how slight compelled him to offer Jonas Corbin's son the only consolation that was within his power to offer.

Grunting at the ache in his bones, Ramsey turned back from the railing. He started to enter the traincar but decided the roof would be quicker than picking his way through the bodies of sleeping Confederates. With one hand on the ladder, he hesitated, reconsidering his decision to let them sleep awhile longer.

Though his men didn't know the details of their present mission, Ramsey knew full well what would happen if the mission failed. Nevertheless, his faithful band of warriors had done every grueling thing he'd asked of them. At present, a few hours of peace was about the only thing he had to offer them in exchange. He climbed the ladder and stepped onto the roof.

No stranger to the rhythm of a moving train, Ramsey strolled along the top, hopping from one car to the next until he reached the stock car. For the second time that day, he cursed whatever idiot thought it was a good idea to build a stock car with no way to get in except through the large sliding doors on the sides. Fortunately, this particular stock car had been shot to pieces at some point in its service, and whoever repaired it improved its functionality by leaving a hole in the side just big enough for a man to slide through.

Ramsey lay on his stomach and dangled his right leg over the side of the car. When his boot struck the bottom of the window, he gripped the edge of the roof and swung down through the opening. The sudden movement and the thud of Ramsey's boots on the floor startled the horses and Cass Corbin, who had volunteered to keep the beasts company.

Cass scrambled to his feet.

"At ease, Corbin," Ramsey said as he patted the thick neck of a strawberry roan with a broken stripe that ran from the top of his head to the tip of his nose. "This is Jack. He's a good horse, but nobody wants him because they think he's bad luck."

Cass rubbed Jack's face and smiled for the first time since the battle. "I'll take him. Anything will be better than that stray plug I've been riding."

A rail thin jumper with an ungainly head and knobby knees snorted and twitched his ears as if he had heard the insult.

"The horse you lost at Shiloh—what was his name?" Ramsey asked.

"That's the funny thing," Cass replied, staring through the beams of sunlight that poured in between the slats of the car. "His name was Shiloh, like the place in the Bible. Reverend Land said it means 'peace.' It's where the people used to meet with God."

" 'Where the people used to meet with God,' " Ramsey mused. "That is funny."

Strange as it might have been to some other soul, one unaccustomed to bloodshed, it was on the battlefield where Ramsey felt most at peace with himself and his Maker. The smell of gunpowder, the sound of artillery that shook the earth, the sight of warriors marching steadily en masse through walls of smoke to their doom—all of it set his Scots-Irish blood on fire.

He had been told all his life that he was Cranston Ramsey made over with a temper as black as his hair—there was no denying the bloodline—but he wanted no part in that side of his family legacy. Cana Ramsey would die before he would play the coward as his grandfather had done. After a year of fighting the war between the North and the South, he still wasn't sure which side was ultimately responsible for starting it and was even less sure about which side was going to win, but as long as he had blood in his veins to burn, he would see it through to the end whether it was the war's end or his own.

Ramsey pulled a flask from his pocket. "Here's to Shiloh." He took a drink and offered the flask to Cass.

Cass took a hesitant sip and returned the flask. "All those men died, and we're drinking to a horse."

"A friend is a friend. Don't matter what form or color they come in." Ramsey ruffled Jack's mane and turned to his own horse, a tall, muscular thoroughbred named Solomon. "Don't you have a sister?"

Cass blinked at what he evidently thought was an abrupt change of subject. "Yes, sir. Alexandra."

"How is she?"

"Same as ever."

Recalling the run-in he'd had with Alexandra at Pop Brady's when she couldn't have been more than seven or eight, Ramsey allowed himself a brief moment of amusement. "I'm glad to hear that."

Cass sifted a handful of hay. "Do you think I made the right decision, sir?"

"About what?"

Cass took a deep breath and dropped the remaining bits of hay. "Leaving my family to fight for a country that isn't even two years old. Heck, we don't know what it's going to become. I signed up because I wanted a chance to do something worth doing, but there's no guarantee the Confederacy will be any better than the Union. If it's not, then what are we fighting for?" He hung his head. "I know I must sound like a coward, but my father always said it was a shame to throw good effort after vanity. Chasing the wind, he called it. I'm willing to shed every drop of blood that's mine to shed, but not for vanity."

Ramsey studied Cass for a moment, surprised at the ease with which the young man confided in him. Cass had fought well at Shiloh and Fallen Timbers, and there was nothing in his manner that would indicate even a hint of cowardice. If there was, Ramsey wouldn't have secured Cass' transfer to his company, and Leonidas Beaumont wouldn't have pitched a fit to lose him. Still, some men were afflicted with a dual nature, men whose public face never revealed the inner man. Maybe Cass Corbin was one of those people, or maybe he was just honest.

At that moment, Solomon snorted and pawed at the floor. Ramsey looked up when he heard boots clomping on the roof. He climbed out the window and peered over the top to see one of his men teetering along the roof. His heart sank; he knew the man by his gait. Ramsey had always been fond of Limpy McGhee, and it wasn't going to bring him any pleasure if he had to kill him.

He waited until Limpy slipped down the ladder at the far end of the adjacent car before he sprang onto the roof in pursuit. Ramsey paused when he reached the top of the ladder. Limpy was standing on the platform outside the rear door of car № 211 tying a red cloth to the railing. Between the wind and the clatter of iron wheels on the train track, Limpy never heard Ramsey coming. He screamed when Ramsey grabbed him, and both men crashed through the doorway of the car.

Limpy was on the floor, squirming under Ramsey's boot when Cass appeared in the doorway. As he entered the car, he stepped on a mound of gold pieces that had spilled out of an overturned powder keg. He drew his revolver and closed the door.

"Move, and you're dead, Limpy," Ramsey threatened, aiming his Colt Dragoon at the crippled man's head.

Limpy nodded his head. Realizing he had moved his head, he shook his head, moving it again. "Wait. I's just noddin'. I weren't movin'."

Cass stayed back as Ramsey jerked Limpy to his feet. "Who told you about the gold?"

Limpy sputtered and whimpered. Ramsey asked again with his backhand. Limpy yelped, "Darby! It was Darby!"

Instead of cursing the bug-eyed ninnyhammer, Ramsey restrained his response to a low growl with which Limpy was already familiar, "Who else knows? Tell me, right now."

Limpy shook his head. Ramsey narrowed one eye. Limpy blurted, "Edwards! Billy Edwards."

At the mention of that name, Ramsey finally let go of at least one swear word before he directed his next order at Cass. "Stay here. If anyone comes through that door, shoot him."

When Ramsey returned with Billy Edwards and Darby, Cass was struggling to free himself from Limpy who was clinging to his leg for dear life. "Don't let Ramsey kill me," the poor wretch begged.

"Shut up and get over here, Limpy," Ramsey ordered.

Limpy scrambled away from Cass and tried to hide behind Darby, the eldest of the perpetrators, but Darby shoved him away. "Get off me, Limpy, you worthless cur."

"How did you know about the gold, Darby?" Ramsey asked with a placid tone that would have terrified a wiser mortal.

Darby glared at him from beneath his thick, dark eyebrows. "I ain't tellin' you nothin'."

Ramsey turned to Billy Edwards who was shaking so badly Ramsey had to hold him against the wall so he could see straight. For a moment, he thought the boy's heart would give out before he could utter a word.

"I d-don't know nothin', I s-swear, Cap'n," Billy gasped, snot and tears rolling down his face. He winced and squeezed his eyelids shut as Ramsey gripped the top of his shoulder muscle.

"Billy, I know you and Limpy and Darby have been fraternizing with the enemy," Ramsey accused, pointing to each malefactor in turn.

Limpy wailed, "We ain't done it, Cap'n, I swear. We been steerin' clear of them bluebellies like you said."

"I don't mean the bluebellies. I mean the yellow ones who've been riding around in gangs robbing their own people." Ramsey glowered at Darby. "You've been working for Prichard Benefield this whole time. I know he's out there layin' in wait. Tell me where."

Darby remained silent until Ramsey shot him in the foot. The rogue collapsed, screaming in pain, but still he refused to give up Prichard. Ramsey holstered his revolver, dragged Darby to the door, and hauled him out onto the platform.

Billy and Limpy clambered after him. "Have mercy, Cap'n! We won't cross you never agin, we swear it!"

Ramsey clutched Darby by the throat. "Tell Prichard that Cana Ramsey sends his regards. He'll know what that means."

Darby jutted his chin in defiance. Ramsey shoved him off the train.

Without bothering to draw his gun, Ramsey snarled at Billy and Limpy. "Where is Prichard?"

Billy shook his head. "I s-swear I don't know, but I-I know he p-plans to stop you b-before you get to B-bridgeport."

Limpy volunteered, "Yes, sir. He's right. I heard Darby say somethin' 'bout laying trees cross the tracks. You know Prichard won't fight 'less he's the one chooses the battlefield."

"I appreciate your cooperation, gentlemen. Now, jump."

They shook their heads.

"Stay here then." He drew a knife from his belt.

Billy and Limpy jumped.

When Ramsey turned back to Cass, he saw that his treatment of the three scoundrels had shocked him, but whatever was going through his head, Cass stuck to his duty when he opened his mouth. "Shall I stand guard in case anybody else figures out what's in these powder kegs?"

Ramsey looked at the floor where Darby's blood had smeared a path to the doorway. He picked up one of the gold coins. As he inspected it, he could feel the blood draining from his face. When he had agreed to escort the gold shipment with the promise that his cut would be enough to clothe and feed his men for a few more months, he had assumed Colonel Whisenhunt and his associates had stolen it from the Yankees. The distinct markings on the reverse of the coin—a phoenix carrying a snake in its talons—revealed the gold's true origins. How Whisenhunt, who was aptly nicknamed Madcap Charlie, had managed to get his hands on gold belonging to the most dangerous organization in the Tennessee Valley, Ramsey could only speculate, but there was nothing to be done about it now except to finish the job, hopefully in one piece.

He tossed the coin into the powder keg. "Cass, go tell Muley to stop the train and keep his head down. A fight's comin'."

Chapter 3

Rivals and Disasters

ALEXANDRA ducked her head as she crossed the street, hoping to avoid the two elderly gentlemen who were sitting on the bench outside Pop Brady's Mercantile. On any other day, she would have been delighted to hear all about the time they went with Old Hickory down to New Orleans to whip the British but not today.

As Alexandra approached, Tate Rollins grunted as he folded the latest edition of *The Marlbridge Sentinel* and used it as a seat cushion. "Wonder how come Beauregard run back to Corinth? Seems like he oughtta chased 'em Billy Yanks clear up to Ohio." He smoothed his breastplate of bushy, white whiskers and leaned back on the well-worn bench.

Cletus Gerry sucked on the few teeth he had left. "Betch-ee Forrest coulda drove 'em all the way to Canada if they'd give him the chance."

"Course, what can a body expect from a gen'ral with a name like Pierre Gustave Toutant Beauregard," Tate mused as he rolled the chaw in his mouth. "I know some folks is fond of him on account of the vict'ry up in Virginny, but I don't know how I feel 'bout some French-soundin' feller leadin' the whole dang army. Now, Albert Sidney Johnston—that's a good name for a gen'ral."

"A dead 'un," Cletus added, sucking his teeth again for emphasis. "Now, what I woulda liked to seen wuz ol' Forrest chasin' 'em Yanks up in Sacramenty, Kaintuck. They say he wuz a-slashin' and swingin', this way and that. Lockin' sabers at a dead gallop they wuz. Why, I heard they laid 'em a trail to Abe Lincoln's door with 'em bluebellies."

"Well, laid 'em a trail they mighta done, but not in no cavalry charge," Tate scoffed. "If ya'd ever seen a real battle, ya'd know sabers is just for show. All ya do in a real battle is stand in a line and shoot acrost the field at the enemy line. Then they make ya march over to the other side of the field and fire at the enemy over thar for a while. Then they tell ya to fall back so's ya can re-form the line and do it all over agin. Ain't nothin' entertainin' 'bout that."

"But I seen 'em. They had sabers and bayonets and all manner of sharp objects, and they wuz stabbin' all 'em bluebellies and blood wuz a-goin' ever'whar."

"Whar d'ya see all that nonsense?"

"In the newspaper."

Tate swatted Cletus on the shoulder. "I done told ya to quit readin' that blasted paper. It ain't good for ya health."

The old codgers spotted Alexandra. "Hey there, Sheriff Corbin's daughter," Cletus hallooed. "D'you hear 'bout Nathan Bedford Forrest whippin' 'em Yanks all by his lonesome? They're callin' it the Battle of Fallen Timbers." He popped Tate on the arm, "Now, you want a name for a battle, that's a good 'un."

Reluctant to get roped into two hours of yarn telling, Alexandra nodded and waved as she scooted through the door at Pop Brady's. She had heard the news from the battle that had taken place in Tennessee and was eager to see if the Huntsville paper had sketches. *The Marlbridge Sentinel* couldn't afford a war correspondent with artistic ability, so if she wanted to see a decent rendering of the battle she would have to go over to Pop Brady's to buy a copy of *The Democrat*.

A full year had passed since Cass had joined Leonidas Beaumont's Volunteers and gone off to war. Alexandra had wanted to go with her brother, and if she had been a man, she would have. It would have been her duty to go, but a girl had no place in the army. Men fought wars, and as good as Alexandra was at pretending to be a boy, Drake was no man.

As a woman, Alexandra had proven herself useless to the war effort, or at least that was the oft-expressed opinion of Mrs. Kilroy, who had assumed the directorship over all the wartime preparations for which the women were responsible. Alexandra couldn't sew, she couldn't quilt, and she couldn't knit-not up to Mrs. Kilroy's standards-so she was assigned to fundraising duty, namely selling pies that other women baked. It wasn't long before Alexandra proved herself to be unsuitable for that task as well. She was promptly discharged from her position after she dumped Mrs. Porter's cream pie in Roger Culpepper's lap for his disparaging remarks against Cass and all the other "secessionist traitors."

After that incident, Mrs. Kilroy vowed that Alexandra Corbin would henceforth be banished from any activity related to the war effort as her participation would undoubtedly do more harm than good. A week later, Mrs. Kilroy repealed her banishment. Apparently, none of the men who had stayed in Marlbridge when the Confederacy called for volunteers would work for Mrs. Kilroy, who had acquired a reputation as a slave driver. Judging Alexandra to be the next best thing to a man, given that she was "tall, skilled in horsemanship, and utterly devoid of feminine grace," Mrs. Kilroy assigned her to transporting the supplies collected from the plantations and small farms scattered across the countryside and depositing them at the church which was serving concurrently as a place of worship, a storage facility, and a meeting house for Unionists and secessionists to accuse and complain about each other to Reverend Land.

While Alexandra relished the opportunity to spend so much time in the saddle, if she was going to do her part for the Cause and be seen doing it—otherwise what was the point, her mother said—she would have to ride as Alexandra, in a dress, and worst of all, side-saddle. As much as she hated to give up Drake, it was a necessary sacrifice and one she was willing to make in order to secure a place for herself in the service of her country. If folks were right in saying this was America's second War for Independence (or third, if one counted the War of 1812), Alexandra Corbin, a true daughter of the '76 Revolution, would not be missing it.

She had just walked through Pop Brady's door and was about to snatch up the last copy of *The Democrat* when she caught Mrs. Kilroy's daughter, Meredith, flirting with Garrett Rainier right in front of her. In Pop Brady's Mercantile! Since she was a child, Pop Brady had been giving her candy sticks every time she came to visit. If Meredith Kilroy thought she was gonna come in Pop Brady's, take Garrett's arm, and employ the same tactics she used to ensnare all the eligible males in town, Alexandra was ready to fight it out tooth and claw. Fortunately, before she lit into her rival, something told her that if she did, she might win the physical altercation and gain a moment's pleasure at Meredith squalling on the floor in a mass of petticoats, but she would lose Garrett forever. No gentleman of any stature would choose for his bride any woman capable of such an unbridled display.

As if she could smell Alexandra's powerlessness, Meredith smiled and stepped closer to Garrett. Refusing to take part in Meredith's game lest she punch the girl in the nose, Alexandra turned to leave, but her hoop skirt whacked into an ill-stocked crate, bouncing her back into a barrel of nails. She rode the barrel all the way to the floor.

If she hadn't been so intent on a masterful fall, she would have noticed Garrett's rescue attempt and would have fallen in his arms instead of landing at his boots. Garrett reached to steady her as she swished to her feet and untangled her long appendages.

"It seems I am too late to be your dashing rescuer. You have righted yourself." He offered her his arm and waited until she realized what she was supposed to do with it. "I promise to dash more quickly in the future," he grinned.

Alexandra smiled when Meredith rolled her eyes, snatched up an armload of fabric, and hauled it to the counter. Mama Brady, a short, stocky woman from Scotland, stepped up onto the little box she kept behind the counter and began sorting through Meredith's expensive, delicate, thin material.

As Meredith began to purchase the items on credit, a vulture-like fellow named Shanks shoved Meredith aside and stuck his hawk nose in Mama Brady's face. "You lettin' this twit buy on credit after you denied me? Looks like only rich folks gets credit at this 'stablishment. All you merchants is in bed with the big planters and their filthy niggers."

Alexandra's eyes widened in anticipation as Mama Brady leaned forward until she was nose-to-nose with Shanks. Alexandra half expected the woman's stubborn, red-gray hair to break loose from her bun like a cat o' nine tails.

"Credit, aye? Is that what ye'll be wanting, then? Weel, I'll no give ye credit this time, Shanks, for ye've never paid what ye already owe, ye wee fiend. Now, give me real coin for that sack o' flour and I'll let ye have it," Mama Brady declared, her face turning redder with every word.

Shanks sliced open the sack and slung the flour all over the counter and the floor, dousing Meredith and her purchases.

If Garrett hadn't acted quickly, Mama Brady would have sliced open Shanks' head with the butcher knife she wielded as she sprang out from behind the counter. "Mama Brady! There is already a considerable mess here. It would not do to add to it."

At that moment, Pop Brady, a thin man wearing spectacles too big for his face, appeared in the doorway that separated the store from the Bradys' living quarters. "Mama, what's the trouble here? And who strewed this flour all over the place?"

Shanks spat on the floor and made a few lewd remarks as he stomped toward the door, his nose turned up so high that he tripped over the threshold on his way out.

"Something ought to be done about Shanks. I've had all I'm gonna take from that ne'er-do-well," Pop Brady grumbled as he took a broom to the mess. "I'd have liked to seen Mama put him in his place, but I reckon it's for the best she didn't. The Lord has His own ways of dealin' with scoundrels, and it don't profit a man to interfere with the Lord's doin's."

Meredith was wailing about her flour-caked dress, so Mama Brady took a dusting rag to it. "Stop ye crying, lassie. It were just a bit o' flour."

Garrett handed Mama Brady enough "real coin" to pay for the flour. Then he led Alexandra to the door. She bumped into him when he halted at the threshold. He was gazing at something down the street. Several townspeople were gathered around Johnsey Carroll who was still sitting atop his winded mount.

Before Garrett could stop her, Alexandra ran out to meet Johnsey and pushed her way through the crowd. As more citizens joined the group, Alexandra reluctantly stepped aside to make room for Mr. and Mrs. Porter who gasped in unison as Johnsey coughed out the news. "The Yankees! They've taken Huntsville!"

Raulston Porter, the largest planter in North Alabama (measured by his person not his produce) exclaimed, "Huntsville? Tell me, boy, does the city still stand or did those demons burn it? Have they cut the rail line? Where are they now? Are they coming here? Well, don't just sit there, boy! Tell us what's happened!"

"They—" Johnsey spit out between gasps for air. "They took the telegraph, the railroad, and God knows what all. It was a disaster, a pure disaster!" Johnsey turned when he spotted Garrett. "Secessionists are being hunted down like dogs and sold into the hands of the enemy by Unionist traitors!"

Garrett contradicted Johnsey. "I doubt they are being 'hunted like dogs.' The president has pursued a policy of reconciliation. It would hardly help his cause to allow such conduct."

"If you don't believe me, Rainier, go see for yourself. If you have the courage, that is, you Yankee-loving, Unionist cur!"

Fortunately, Mrs. Porter, a boisterous, heavy-set woman who had eight sons of her own, prevented any further hostilities between the two young Southern men by handing Johnsey a handkerchief and ordering him to wipe the dirt and sweat off his face.

Shanks came bounding up, hooting and hollering. "Hee-hee! Serves y'all right for wantin' to secede from the Union. All your big talk about rights when us workin' men knows all you secessionists is in with the big planters. Now, y'all gonna git what's comin' to ya. I'm gonna be right there on the courthouse steps with my pencil, ready to write down the names of all you 'secesh' and hand y'all over to the enemy. And I'm gonna be rejoicin' when y'all's hangin' from the nearest tree."

"Fiddlesticks!" Mr. Porter replied. "We all know you can't write, you filthy creature."

"Reckon there ain't no tree big enough to hang you on, Raulston," Shanks sneered.

Arliss McKinney, a freckle-faced terror beyond his ten years, punched Shanks in the stomach and yelled, "Ain't no Yankees gonna take my town! Captain Ramsey's gonna come with the whole Rebel Army and kill 'em all!"

"Cana Ramsey?" Mrs. Porter scoffed. "Why, that boy wouldn't dare show his face in this town after what his scoundrel of a father did."

"Boy?" Mr. Porter argued with his wife. "He's a grown man now and a cavalry commander. Why, he and his men could swoop down upon us any minute, if they had a mind to."

Cana Ramsey's here? And he's a captain of cavalry? As Alexandra contemplated the possibility that Cana Ramsey might return to Marlbridge, she didn't notice that Elias Kelson had ridden up until he parted the crowd, urging his horse to the front.

"Y'all know as well as I do that Cana Ramsey isn't coming back," he avowed. "As for the enemy, there's only one thing we can do. We must ready ourselves to meet them."

Alexandra's heart pounded at his words. They would see the enemy and confront them! Elias was wrong—Cana Ramsey would come back this time. She knew it in her heart. He wouldn't let Marlbridge fall into the hands of the enemy. All the battle scenes she had envisioned from her childhood forays into her brother's books on military history and tactics sprang up in her mind: Ethan Allen and the Green Mountain boys storming Ticonderoga, Andrew Jackson smashing the British at New Orleans, Sam Houston sending Santa Anna running back to Mexico in a dress.

Mr. Porter's velvety tone sliced through Alexandra's visions of battlefield glory. "We can't fight off an invading army! We barely have enough able-bodied men to keep Prichard Benefield and his band of rogues at bay," he fussed as he wiped beads of sweat from his chins.

Elias coolly replied, "I said meet them. Rest assured, gentlemen, I have no intention of fighting them."

Alexandra's heart sank as Elias wheeled his horse around and cantered away. She stood horrified as the other men seemed to agree with Elias, nodding to each other as they dispersed. Were there no Francis Marions among them? No Davy Crocketts? No Andrew Jacksons? If the men of Marlbridge weren't going to fight the invaders…

"Alexandra," Garrett interrupted her thoughts. "Did you hear me?"

She hadn't noticed that Garrett had walked her back to Pop Brady's. Evidently, he had been speaking to her the whole way, but she hadn't heard any of it.

Garrett took her hand. "Do not let this news frighten you. I am certain that the Union Army will not come here."

Alexandra stared at him for a moment. Sometimes he acted as if he didn't know her at all. She jerked her hand away from him. "I wasn't frightened. There's an invader at our door, and I want to know what the men in this town are gonna do about it!"

He didn't fight to get her hand back, but instead tried to reason with her. "Just over a year ago, the army that you now decry as 'an invader' was the very same army in which Beauregard, Johnston, Jackson, and even your own father served. It is hardly fair to despise the institution merely because a handful of men in Montgomery decided that Alabama should leave the Union. Besides, why would the Union Army harm civilians? The federal government is endeavoring to bring us back into the Union not drive us further away."

"The federal government sent an army to kill us! Return to the Union or die!"

Garrett removed his hat and rubbed his forehead. "You are not going to like what I have to say, but it is the truth, so please hear me. If the Union Army invades there is nothing you or I can do about it."

Alexandra was about to protest, but Chance Mullins beat her to it. He marched up to Garrett, inches from his face. "The hell, you say! No Yankee, or Yankee-lover, who wants to keep his life better set foot in Marlbridge. If you ain't gonna do somethin' about it, Rainier, I will. There's a few of us left who ain't cowards."

Chance turned to Alexandra, "Don't you worry, Miss Alexandra, and pardon my language. Me and the rest of us *men* are gonna form a Home Guard. Maybe we can't stop the Yankees from comin' down here, but we can sure make 'em wish they hadn't."

He whirled on the heel of his expensive, patent leather, stove pipe boot and trotted off to join Bryce Calhoun, Quinn O'Dell, and a few other young men who had been exempted from military service for various reasons.

Quinn had been declared unfit because he wasn't quite right in the head. The others were excused because they were the heads of their respective families, all of whom owned farms, businesses, and other enterprises that were deemed too important to the local economy to risk their collapse should their young masters go off to war and get themselves killed.

By the time Chance and his cohort mounted their steeds and galloped away, Meredith had stepped out of Pop Brady's where she had been hiding. She ran up to Garrett all a-fright and latched on to his arm. "The Yankees are coming! Whatever will we do? Has our own army abandoned us?" Meredith jabbered on until she finally wheedled Garrett into escorting her home.

After Garrett hoisted Meredith into his buggy, he extended his hand to Alexandra. "May I have the honor of escorting you as well, Miss Corbin?"

Alexandra cut her eyes at Meredith who was smirking at her in triumph. Not a trace of fear remained on the girl's face. As much as Alexandra relished a long buggy ride with Garrett Rainier, she refused to share a seat with that lying, spoiled, hateful Meredith. She wondered what Warren Lydell would think of his fiancée flirting with another man while he was away from home fighting for his country.

"I don't need an escort, thank you." Alexandra turned away from Garrett, but before she retreated to Pop Brady's to hide her red face in the newspaper, she goaded her rival, "Oh, Meredith, in your next letter to Warren, do tell him how much we all appreciate his sacrifice." It pleased Alexandra to see Meredith scowl.

Chapter 4

Remember the Alamo

Ramsey peeked between the slats of the rail car. He hoped his plan would work. If it didn't…

Gunfire erupted as Prichard Benefield and his gang, numbering close to forty, came tearing out of the woods. They fired several rounds into the stationary train before they realized no one was firing back. Prichard ordered his men to cease fire. He urged his horse closer to the train, slowly at first as if he wasn't sure the train was occupied.

Ramsey had hoped Limpy and Billy Edwards would run tell Prichard that he was waiting for him and that the information would deter Prichard, but evidently they hadn't told him, or he didn't care. It wasn't that Ramsey didn't want to put an end to Prichard Benefield—he just didn't have the time. The gold had to be delivered to Chattanooga, and they were already late.

He grimaced when Prichard rode past the car where he was hiding. None of the Confederates who were hiding on the rest of the train made a sound. The mounted Confederates Ramsey had stationed in the woods likewise remained out of sight.

Prichard waved his hand and two of his men rode up, dismounted, and climbed into the car Limpy had marked. They emerged a few seconds later toting a barrel.

"Open it," Prichard ordered.

The balding one named Jenkins hesitated. "He's gwone know we open'd it."

"You willin' to risk bringin' him the wrong barrel?" Prichard asked as he continually scanned his surroundings for any threats.

Jenkins opened the barrel and jumped back, letting loose a string of swear words.

Prichard looked into the barrel, but remained calm. "Stick your hand in it to make sure."

"You do it!" Jenkins protested.

Prichard dismounted and shoved Jenkins aside. Without hesitation, he stuck his hand into the fresh horse manure and dug out about half of it before he decided the gold wasn't in there.

"Ramsey," Prichard spat the name out of his mouth like rotgut. "Limpy, get over here!"

Limpy cowered as he approached Prichard. "Now-now, Prichard, I did like you told me. I marked the car and I told you Ramsey was the one guardin' the train, so it was him that fooled you not me."

Prichard roared and dumped the rest of the manure on Limpy's head.

"Wonder whar Ramsey's at?" Jenkins muttered. "Reckon the Yanks got him? They done took Huntsville, and last I heard, they was headed this way to secure the railroad. I bet ol' Ramsey's done got hisself captured. That's what I think."

Prichard kicked Jenkins in the leg. "Shut up about Ramsey and get to searchin' the train."

Ramsey waited until one of Prichard's men opened the door of the car where he was hiding. The man froze like a scared rabbit when he saw Ramsey standing in the doorway. Ramsey fired, and the man fell backwards with a bullet hole in his head.

The rest of Ramsey's men opened fire. Mounted Confederates poured out of the woods. Prichard sprang onto his horse and might have escaped, but he was cut off by a force of over two hundred Yankees who came charging in at the last minute, raining bullets down on anyone not wearing a Federal uniform.

Ramsey cringed when he recognized the man who was leading the Federal onslaught. Joab Barrymore rode his horse like a wraith, cutting down every mortal in his path. Prichard and his gang fled in the opposite direction.

Lieutenant St. Clair, who was leading the mounted contingency, re-formed the Confederate line and repelled the Yankee charge long enough for Ramsey and the rest of the men to escape to the other side of the train where the holders had secured the horses. Ramsey leapt onto Solomon's back and took off in the direction he had sent Cass Corbin with the gold.

When he reached the place where he was supposed to meet Cass, Ramsey pulled Solomon up abruptly and jumped out of the saddle. Filled with dread, he rushed over to the body sprawled on the ground. From the looks of things, Cass Corbin was dead.

* * *

Alexandra had spent nearly twenty minutes perusing the newspaper before she left Pop Brady's and marched toward home. She had always known that if she had lived back in the days of the first War for Independence, she would have joined the Patriots, her people, without a moment's hesitation. She was certain she would have hated all the Tories who remained loyal to the British monarchy, but curiously, she found herself not hating the people in her own town who refused to take up arms against the Union, people like Garrett.

Even before the war broke out, Marlbridge had been divided on the issue of secession. While the majority had gone all in when the Confederacy called them to arms, there were still many folks who thought leaving the Union was foolhardy and perhaps even traitorous. They accused their secessionist neighbors of rebellion toward God who had established the Union of the American colonies through diverse miracles.

The secessionists emphasized that God had also led their forefathers to revolt against tyranny back in '76 and form their own country, which was what the South had done. Moreover, no president from Illinois or elsewhere had the right to force the sovereign state of Alabama to remain in a political union that no longer respected the rights of its people to own property and to take their property with them wherever they had a mind to go.

As for the U.S. Constitution, at least one secessionist in Marlbridge denounced the compact as a Federalist plot conjured by the likes of Alexander Hamilton, a man who had gone so far afoul of godliness as to propose a national bank, the surest instrument to enslave a free people to debt and speculation. However, Reverend Land was careful not to disseminate his views from the pulpit as many of the faithful tithers among his congregation were Unionists.

While Alexandra admired certain people on both sides of the conflict for holding to their principles, she wasn't sure holding to one's principles out of stubbornness and pride was any better than sending one's principles to the Devil whenever the defense of life and liberty seemed to call for it.

Lost in her thoughts, Alexandra paid no mind to the storm clouds forming above her head until large raindrops began pelting her face. She yelped when lightning struck a tree further down the road. Gathering her skirts, she ran for home, chiding herself for letting her pride get in the way of a ride home in a covered buggy with the handsomest man of her acquaintance.

Eventually, the weight of her rain-soaked garments made it impossible to run. Tripping along as best she could, she struggled to shield her eyes from the rain. She hadn't gone much further when she stumbled and fell into a muddy stream the downpour had formed in the middle of the road.

It wasn't in her nature to accept a misfortune without a valiant effort to overcome it, yet she made no move to extricate herself from the mire. A bucketful of tears might have done her good, but after all she had overcome without resorting to tears, she would not allow herself to waste them on anything as silly as getting caught in the rain.

With new resolve, Alexandra struggled to her feet. Shoving the past from her mind, she forced her attention to present troubles. The Yankees were coming, the men in her town weren't going to do anything about it, and Cass might be lying dead on a battlefield somewhere. In light of all that, losing to Meredith Kilroy, walking home in the rain, and muddying her dress were trifling matters. Furthermore, there was not one thing she could do about any of it: not the Yankees, not the cowards, not the rain, and not Meredith. Although, surely there was something she could do to get back at Meredith.

Before she had time to devise a suitable plot of revenge, she heard the sound of a horse and buggy coming around the bend. As the buggy came into view, she couldn't see the driver's face, but she recognized Dumplin, the chunky dun hauling the buggy.

Moments later, Reverend Land pulled up beside her. "Miss Alexandra, what are you doing in the rain?" He patted the seat next to him, then held out his hand and pulled her up. Seeing her muddied dress, he asked, "What has happened? Are you hurt?"

"No, sir, I'm not hurt."

Once she was safely inside the buggy, Reverend Land popped the reins and Dumplin lurched into a sloppy trot.

Alexandra's wet hair hung in tatters around her shoulders, and her dress was ruined. Someone else would have scolded her for allowing herself to get into such a mess, but not Reverend Land. Besides Lellen, the middle-aged slave woman who had been Alexandra's nursemaid and confidant for most of her life, Reverend Land was the only person she knew who worried over the soul of a person more than the look of her.

"Well, I'm happy I came along when I did. I would hate to think of you having to walk the rest of the way home by yourself and in such disagreeable weather." Reverend Land offered her his handkerchief to wipe her face. "I suppose you have heard the news about Huntsville?"

Rather than respond with words that a girl shouldn't utter, especially in front of the preacher, Alexandra frowned and kept her mouth shut. Not yet ready to relinquish her dark mood, she hoped the reverend wouldn't try to cheer her up.

"Now, we mustn't get discouraged," Reverend Land began. "Christ has said we are more than conquerors, but that doesn't guarantee the enemy won't bloody our noses every now and then."

Alexandra had no trouble thinking of the Yankees as the enemy—as much as she would think of the British or the French or the Spaniards if they were planning to invade her newly independent country—but she imagined there was probably at least one Yankee somewhere thinking the same about her. "I suppose if God turns out to be for the Union, there's nothing I can do to talk Him out of it no more than I can talk Garrett Rainier into being for the Confederacy." She could feel Reverend Land's eyes studying her much the way her father used to do when he was deliberating on whether or not to scold her.

He raised his eyebrows. "Alexandra Corbin, what's this I'm hearing?"

"Nothing of any consequence," she mumbled.

"Sounds like doubt to me, and that is never without consequence."

"We lost the battle! Cass is probably dead! Now the enemy is coming to take us over, and no one is gonna do anything about it," she replied more forcefully than she had intended.

Her outburst did not seem to offend Reverend Land. "We have lost *a* battle. There is every hope in the world that your brother is alive and well and ready for the next one. As for the enemy, they have not come yet, and if they do, the Lord has already prepared us."

He drove past the turn off to the Corbin farm. When Alexandra looked at him in confusion, he held up his hand. "I know I missed the turn, but I have something to show you."

Reverend Land drove on for several miles until they reached the bend in the road where the gate to the old Ramsey plantation lay tangled in a web of poison ivy and cow itch vines. The abandoned house wasn't visible from the road, and it remained hidden until they were halfway up the drive where the dense woods abruptly ended.

It had once been a beautiful mansion and aptly named Storm Chase. Cranston Ramsey, the long-gone patriarch of the Ramsey family, had built it on the very spot where the worst storm ever to hit that part of Alabama struck down a great many trees, leaving a choice flank of the hillside stripped bare. The moment he'd set eyes on the property, Cranston had claimed it as his Promised Land, joking that Providence had gone ahead and cleared it for him.

As Reverend Land drove closer to the house, Alexandra recognized the horses that were grazing in the front yard. The front door opened, and Bryce Calhoun stepped out onto the porch, gun in hand. "Glad you could make it, Reverend," he said. "Is that you, Miss Alexandra?"

Reverend Land answered as he hopped out of the buggy, "I thought a representative of the Corbin family should be present."

Something stirred in Alexandra's chest, and she didn't know what to make of it. Without waiting for Reverend Land's assistance, she climbed out of the buggy.

The grass was tall, and she almost plunged right into a bed of fire ants. Side-stepping the ant bed, she trod on streams of disemboweled pecans and walnuts as she picked her way to the front porch. Whatever other critters had come and gone, the squirrels still had run of the place.

Alexandra halted at the bottom of the porch steps and stared up at the massive oak door. Laura Catherine had forbidden her daughter to ever set foot on the Ramsey estate. Everyone said it was cursed. Yet here she was, and with Reverend Land right behind her. Surely his presence would alleviate any disfavor she might incur as a result of her disobedience.

Bryce led them into the parlor where a number of secessionists were gathered. When Alexandra appeared in the doorway, they all fell silent and gawked at her. She didn't know if it was because they hadn't expected to see a girl or because they hadn't expected to see a girl who looked as if she'd just come up out of a swamp.

Quinn O'Dell seemed not to notice her muddy dress or her disheveled hair. He blushed and gave her a shy smile. "Hey, Miss Alexandra."

Chance Mullins rolled his eyes. "Quinn, stop makin' a fool of yourself."

Quinn hopped out of his chair and offered it to Alexandra.

"What's Miss Alexandra doin' here anyhow, Reverend?" Chance asked. "Don't tell me Marlbridge is so overrun with cowards that we've resorted to armin' the women."

Reverend Land repeated what he'd said to Bryce. "What we are planning to do will affect everyone, so I invited Alexandra to represent the Corbin family."

Chance scoffed, "Yeah, with Cass gone off to war, she's the closest thing they've got to a man."

Several of the young men snickered.

Alexandra hated to admit that she had always been a little ashamed of her stepfather. Wilson Metcalf was a smart man and had always treated her with kindness, but when it came down to fighting, he was no Jonas Corbin. Nevertheless, he was a family member, and she couldn't allow the likes of Chance Mullins to ridicule him, especially when Chance's own father had shown himself on more than one occasion to be as yellow as Tate Rollins' teeth.

Alexandra arched her brows and lifted her chin. "We women aren't looking to Wilson Metcalf to do anything about the enemy. We want to know what you *all* are gonna do about it." Satisfied with Chance's angry blush, Alexandra marched across the room and claimed the seat Quinn had offered her.

Chance smarted off, "Well, we ain't here to plan no prayer meeting. No offense, Reverend."

"None taken, though perhaps it would be wiser to plan a prayer meeting than to continue with this crusade." Reverend Land shook his head and looked at the ceiling.

"Huh, you ain't no Quaker, Reverend," Chance retaliated.

Suddenly, Bryce clapped Chance on the shoulder. "Chance, you're wrong. Alexandra is not the only man left in the Corbin family." He grinned at their bewildered faces. "We forgot about Drake."

Alexandra tried not to let her surprise show on her face. "Who?"

"Bless you, Miss Alexandra, you will save us all. Come with me."

Bryce led her to the library. He threw back the floor rug to reveal a trap door. Chance held out a lantern, and Bryce descended the ladder. When he got to the bottom, he reached up for the lantern and with his other hand helped Alexandra down into the dark hole. The light revealed a large wine cellar with a cache of weapons and supplies piled in the middle of the floor: half a dozen muskets, three single-shot pocket pistols, a mace (for all the good that would do against a rifled musket), blankets, canned goods, two water canteens, and several mismatched shoes.

Alexandra picked up the mace. "What does all this have to do with me?"

Chance, who had followed them to the cellar, jumped back when Alexandra swung the mace. "Bryce, take that thing away from her before she kills somebody!"

"Uh, here, better let me have that." Bryce carefully took the mace out of Alexandra's hand and returned it to the stash. "All we need you to do is get a message to your cousin right away. Does he live close to here?"

"My cousin?"

"Yes, didn't Drake nearly beat Cass in the county race last year? Anybody who can ride as good as your brother is somebody we need for the Cause."

Alexandra scrambled back up the ladder to the library where Reverend Land was waiting. Bryce and Chance came up after her.

"We didn't mean to frighten you, but if Drake is truly for the South, we need him," Bryce pleaded.

"I'm not frightened, I just, well, what is it that you want Drake to do, exactly?" Her voice quivered with excitement, more than fear. It was one thing for a woman to take up arms and talk about fighting off the invaders if her intent was to shame the men into doing it, but it would have been grossly inappropriate for a girl to be openly enthused about going to war herself. "Reason I ask is, well, Drake is…shy and whatever it is you want him to do, he would need to do it without being seen."

"That's the plan," Bryce replied. "We need someone who can collect arms and munitions from the other secessionists and deposit them here without being seen. The enemy has spies everywhere, even amongst our own kin. We can't trust anyone, and none of us must be seen engaged in subversive activities. Were any one of us to be recognized, we would hang."

"And God knows what the invader would do to our women and children," Chance added.

Bryce continued, "Miss Alexandra, we need you to convince Drake to do his duty for the Confederacy."

"And for the liberation of Huntsville," Chance declared.

Chance couldn't have received a more enthusiastic response if he'd said "Remember the Alamo." Everyone present, except Alexandra, sent up a hearty cheer. What Alexandra remembered about the Alamo was that everyone died.

Chapter 5

A Double-Dealing Rogue

Behind the carefully constructed mounds of loan documents, maps, and shipping schedules that covered his desk, Elias sat with his feet propped in the only available square foot. Engrossed in a shocking work of fiction, he ignored whoever was banging on the front door. A few seconds later they banged again, this time so forcefully that it rattled the collection of swords and daggers that decorated the walls of the library. Elias yelled for Melissa, one of his house slaves.

A skittish girl appeared in the doorway. "Yessuh, Massa Elias. I'm gettin' it." She scampered into the foyer and opened the front door to a hailstorm of swear words.

Recognizing the voice of Prichard Benefield, Elias chuckled, highly amused that the ape would appear just as he was reading Darwin's hogwash. He tossed *On the Origin of Species* into the wastebasket as Prichard burst into the room.

"I take it you were unsuccessful," Elias quipped, keeping his feet propped on the desk.

"Unsuccessful? Me and my boys barely escaped with our lives. We'd all been goners if them bluebellies hadn't a-showed up and drawed the Confed'rate fire off us. They come outta nowhere, and them graybacks kept pouring outta them train cars like we'd stepped on a far ant bed."

Before Prichard could draw enough breath to continue his tirade, Luke entered the library, his face pale and taut. He plopped onto the chair in front of the desk. "I've never seen such a mess. The Rebels must have known we were coming for the gold. Then the Yankees showed up, and everybody was shooting at everybody."

"How come you seen all that when you was hidin' in the woods like a little coward," Prichard snorted.

Luke's face flushed. "*You* are calling *me* a coward? You skedaddled the second you laid eyes on Cana Ramsey."

Elias moved his feet off the desk and sat up straight. "Ramsey?"

Prichard curled his lip at Luke. "Him and a hunnerd other graybacks," he clarified, shifting his malevolent gaze to Elias. "If you want me to rob trains for you, that's one thing. I'll steal as much gold as you like, but I ain't gonna fight Ramsey for it. It's too risky."

Luke dismissed Prichard's declaration with a wave of his hand. "Prichard here has been listening to all the rumors going around that Cana Ramsey can't die."

"It ain't no rumor. I seen it for myself. That devil cain't be kilt with no mortal weapon."

Elias grimaced as he got out of his chair and took Old Wristbreaker down from its berth. He raised the saber to eye level and inspected the blade. The heavy cavalry saber had lopped off a variety of appendages since it had come into the Kelson family. "I assure you, Prichard, Cana Ramsey is as mortal as you are." He pointed the saber at Prichard's chest.

Prichard puffed his chest out, daring Elias to draw blood. When Elias didn't cut him to ribbons, he shoved the blade away. "I'm done taking orders from you, Kelson. You and your lily-livered offspring can go to the Devil!" He stormed out of the library.

Elias waited until he heard Prichard slam the front door before he placed the saber back on the wall. When he stepped into the foyer he saw that the portrait of Montague Kelson had crashed to the floor, face-down. Melissa was struggling to restore it, but she was too short.

"Leave it," Elias ordered. Melissa nodded and escaped into the dining room. While Luke bolted the front door, Elias picked up the fallen portrait and examined it for several moments before he stuffed it in the closet under the stairs.

Luke glanced around the foyer to make sure no slaves were listening. "The gold is gone. I don't know if the Yankees took it or the Confederates, but it's gone. What are we gonna tell the Council?"

Elias leaned against the closet door. "I'll deal with the Council. I need you to go to Huntsville. Ormsby Mitchel is the Union general in charge there. I want to know everything about him and what his intentions are toward Marlbridge."

"But Father, what about the gold? If we don't get it back—"

Elias strode to the door where Luke was standing and grabbed his shirt collar. "Now, how am I to trust you to get it back when you were the one who lost it to Charlie Whisenhunt in the first place?" Satisfied with the fear he saw in Luke's eyes, he released him. "We'll discuss the gold when you get back."

Luke stepped away from Elias and stalked off toward the back of the house. He paused at the end of the foyer and looked back at Elias, who was still within earshot but at a safe distance. "I know you don't love me, Father, but I do expect to be treated better than a slave." Without waiting for a response, he disappeared into the hallway.

Elias remained in the foyer until he heard Luke slam the back door. He had never loved the boy—he looked too much like his mother—but he was his heir, and Elias intended to make a cunning businessman out of him yet, even if it required beating some sense into him.

Returning to the library, Elias halted in the doorway. The front window was open, and Cana Ramsey was sitting in his chair, smoking one of his cigars. His feet were propped on the desk in the very spot Elias had previously occupied.

When Ramsey didn't volunteer an explanation for his presence, Elias stepped over to the window and closed it. "You swore an oath that you'd never come back to Marlbridge."

Ramsey exhaled a cloud of smoke. "From where I'm sitting, I've kept that oath, or does the town border now include your palace?"

Elias gritted his teeth. "What do you want?"

Ramsey rolled the cigar between his thumb and index finger. "Well, I thought it would be rude for me to stop by the Corbin place and not pay you a visit while I was in the area."

"What business do you have with the Corbins? I'd say they've suffered enough grief on your account."

"My account? It was *your* actions that almost got Cass Corbin killed today."

"What?"

"Oh, you haven't heard. The boy nearly got his head blown off in that train robbery you masterminded."

Elias poured himself a glass of brandy. Ramsey had already helped himself to a glass. "I didn't know the boy was on the train. Where is he?"

"I took him home. I don't know how safe he'll be now that Joab Barrymore has taken an interest in your town."

"Barrymore?"

Ramsey peered at Elias over the rim of his glass. "Don't act like you hadn't already heard that name from one of your many informants."

"What makes Barrymore of any interest to me?"

"He believes Prichard Benefield and his gang are the ones who murdered his family. If he finds out that you and Prichard are in league, you're a dead man." Ramsey finished his drink and set the glass down on top of Elias' cigar box.

"We are not 'in league.' Whatever Prichard may have done to the man's family, I had nothing to do with it. As for the train robbery, I was simply trying to recover stolen property and return it to its rightful owner. You're the one who's ended up on the wrong side of this thing, so I'm betting you'll be dead before me." Elias lifted the lid of the long rectangular box that contained his dueling pistols. "I wonder how much the Council would pay for your head."

"Evidently not enough or else it would already be mounted on their wall. Besides, you can't kill me, Elias. You swore an oath, too, that night at Storm Chase."

"Is that why you're here? To make sure I haven't forgotten?" Elias replied with a bitter edge to his voice.

Ramsey relinquished Elias' chair, came around to the front of the desk, and closed the lid of the gun box. "I came here to warn you."

Long after Ramsey left, Elias sat at his desk, flipping through the deck of playing cards that he always kept within reach. He had never thought of himself as the savior of Marlbridge, and he would reject the anointing right up to the end. As he mulled over his schemes, he concluded that the job might fall to him anyway. As twilight began to set in, Elias extinguished the nub of his cigar and hollered for Melissa to put more oil in the lamp.

Chapter 6

Man of War

THE sun was beginning to set as Alexandra stared down the long, dark drive. If she hadn't believed her mission was necessary to save her town, she would have turned her horse around and headed straight for home as fast as Shadow could run. Storm Chase was the last place on earth she wanted to be when the sun went down.

Shadow ducked his head and turned his ears out as was his custom whenever Alexandra asked him to go somewhere he didn't want to go. He started to back away, but Alexandra turned him in a circle and gave him a firm kick. He snorted and shook his head. Alexandra hated using the crop on him, but every once in a while a good crack on the rump was the only tactic that worked.

Shadow sprang into a gallop. By the time they reached the front of the mansion, Shadow was so out of sorts that he didn't wait for Alexandra to dismount before he buried his head in the nearest clump of grass.

Alexandra tied Shadow to the hitching post and retrieved the large sack she had strapped onto the saddle. She heaved the sack over her shoulder and stepped onto the porch. The humidity had caused the door to swell, and it took her full weight to push it open. As the heavy door swung inward, a gust of wind swept through the foyer. The mansion creaked and groaned like an aged man-o-war left too long at sea. Alexandra crossed the threshold, keeping her eyes on the floor so as to avoid the gigantic portrait of Cranston Ramsey that loomed over the foyer.

Thus far, her first mission as Drake had not been difficult except that her backside was a little sore from spending the whole day riding all over the countryside collecting weapons and munitions. Any secessionist who wanted to contribute to the growing arsenal at Storm Chase informed Pop Brady by way of a note with the location of their contribution. No items were listed in case a nosy Unionist intercepted the note. They hid the note in the bills they handed Pop Brady when they made purchases. Pop Brady gave Alexandra the note hidden in a sack of candy sticks. Everyone assumed Alexandra delivered the note to Drake, so Drake could pick up the contribution and deliver it to Storm Chase.

The most difficult problem for Alexandra had been concocting a believable story to explain her whereabouts. While it wasn't unusual for Alexandra to go for a ride in the late afternoon, she always returned before dark. Anticipating that it might be later in the evening before she completed her mission, she had told her mother that she was going to a prayer meeting. It didn't occur to her until later that Laura Catherine could easily catch her in the lie the next time she paid Mrs. Land a visit. Mrs. Land was not one of Laura Catherine's preferred confidants, but being associated with the preacher's wife was good for keeping up appearances.

Alexandra took a deep breath as she opened the trap door in the library and descended the ladder. It was too late to worry about getting caught now when she was so close to fulfilling her duty. She placed the weapons with the rest of the stash in the cellar and climbed back up to the library floor.

When she started to pull the rug back over the trap door, she noticed the large blood stain on the bare floorboards in front of the desk. It was so large that she wondered how she hadn't seen it the last time she had been in this room. She wished she hadn't seen it because she knew whose blood it was. In all the years that had passed, she had not allowed herself to grieve over the loss of something that she couldn't bring back, and she resisted the impulse to grieve now. She secured her resolve with a deep breath and threw the rug back in place.

She thought she heard a noise outside, so she walked around the desk to the window. There she saw a second blood stain. Someone had replaced the window years ago, but fingers of dried blood still darkened the wall beneath the sill. This must have been where Miles Ramsey was standing when he shot himself. Everyone thought Miles was a coward for taking his own life, but it was a small comfort to Alexandra to know that Miles at least had the decency to admit he had no right to live after he murdered her father. She was glad there hadn't been a trial. She couldn't bear the thought of Miles Ramsey begging her to forgive him. It would have disgusted her to see her father's murderer pleading for mercy and then swinging from a rope like a hog shank. A man such as that could not have gotten the best of Jonas Corbin.

Alexandra eased down onto a settee and leaned her head back. She hadn't cried since she was eight. It was that last day in the cotton field when her father, the sheriff, told her to be a big girl and not cry. He was going out to settle a dispute between the Kelsons and the Ramseys, but she need not worry. He would be back in time for supper, and he just might tell a war story or two afterward, if her mother allowed it.

The neighbors must have thought her a strange, hardhearted little girl who did not weep at her dear father's funeral. It wasn't that she resisted the urge to cry; the tears just never came, and they didn't come now.

In the quiet, she heard Shadow snort, and it wasn't the snort he made when he was happy. She slipped into the parlor to peek out the front window. Another horse was standing in the yard. As striking as he was with his black mane and tail offsetting his light gray coat, it was his demeanor that drew Alexandra's attention.

Shadow was not the kind of horse to spook easy, but even he was a little nervy around the Ramsey premises. This horse remained at ease even when an owl flew out of the trees and perched on the exposed rafters of the chicken coop. The flex of his muscles, the expression in his eyes, and the way he held his head gave Alexandra the impression that no matter what sort of man or beast came after him, he would sooner charge than run. He reminded her of her father's horse, Ginger. The saddle and tack confirmed it. He was a war horse.

A floorboard creaked. Alexandra drew her Colt pocket pistol and stepped lightly toward the foyer. She hoped that the horse belonged to Bryce or Chance or one of the other young men from Marlbridge, but that was unlikely. He was too calm to be of interest to her men-at-arms who preferred mounts with more "spirit" than sense.

Alexandra had never been afraid of any man, but she also hadn't been around enough of them to be a good judge of their intentions. If the stranger in the house was a Yankee, he might be out for vengeance against any Southerner, male or female. Especially a female. A helpless female. Then Alexandra remembered that she was wearing pants and carrying a gun. If he attacked her, she could just shoot him.

Her confidence abandoned her the moment she stepped into the foyer and felt the cold barrel of a revolver settle into the back of her neck.

"Who are you, and what are you doing in my house?" the man growled close to Alexandra's ear. When she didn't answer, he shoved her so hard that she fell.

The impact of the fall knocked the gun from her hand. She reached for it.

"Leave it," he warned.

She pulled her hand away from the gun.

"Get up."

Alexandra struggled to her feet, trying not to appear as scared as she was feeling. Before she faced him, she tucked a loose strand of hair back into her hat, praying that he hadn't seen it. When she finally turned around, she didn't know what face she had been expecting to see, but she had not expected the one she saw. Beneath the dirt and blood, he was almost as striking as his horse. He had coal-black hair and close-set blue eyes, one of which was just a hair off-centered, adding a sinister glint to his appearance. He was wearing Confederate gray, a cavalryman by the cut of his boots. One of the captain's bars on his shoulder had come loose, and the front of his uniform was covered in blood; though, he didn't appear to be wounded.

Alexandra's heart beat with greater force as he walked toward her, but it wasn't outright fear that kept her in her place. She had revered Cana Ramsey ever since that day she had run into him at Pop Brady's when she was a kid. He had been standing at the counter. She had been running from her brother's stick sword, and Cana Ramsey had caught her when she tripped and almost fell at his feet. Then, he had bought her a candy stick and smiled at her before he left the store with that brand new Colt Dragoon.

Despite the fact that it was probably the very same Colt Dragoon he was now aiming at her chest, she felt relieved. It was as if she was eight again and he was sixteen and her father was alive and Cass was with her and everything was as it should be.

Keeping his eyes on her, Ramsey reached down and picked up her gun. "You ride with Prichard Benefield?"

Taken off guard by the absurdity of the idea and wondering what Prichard Benefield had to do with anything, Alexandra crinkled her nose and huffed, "If by 'riding with him' you mean beating him in the county horserace then I guess so, but that's the extent of it."

Apparently satisfied with her answer, he released the hammer of his revolver. "What are you doing out here?"

She hesitated. If she told him the truth, he would certainly take the weapons for the army, and the town would be defenseless. If she lied, he would probably know it, and she would be defenseless. Figuring that he would take the weapons no matter what she did, she proceeded with the truth. "I've been helping the Home Guard store arms under the floor in the library. There's a secret door."

"I know about the door. This was my house."

"Then why did you abandon it?" she snapped. Alexandra had thought about this moment for twelve years: what she would say to Cana Ramsey the next time she saw him. He had run away the night her father died. When Marlbridge needed him, he had run away. She had overheard her father tell her mother on more than one occasion that Cana Ramsey would make a fine sheriff when he grew up. Well, he was grown now, standing there in the dark with his gun in her face. It never entered her mind that he might shoot her.

"Do you know who I am?" he asked.

Alexandra jerked her head at the portrait of Cranston Ramsey.

"I'm not Cranston Ramsey."

"I meant, you are obviously a Ramsey. Since Cana is the only one left, you must be him."

He lowered his revolver as he circled her, but he didn't holster it. "You're a healthy-looking lad. Why aren't you fighting for your country on the battlefield instead of riding around playing Swamp Fox?"

Alexandra had almost forgotten she was supposed to be a boy.

Until Ramsey called her out for not fighting like a man, she had never felt like a coward. Of course, Ramsey wouldn't have expected such a thing of her if he had known she was a girl, but that didn't make Alexandra feel any less ashamed. That day at Pop Brady's when she'd told him how she got her black eye in a schoolyard fight with Braxton Benefield, Prichard's youngest brother, Ramsey had been impressed by her fighting spirit. She wanted to impress him now, but the look on his face convinced her that would be impossible. Yet, she still had one last hope to prove she wasn't afraid to fight. "I've heard the enemy is coming to subjugate us."

She waited for him to tell her how he was going to save their town from the invaders, so she could volunteer to join him. When he didn't say more, she prompted him. "Well, aren't you here to stop them?"

He walked toward the library but paused at the door. "No."

Surely he didn't mean that. "Captain Ramsey—"

He disappeared into the library.

Alexandra went in after him. "Captain Ramsey, there are some still here who want to fight, and I'm one of them. We've been storing up arms and supplies—"

As if he hadn't heard her, he asked, "Did you know Jonas Corbin?"

"He was my—" Alexandra caught herself. "My uncle. I'm Drake Corbin."

Ramsey looked down at the rug. "Sheriff Corbin was a good man."

Giving in to a little more honesty than she intended, she replied, "I wish he were here now."

He acknowledged her statement with a slight nod. If she hadn't been so desperate to prove herself, she would have realized sooner that standing in the room where his father had killed hers must have had some effect on him.

Ramsey kicked the rug back and opened the trap door. "Bring the lantern."

Alexandra obeyed and followed Ramsey into the cellar.

Seemingly unimpressed with the small stash of weapons and supplies, Ramsey turned his attention to the wine cupboard. While Alexandra held the lantern, he began sorting through the bottles, examining each label before he returned the bottles to the cupboard. He was about to go to the next shelf when he stopped, cocked his head, and peered into the back corner of the cupboard. He reached in and retrieved a sack. The sack caught on a nail and several oddly marked gold pieces spilled out onto his boots.

Before Alexandra could react, Ramsey dropped the sack and seized her by the throat. "You lied about riding with Prichard Benefield."

Not knowing what he was talking about, Alexandra declared, "I wasn't lying. I really did beat him in the race last year. Ask anybody."

Ramsey loosened his grip, but not enough to make Alexandra feel any safer. "Where did you get the gold?"

"I don't know where it came from. I've never seen it before."

He shoved her against the wall. "Tell me where you got the gold, or it will be your name on the next casualty report. *If* they find your body."

When Ramsey placed his Colt under Alexandra's chin, an action that should have frightened a girl witless, a well of anger burst open and flooded her chest. She grasped the gun barrel and shoved it away from her.

"Don't you threaten me!" she snarled. "The only reason I'm doing any of this is because there was no one else man enough to do it!"

Evidently her reaction stunned him. After staring at her for a moment, he released her and holstered his gun. He picked up the gold pieces and stuffed them in his pocket. Carrying the sack upside down so the rest of the pieces wouldn't slip through the tear in the bottom, Ramsey climbed the ladder and waited for her to climb up after him before he slammed the trap door and threw the rug over it.

Alexandra waited as Ramsey set the sack on the desk and paced the room. Finally, he stopped in front of the bookcase. After staring at the middle shelf for a moment, he picked up the book that was sitting by itself on the top shelf and swept the dust off the cover. As he thumbed through the small volume he asked, "You Alexandra's kin?"

It surprised her that he remembered her real name after all those years. "Cousins."

"How is Alexandra?"

Alexandra thought she saw a hint of a smile on his lips. "You know her?" Surely he didn't remember that day at Pop Brady's.

"A long time ago." This time his smile was evident, but it faded before Alexandra figured out what it meant. What he said next snuffed out any importance that the past might have had.

Ramsey closed the book and returned it to the shelf. "Well, Alexandra's your responsibility now, so you take good care of her."

Dread seized her. "What does she need me for? She has Cass."

"Cass was wounded."

She took a couple of breaths, struggling to keep her voice steady. "Is he—?" She couldn't bring herself to say the word.

"He's not dead. I took him home, but he won't be safe there much longer. Neither will you."

Alexandra could feel Ramsey watching her, but she didn't look up until he handed her gun back and said, "A lot of good men were lost at Shiloh, and they'll have to be replaced one way or another. Go tend to your family. When you're done with that, report to Bolivar's Tavern. Talk to no one except the Negro who lives in the back. His name is Mose. He'll know where to find me."

Alexandra did not wait for further instructions. She bolted from the premises, leaving Storm Chase and all its curses to Ramsey.

Chapter 7

Ain't No Cause

NIGHT had already set in when Alexandra finally made it home. She hesitated at the turnoff to the Corbin plantation, another dark oblivion stretching before her. Anyone traveling along the drive during the day felt protected by the oak sentries that lined the way, but at night the trees closed in on the path, some of their branches so low that they raked back and forth across the ground with a ferocious screech as the wind sent shrouds of leaves howling after any intruder. If she hadn't been in such a hurry, Alexandra might have waited a little longer to see if the dogs would come to greet her, but she pressed on. Shadow, who was eager to get back to the barn, offered no resistance.

As Alexandra reached the end of the drive, the moonlight broke through the trees and bounced off the white surface of the Corbin house. In truth, no one but Laura Catherine thought of the modest house as a bastion of gentility, but that was how Laura Catherine pretty much saw everything—an expression of the way life was supposed to be, dictated by the unseen hand of civility, rather than by reality.

Matthew met Alexandra at the barn door and took Shadow's reins. "Best gwone in, chile. Dey's all waitin' fo' ya. I see to da hoss."

Without bothering to change her attire, Alexandra rushed into the house. She paused at the door to Cass' bedroom. Most of her prayers of late had been snippets in the heat of the moment: *Lord, don't let Mama catch me riding in public; Lord, don't let Garrett see me wearing pants; Lord, help me not to punch Meredith Kilroy in the face even though she deserves it.* She had gotten out of the habit of praying about important things. She wanted to ask God to do something, but she wasn't sure what she ought to ask Him to do. If the Lord had a mind to take her brother away from her, what could she do about it? Maybe this was God's punishment for her not staying in her place. Maybe her mother was right: Maybe God doesn't think too highly of girls who don't honor their parents and mind their manners.

Figuring that God was going to do what He was going to do whether she had anything to say about it or not, Alexandra went ahead and opened the door. Lellen, a stalwart black woman whose freedom of mind and soul typically lay undisturbed by her circumstances, was bustling about the room, fussing over Cass who was in the bed.

Alexandra moved closer to the bed and spoke to Cass, but he didn't move nor open his eyes. Upon closer inspection, Alexandra was relieved that the wound didn't appear to be mortal. A bullet had grazed the side of his head, leaving an ugly gash, but due to Lellen's skill in the healing arts, the bleeding had already stopped.

Lellen pulled a quilt up to Cass' neck. "I cleaned the wound and sent Clarence to fetch the doctor, but it might be tomorrow before he gets here. Your brother wasn't the only one hurt in that train robbery." She shook her head. "A train robbery! In this county! I just can't believe it. These times we're livin' in. Lord, help us." Alexandra glanced at the bloody dressing Lellen had piled in the chamber pot. "Child, there's nothin' you can do for him right now. Best let him rest."

"Where's Mama?"

"I put her to bed. She was beside herself when that Ramsey boy brought Mister Cass home. And then you were nowhere to be found. I reckon in the mornin', Miss Laura Catherine'll be givin' you a good talkin' to. Somebody's got to. Ain't right, Miss Alexandra. Lyin' about goin' to a prayer meetin' then ridin' off doin' God knows what."

Lellen froze. Her eyes grew wide as she drew in a sharp breath, staring at Alexandra in disbelief. "You didn't! Don't you tell me you did!"

"Did what?"

Lellen brought her voice down. "Don't tell me you had anything to do with that train robbery because if you did—"

Alexandra gasped, "Lellen! How could you even think such a thing?"

"Because I know you like I know my own daughters."

Taken aback by how quickly Lellen answered, Alexandra huffed, "I know I've done some reckless and unladylike things in my lifetime, but I can't believe you would think me capable of robbing a train." She didn't dare tell Lellen the thought had crossed her mind when she first heard that the Yankees had captured the railroad. "Besides, do you really think Cass would let me be involved in something like that?"

Lellen seemed to be satisfied that Cass, who had never caused half as much trouble as his sister, would certainly not allow such a thing. "Still ain't right to worry folks sick. Shame on ya."

"I was doing my part for the Cause."

"Ain't no cause for a young woman to be out ridin' around at night. And dressed like a man. What do you think your brother's gonna say about you? Him out there on the battlefield where he's 'sposed to be and you everywhere you ain't 'sposed to be. You think he'd be proud to have a sister who doesn't know her place?"

Alexandra could have said a thing or two to Lellen about place, but instead she kept to the matter at hand. "What did Captain Ramsey say?"

"Not much. That boy never was much of a talker. He said he was sorry for everything that'd happened. I 'spect he meant he was sorry about Mister Jonas, too."

"What did Mama say to him?"

"She just cried and thanked him for bringin' her boy back to her."

As much as Alexandra wanted to confide in another woman about what she had been doing, she couldn't risk it. In many ways, Lellen had been more like a mother than Laura Catherine had ever been. Yet, as much as Lellen cared for her and Cass and would never hurt them intentionally, she was still a slave, and Alexandra couldn't risk the possibility that she might tell the Yankees about the Home Guard's activities if it meant her freedom. She felt ashamed for thinking Lellen would betray her when Lellen had always taken care of her whenever she was hurt or sick and taken up for her whenever Laura Catherine scolded her unjustly. Nevertheless, Alexandra decided that if expelling the invader was more important than her own freedom it was more important than Lellen's, too.

After changing her clothes, Alexandra made her way back to Cass' room. As she crossed the hallway, a man's voice called her name. Elias was looking up at her from the foyer. He laid his hat and riding crop on a nearby chair and leaned on the gooseneck railing at the foot of the stairs as if he owned the place.

"I would say good evening, but, well, it isn't," he admitted.

Not wishing anyone to overhear her talking to Elias in the event that unladylike speech came out, Alexandra descended the stairs until she was eye-to-eye with Elias. "What are you doing here?"

"I heard your brother was wounded, so I came to pay my respects."

"Keep your respects. He's not dead." Alexandra moved to leave, but Elias caught her wrist and pulled her back. When she tried to jerk loose, his grip tightened.

"I also heard a rumor that a group of rebels are planning to make trouble for the Yankees when they arrive," he said. "I've even heard a few names mentioned."

Alexandra raised her chin, hoping a show of pride would mask her fear that the name Drake had been mentioned or worse, Alexandra. "What does that have to do with me?"

"Oh, nothing. I'm sure it's only a rumor. Imagine a handful of rebels planning to take on a whole Yankee regiment by themselves. A regiment is a thousand—"

"I know what a regiment is," she snapped.

"Then you also know how foolish it would be to resist them."

"I'm sure caring for my brother won't afford me the time or opportunity to bother with the Yankees. As long as they stay out of my way, I'll stay out of theirs. Good night, Mr. Kelson." She headed up the stairs, leaving Elias to see himself out.

As far as Alexandra knew, she had no reason to dislike the man other than it was as much his fault as it was Miles Ramsey's that her father was dead. Miles had aimed for Elias, but Jonas pushed Elias out of the way. Protecting that sorry gambler had cost Jonas his life. If her rudeness offended him, she was sure to get a good night's sleep.

She was halfway up the stairs when someone pounded on the front door. She came back down to see Wilson emerge from the library and open the door.

Elias had gathered his hat and riding crop, but was still standing in the foyer when Johnsey Carroll burst through the door.

"Beg your pardon for calling so late, Mr. Metcalf, but—" Johnsey cut his words short when he saw Elias.

Wilson finished for him. "I suppose you've heard about Cass. We appreciate your thoughtfulness, but my wife and Alexandra have already retired."

Alexandra appeared at the bottom of the stairs. "I'm here."

"Might I have a word, Miss Alexandra?" Johnsey glanced at Elias and continued, "Privately."

Alexandra ignored the suspicious look Elias gave her as she left him and Wilson in the foyer and ushered Johnsey into the parlor. She sat in one of the wingback chairs and waited until she heard Elias leave before she let Johnsey talk. She watched him closely, finding it odd that he would call on her at this hour even to inquire after Cass' wellbeing. Of her brother's friends, Johnsey was the only one Cass had never fully trusted, and he had said as much to Alexandra on several occasions.

"How's Cass?" Johnsey asked.

"I can't say for sure, but I think he'll live," Alexandra replied, guarding her words.

"Good. I'm glad to hear it," he stammered as he plucked at a tear in his sleeve. "Where's Drake?"

Alexandra hesitated. Still unsettled by Ramsey's insinuation that Drake was a coward, she hated to put Drake's reputation in further jeopardy, but neither could she commit Drake to any more missions while Cass needed his sister. "Drake's gone."

Johnsey's dark eyes flashed. "What do you mean he's gone?"

"I mean, he's gone, for awhile at least. He has a family to tend to."

"I thought you and Cass were his family."

"We are, but—"

"Miss Alexandra, we need every man at his post. I can't believe Drake has turned out to be a coward. You have to convince him to come back and fight with us."

As much as she hated to admit it, Elias Kelson was right. "We can't fight a thousand men, with or without Drake."

Johnsey knelt in front of her and took her hand. "Miss Alexandra,

I know you can't bear the thought of losing another loved one, but you can't save Drake from this war. We need him. Look." Johnsey pulled a handful of gold coins from his pocket.

Alexandra gasped. "Where did you get that?"

"It doesn't matter where I got it if it can buy our freedom from our oppressors." Johnsey got to his feet and began to pace the room.

"It does matter where you got it. I just came from—" She stopped. She couldn't tell Johnsey she'd just come from Storm Chase. "It matters."

His reluctance waning somewhat, Johnsey propped his elbow on the fireplace mantel. "I was on my way home when I came upon a Confederate train under attack. I would have gotten caught in the crossfire, but Cass saved my life. He told me about the gold and asked me to help. That's when the Yankee cavalry showed up and Cass got shot. I thought he was dead, so I took the gold to keep it from falling into the wrong hands. Don't you see? We can use it to put an end to all this."

"What did you do with it?"

He hesitated. "Don't worry. I didn't hide it all in one spot." He stood to leave. "Tell Drake we still need him."

Alexandra nodded.

Johnsey took her hand. "Thank you, Miss Alexandra. Your country owes you a great debt."

As Johnsey left the parlor, Alexandra walked over to the fireplace and picked up the framed portrait of her father. Johnsey's words haunted her. Until now, Alexandra had never found it difficult to be herself and to do whatever it was she thought was hers to do, whether she was dressed as Alexandra or as Drake. Now, she was torn between what was expected of a man—to go out and fight—and what was expected of a woman—to stay home and care for her loved ones. In the end, she decided it didn't matter what folks expected of Drake. Let them think Drake was a coward for not showing up for duty. Alexandra would take care of her brother, for now.

* * *

The moment Johnsey left the Corbin house, Elias stepped back into the hall from the dining room. He smiled at his good fortune. He had ridden out to the Corbin plantation with no other motive than to see about the boy. Not that Elias blamed himself for the boy's injury, but Jonas Corbin was the only genuine friend Elias had ever known. He had promised Jonas the night he died that he would look in on Laura Catherine and the two children and do what he could for them should any misfortune befall them.

Introducing Laura Catherine to Wilson Metcalf soon after Jonas' death had turned out to be one of Elias' most brilliant moves. Laura Catherine was no doubt a source of amusement for Wilson, and Wilson's knack for sniffing out a good business venture ensured a higher level of financial stability than Jonas had been able to provide. Not once had he felt obliged to offer Laura Catherine any assistance. Until tonight. Moreover, it delighted him that his show of altruism had been so quickly rewarded with information about the missing gold that might save his life and Luke's. All he had to do now was play the right card, and all would be forgiven.

Keeping his eye on the parlor door, Elias made sure Alexandra didn't see him go upstairs to Cass' bedroom. He slipped into the room and clamped his hand over Lellen's mouth. Lellen struggled to get away, but Elias wouldn't let her go. He held her against the wall. "One word and I'll tell Alexandra the truth—all of it. You don't want that, do you?"

Lellen shook her head.

"So, are you gonna do as I say?"

She nodded.

"Good girl. Now go downstairs and distract Alexandra until I leave." Elias patted her shoulder as he released her.

Paying no mind to her place or his, Lellen smoothed her hair and her apron as she looked Elias in the eye and said in her usual deep, steady voice, "The only truth you best be concerned about is this: You touch me again, and I'll kill ya."

When Lellen marched to the door and flung it open, Elias chuckled. "You know, Jonas and I nearly came to blows when Grandison Kilroy put you on the market and Jonas outbid me. Why, I was willing to pay more for you than I'd ever paid for a champion thoroughbred."

Lellen raised her eyebrows. "Am I supposed to appreciate that?"

"Yes," Elias replied in all seriousness. "Because it means that you are worth more to your masters than I am to mine. Now, go on and do as I say."

The moment the door closed behind Lellen, Elias began searching through Cass' belongings to see if the boy had taken any of the gold. After a fruitless search, Elias was satisfied that the boy didn't have any of the cursed metal on him when Ramsey brought him home—unless Ramsey took it—but Elias couldn't imagine, even as reckless as Cana Ramsey could be at times, that he would be fool enough to make the situation worse than it was already. As much as Elias hated the Ramseys and all their offspring, he almost felt a little pity for Cana who, more often than not, gave his best effort to avoid trouble, but trouble just wouldn't let him be. As it stood now, Ramsey would be lucky if he finished out the summer with his head still on his shoulders.

Elias was about to leave the room when he spotted the framed daguerreotype of Jonas and Laura Catherine that was sitting on the dresser. He picked it up and studied it for a moment, wondering what Jonas would have to say about all that had happened over the past twelve years. He would no doubt accuse Elias of dereliction, but Elias was certain Jonas wouldn't have fared any better had he lived. The whole nation was rushing headlong into disaster, and no one, not even Jonas Corbin back from the dead, could stop it.

Elias set the framed image on the nightstand. As he did so, he looked down at Cass, and for the first time, he noticed how much the boy favored his father. He never thought he'd see that face in the flesh ever again, and the shock of it almost made him wish he could go back and set things right. Then, as quickly as the sentiment came, it vanished, and Elias was himself again. It was at that moment that an idea came to him, a solution that might take care of several problems at once. It was dangerous, but if Cass' resemblance to his father ran deeper than his face, it just might work.

Chapter 8

Invasion

ALEXANDRA opened her eyes when she heard a man yell out in pain. Garrett was kneeling next to her on the picnic blanket, blocking her swings with one hand and holding a bloody handkerchief to his nose with the other.

"Oh, Garrett, I'm so sorry. I was dreaming and didn't know what I was doing. Why did you let me fall asleep?" Alexandra pulled the handkerchief away from his nose. Underneath all the blood, it didn't look too bad.

"Lellen told me you have been sitting up with Cass for the past week, so I thought you needed the rest."

Alexandra gave him an appreciative glance. When Garrett had invited her to his family's estate for a picnic in the garden, she had at first declined, but Laura Catherine had insisted that she accept the invitation. For once, Alexandra was glad she had listened to her mother. Garrett's mother had spent a fortune on the construction and maintenance of the garden. The colors and scents of the spring flowers made Alexandra feel somewhat at peace in spite of her circumstances.

Her concern for her brother had worn her down more than she wanted to admit. While the wound itself was healing, Dr. Mills had said there was nothing he could do to cure the lingering mental incapacity. Cass rarely made eye contact with anyone but Alexandra, he only moved when he had to, and he never spoke or smiled. Heartbroken over her brother's condition, Alexandra had spent every possible hour at his side. She fed him, read to him, took him for walks in their mother's garden, hoping that she would say or do something that would bring Cass back. Yet, none of her efforts had made a difference. With each passing day, it seemed more apparent that Cass would be an invalid for the rest of his life.

Forcing her attention back to Garrett, Alexandra again apologized for the accident. "Does it hurt?" she asked.

"Yes."

"I'm sorry."

"What on earth were you dreaming about?"

She hesitated to tell him the truth, but considering that she had already punched him in the nose, she might as well. "It was the bear dream."

Garrett said nothing for a long time, and she didn't expect him to respond at all. He wasn't the sort of man who responded right away to bad news. After a few minutes, he reached for his hat. "It does not mean anything. Last time was a coincidence. Come, I will drive you home." He held out his hand to help her up.

Garrett and Alexandra remained silent for most of the drive back to the Corbin plantation. Alexandra could think of nothing to say except to apologize again for punching him in the nose, but as she had already apologized three times and he had forgiven her three times, she decided that apologizing again would do neither of them any good.

They were approaching the turnoff to the Corbin plantation when a carriage overtook them. As the carriage passed, Alexandra recognized Mrs. Porter.

The corpulent replica of Dolly Madison pounded her driver on the back and ordered him to stop when she spotted Alexandra and Garrett. "Miss Alexandra! Young Mr. Rainier! Have you heard the news?" she sputtered as she fanned herself with great enthusiasm. "There are a swarm of them, a mighty host, I tell you! They came in on the road, on the train, pouring into town from all directions! They are everywhere!"

"The Yankees?" Alexandra exclaimed.

"Yes, dear girl. The invader has come at last!" Mrs. Porter snapped her fan shut and brandished it like a dagger.

"Has there been any bloodshed?" Garrett asked.

"Bloodshed?" Mrs. Porter chuckled. "Of course not! Bloodshed only comes of fighting, my dear boy. I'd rather Mr. Porter be a coward than a fool. Can you imagine my dear husband standing in the line of battle?" She burst into a fierce cackle. "He would take up the whole thing! Why, the worst marksman on the earth couldn't miss him if he tried!" She wiped her eyes with her glove, and let out a heavy sigh. "Oh, thank you, Lord. I needed a good laugh. 'A merry heart doeth good like a medicine.' Well, I must be off. The world is coming to an end. Onward we must go. Goodbye!" She waved as the four winded carriage horses hauled her away.

Alexandra ordered Garret to take her to Marlbridge to see if what Mrs. Porter had said was true. He refused, thus dooming their excursion to end in a quarrel that ceased only when Garrett stopped the buggy in Alexandra's front yard.

"Does your mother have company?" he asked.

Shielding her eyes from the sun, Alexandra looked to see Laura Catherine standing in the yard giving orders as Lellen helped a strange woman tie on a bonnet. Alexandra hopped out of the buggy and made her way over to where the three women were standing.

Horrified, Alexandra dropped the blanket she was carrying. The strange woman was Wilson, disguised in one of Laura Catherine's old dresses. "Mother! What are you doing?"

Apparently unperturbed by the ordeal, Wilson stood quietly even when Lellen tied the bonnet a little too tight. "Good day, Alexandra. I told your mother it is highly unlikely the Yankees would bother with me when there are so many more nefarious rebels running about, but she insisted, of course."

"Mother!"

"Hush, Alexandra! Have you not heard the news? The Yankees have taken over Marlbridge." Laura Catherine continued to fiddle with Wilson's attire. "I won't allow them to take your stepfather captive."

"I heard the news from Mrs. Porter. Not one person tried to stop them," Alexandra grumbled.

Laura Catherine huffed, "Oh, I'm sure the McKinney boy left no mischievous deed undone. I hope you'll stay the rest of the afternoon with us, Mr. Rainier. I haven't yet decided if we will stay here and weather the storm or if we will go into exile with the other prominent families of Marlbridge. The Carrolls and the Beaumonts have left for Atlanta, but we have no family in Atlanta, so if we go, we will most likely go to Chattanooga, though I've heard General Mitchel has designs to take Chattanooga when he has completed his ravaging of North Alabama. I assume the Rainiers will stay? As you all are Unionists, I'm sure you have nothing to fear from the enemy."

"My apologies, Mrs. Metcalf, but I must return to town to ensure the safety of my family," Garrett replied. "Good day, ladies, Mr. Metcalf."

Alexandra snatched the bonnet off Wilson's head and chased after Garrett when he returned to his buggy. "I'm coming with you!"

"No! It is too dangerous," Garrett objected as he climbed into the buggy.

"What if they come and take Cass prisoner? He would die in a prison camp."

"Nothing is going to happen. The Union Army did not come down here to rob us or take our land or hurt us. Besides, if you are so concerned for your brother, how will you protect him if you abandon him to go off chasing your enemies elsewhere?" He leaned close to her face and whispered harshly, "Do you intend to leave your stepfather behind to man the home front?"

Alexandra glanced back at Wilson who was struggling to disentangle himself from the dress. Garrett was right. If she left now, there would be no one to protect Cass if the Yankees tried to take him. They might not care that he was an invalid. He had fought for the Confederacy and had surely killed some Yankees at Shiloh. She had already hidden his uniform in the false bottom of her wardrobe, but she had not thought to hide her own manly garments and her revolver, and she would need to hide the horses. The number of preparations she had failed to make in her initial efforts to conceal anything of value sickened her. She had no choice but to stay behind.

Chapter 9

Backwoods Caesar

Elias lit a cigar as he leaned against a column of the gorgeous Main Street home that had been chosen for Union headquarters. The Commodore Mansion was the second most glorious house in town and would not have been selected as Union headquarters if the Rainier Mansion, though superior in splendor, space, and proximity to all of Marlbridge's greatest amenities, had not been conspicuously spared the honor.

Marlbridge itself was of no consequence to the Union war effort except that it happened to sit right in between Huntsville and the town of Bridgeport, named and prized for the rail bridge that connected the town with Chattanooga. Elias had hoped to use his influence in Huntsville to keep the Union Army out of Marlbridge altogether. However, no sooner had the Yankees captured the Memphis and Charleston Railroad than small bands of Confederate cavalry and their civilian counterparts began attacking Union supply lines, firing into trains, and committing whatever other actions they could think of to harass the invaders. Their ongoing belligerence had convinced General Mitchel that Federal presence was required at all stops along the railroad.

Elias smiled as Colonel Manfred P. Heppinstahl, a rotund Federal with enormous muttonchops and mustache, flopped out of his carriage and bobbled up the porch steps. Yankee privates staggered behind with a load of trunks.

Across the yard, a horde of schoolboys led by Arliss McKinney darted by and blasted the invaders with rocks from their slingshots. Schoolgirls looked at each other to determine if they, too, were supposed to participate in the uprising. One of the girls picked up a pebble and tossed it at a passing Yankee, but it might as well have been a flower as it landed on the man's boot.

Arliss then unleashed the deadliest of all curses known to him, "Wait 'til Captain Ramsey comes! He'll show all you Yankee cowards what us Southerners are made of!"

One of the officers, Major Fontaine, dodged the kick that Arliss aimed at his shin. Fontaine, who seemed to take in the whole world and all its wars as if he were a serious university student caught in the midst of a tavern brawl, jerked the boy up by his suspenders and set him out of the way. The major brushed past Elias, scowling as he strode into the house.

Following Fontaine, Elias stepped into the foyer as the Commodore's grand library was being transformed into Colonel Heppinstahl's private office. He found the colonel pining over a map of Virginia while his underlings unpacked the trunks, removed the Commodore's extensive collection of books, and piled them in the closet under the stairs to make room for Heppinstahl's collection of presidential busts.

"No, no, no!" Heppinstahl wailed when a young private disrobed the bust of Lincoln. "Not that one. Put it away. You saw what happened last time. It took that wretched maid three days to get the tar off. Hide it in the cabinet over there. We'll display it if General Mitchel comes for inspection, but not a moment before, do you hear? And move 'Backwoods Caesar' to the forefront. These barbarous people love all the wrong presidents for all the wrong reasons. It seems they will forgive any man his sins so long as he saves them from the specter of the national bank."

The private stared at him in confusion. "Which one is 'Backwoods Caesar'?"

"Jackson!" the colonel barked. "When I was your age, I spent every minute studying the great men who built this nation. You should do the same. Now, hurry up with the presidents and after you've unpacked everything, report to Major Fontaine. He'll assign you the rest of your duties."

The boy sighed with exhaustion as he hoisted Andrew Jackson to a prominent position on the shelf and hid Lincoln in the cabinet.

Elias was delighted that the Union chieftains had selected Heppinstahl to pursue Federal interests in Marlbridge. He had the look of a man accustomed to luxury and ease. Before the colonel had a chance to burrow into his new office chair, Elias had already devised multiple scenarios in which the fellow could be maneuvered to best suit his own interests.

He dislodged a set of leather-bound documents from his coat pocket as Heppinstahl bustled about, wagging his finger. "I tell you, Elias, you must use your influence to keep these people under control. The president has invested me with the proper authority to carry out his policy of reconciliation, but these people will have none of it. Ungrateful savages. General Mitchel is none too pleased with how they've acted. And the women! I am appalled. If there is any greater proof of the evil of secessionism, it is the effect it has had on the secessionist women. I have even heard them speak profanity. To my face. And I mean to put a stop to it. If it is perceived that I have failed here in this dejected part of the country, the gates of Washington will forever be closed to me."

Elias glanced around at the pile of trunks already crowding the room before he responded, "But, then again, Washington is such a small area. Much too small for a man of your...social standing." He laid out the documents on the desk.

After studying them briefly, Heppinstahl raised his brow in conspiratorial amusement. "Elias, you put all the Caesars to shame."

As Elias finished off his cigar, Heppinstahl took out his spectacles and perused more carefully. After a moment, he looked up from the documents and sent his underlings out of the room with a wave of his hand. "All the estates listed here belong to rebels, you say?"

"Most of them."

Heppinstahl removed his spectacles. "As you know, the president's current policies won't allow inappropriate seizures of whole estates, unless there were to be an incident clearly demonstrating the waywardness of the vast majority of the citizens here in which case I would have to declare martial law. Even then, possession would be somewhat dubious." He patted the documents. "Now, I assume you've provided me this information with the intent of getting something in return, but if I were to obtain these properties by seizures within my own right what need would I have of you?"

Elias smiled. "I can make arrangements for all the beef, cotton, lumber, horses, whatever you need to maintain a comfortable presence. And, unless you have any inclination to live in Alabama after the war, which I doubt, you'll be needing a buyer for all these properties. Of course, the economy will be in shambles, so you'll have to sell for well-below market value. Even at that, it will still be a fat profit for you since they cost you nothing."

Heppinstahl snorted, "Cost me nothing? Do you realize what I've sacrificed to serve my country, traipsing around in this backwoods squalor of a state? If it were up to me, I would just as soon bid you Southerners good riddance, polluting the Union with your backward habits and parochial interests. My associates and I have a nation to build, for God's sake, and cotton can be grown elsewhere."

Both men flinched when they heard a loud pop. Heppinstahl scooted to the window, huffing and puffing as a light stream of smoke drifted in.

Soon after, Major Fontaine appeared in the doorway, tugging Arliss along by the ear. "Only a harmless school boy, sir."

Arliss puffed his chest out and declared, "Captain Ramsey's gonna whip you Yankee cowards to Kingdom come!"

Heppinstahl turned to Fontaine. "Who the devil is Captain Ramsey?"

Elias grimaced, "He *is* the devil, Colonel, but don't trouble yourself on his account. If Cana Ramsey becomes a nuisance, I'll deal with him myself."

With angry tears beginning to surface, Arliss hollered, "He *is* coming! You wait and see!"

Heppinstahl loomed over the troublesome waif. "You listen here, young man. I represent the full force of the United States government, and neither you, nor this Captain Ramsey nor the resurrection of George Washington himself can dislodge my foot from wherever I choose to set it. So you mind your ways."

Arliss sneered, "I know somebody."

"Somebody who?"

"Somebody who can make you leave this town whenever he wants just by signing a little ol' piece of paper."

Heppinstahl glared at the impertinent whelp more intently as he repeated, "Somebody who?"

Arliss paused to heighten the suspense before he spat, "Abe Lincoln!" He wriggled free and stomped Fontaine's toe. He delayed his escape just long enough to stick out his tongue.

Elias chuckled and picked up the documents. "I'll do what I can to alleviate your suffering while you're here, Colonel. This is my town after all. If you play nice, I might let you stay."

"Mr. Kelson, your assistance was recommended to me by a trusted colleague. That is the only reason I'm going to take your proposal under advisement." He snatched the documents out of Elias' hand and dismissed him.

Chapter 10

Joab Barrymore

April 19

Just before dawn, Elias had woken from a dream, or at least he decided it must have been a dream. He hadn't had a bona fide vision since he was seventeen—the last time he'd had words with the Creator. From that point on, Elias and God had gone their separate ways.

Yet, as he rode into town early that morning, he couldn't get the images out of his mind. From a logical viewpoint, none of the images made sense, and Elias could have easily disregarded the dream as a bad reaction to something he'd eaten or drunk or smoked. He pulled a cigar out of his coat pocket and sniffed it. Nothing seemed amiss, but he wasn't satisfied, even though he had every reason to be: all of his plans were coming together nicely and no one had died in the process. Not yet anyway.

The closer he came to town, the stronger his uneasy feeling became. No one was on the streets, not even Arliss. The few Union soldiers who were milling about seemed nervous as they spoke to each other in hushed tones. Another group of soldiers with strained looks on their faces were hurrying away from Union headquarters. The source of their apprehension seemed to be the cadre of irregular cavalry assembled in the street where several civilians were lined up. Elias had made it a point to know the face of every soul that came into his territory, but these cavalrymen he had never seen before. The civilians protested as the soldiers searched and interrogated them.

Elias dismounted and strode closer to the mansion. He could hear Heppinstahl's blustering, but couldn't make out what he was saying.

Cletus and Tate were leaning on the short stone wall that surrounded the premises. Cletus spat a stream of tobacco juice nowhere near Elias' boots, but Elias paused anyway. Cletus drawled to Tate, "Yep. Won't be long now 'fore Ramsey comes back and takes vengeance on all his enemies in this town, and boy, does he have a passel of 'em. Wouldn't you say, Elias?"

"I don't think Cana Ramsey is fool enough to try it, and you're a fool for mentioning that name under the circumstances." Elias pulled the can of snuff from Cletus' shirt pocket and scattered the contents to the wind.

Tate croaked, "Who keers 'bout that Ramsey boy! We got ourselves a Yankee problem in this town, and we all want to know what you're a-gonna do about it, Mr. High and Mighty. You for the Confed'racy, or ain't ya?" He poked the air with his cane as if he was ready to run the Yankees through.

Elias caught hold of the cane. "I don't care about the Confederacy. It's money that rules the world, and as it stands, the Yankees have more of it." He left Cletus and Tate to their incessant jawing and disappeared into Union headquarters.

He had been pleased with how quickly Heppinstahl had become comfortable in his new post. The colonel had spent a great deal of his time as the commandant of Marlbridge experimenting with how he preferred his grits, and his appreciation for the culinary arts had gained him a small amount of favor, even from some of the secessionist women who were the first to figure out that as long as the Yankees were fat and happy in Marlbridge, they would be less enthusiastic to go out and hunt down their rebel menfolk.

As he entered the foyer, Elias spotted Major Fontaine sitting in a chair, holding his head in his hands. "What the devil is going on here, Major?"

The young man's face was pale and weary. "The Devil is what's going on here," he muttered. "We had a chance to diminish the hostilities among the populace. The colonel was even making headway with some of the women, convincing them we aren't merciless scoundrels."

Fontaine seemed genuinely despondent. Elias found that more alarming than the presence of more soldiers. The major was about as levelheaded a soldier as he had ever run across. If Fontaine was worried, it must be something worth worrying about.

Elias leaned forward to catch the heated argument going on behind the office door. The door was cracked just enough for Elias to see Heppinstahl slam his fist on the table, jarring his cup of coffee. "No! I will not stand for it!" he bellowed.

A tall, gaunt officer was standing at the window. Elias had never seen him in person, but he had heard enough stories to get a pretty good picture of what Colonel Joab Barrymore was like and what his presence would mean to the success of Elias' agenda.

Although the colonel's band of irregular cavalry sometimes served as a detachment of the U.S. 1st Alabama, they rarely engaged in anything beyond tracking down secessionist guerillas and "bringing them to justice," which usually involved a rope.

In the face of so large a force and in light of Barrymore's reputation, Elias watched Heppinstahl's fortitude begin to disintegrate. In an instant, Elias finished his calculations and concluded that to resist Barrymore openly would be ill-advised. He wasn't greedy, nor was he susceptible to the temptations that could be used to lure less determined men. Neither Heppinstahl nor Elias would have any leverage with him. There would be no negotiating, no alliances to forge, no deals to arrange. Barrymore's purpose was singular—vengeance.

The colonel turned from the window and peered down at Heppinstahl, disdain dripping from his jowls as he smiled curtly. "I assure you, Colonel, these methods that you find so odious are necessary. Johnsey Carroll, a resident of this county, is known to be involved in a plot to assassinate General Mitchel. The general has sent me to investigate. I have already discovered several of his known associates. They are being questioned as we speak."

Heppinstahl's mustache twitched. "Now see here, I have gone to great lengths to keep the peace in this town. So far, there have been no incidents that would jeopardize my accomplishment. If you stir up trouble—"

"I assure you, my intention is to eliminate it," Barrymore avowed as he returned to the window.

Elias retreated from the door and leveled his riding crop at Fontaine. "Don't tell me you all intend to let that madman loose in my town."

Fontaine flicked the crop away from his face. "That madman wouldn't be here if Johnsey Carroll hadn't been such a fool. So, perhaps, it might not hurt for the secessionists to get a little taste of what the rest of the country thinks they deserve for starting this whole bloody mess."

"Major, the people of Marlbridge are reasonable, and they can be persuaded with reasonable measures, but I know what it will take to break them and the rest of the South. I don't believe you all are willing to go that far. If you are, well, you might win the war, but you'll lose the South and possibly your souls. The men running this show don't care about that. What they do care about are power and money. Now, isn't that the real cause of this 'bloody mess'?"

Elias turned when a young man's voice called out. "I thought it was the Knights of the Golden Circle who are to blame."

In the parlor across the foyer, a teenage boy sat under a window. A light-skinned slave woman sat next to him, mending a tear in a suit coat that was so worn and faded it wasn't worth the effort. The boy turned his head when Elias crossed into the room, but his eyes stared off in the distance. Even when Elias approached, he didn't move his eyes until Elias stepped on the creaky board that was buried under the plush carpet. "You've been reading too many Yankee newspapers, boy." Elias waved his hand in front of the young man's face as he asked the slave woman, "Is he blind?"

She neither answered nor looked up from her mending. Her fingers moved faster, but they were too skilled to shake despite the tension evident in the rest of her body.

"My name is Thomas," the boy declared, "and I'm blind, not deaf."

"Oh, so she's the deaf one," Elias snapped, irritated that the woman hadn't paid him proper deference.

"Her name is Winnie, and I don't require her to speak to people she doesn't know."

Winnie's fingers were moving so fast that Elias failed to notice the discolored burn marks on her hands until she double-knotted the thread and snipped the excess with a pair of shears that had been concealed in the folds of her skirt. She eyed Elias for a moment before she placed the shears and the coat in her sewing basket.

Elias growled, "Suits me. I doubt I'd like what she has to say."

Winnie looked as if she was tempted to smile in agreement, but her amusement quickly dissolved when a shadow fell across the room.

Elias turned to see Barrymore standing behind him. He could feel Barrymore's mind analyzing every word, every move, every expression. He had seen that phony placid face many times on less intelligent men who had dared to sit down with him at the poker table. "You must be the fabled Joab Barrymore, professor of ancient history and dead languages. Surely, you must miss the confines of Tuscaloosa. I hear the University has one of the largest libraries in the South, if I'm not mistaken."

Barrymore smiled. "Our corpulent colonel informs me you are the man with whom I should consult in the identification of secessionists and their sympathizers. You are, for lack of a more suitable phrase, the chief public servant in town, if I'm not mistaken?"

"Mistaken, indeed. I am no one's servant, as anyone in town will readily testify, having witnessed for themselves my disavowal of civic responsibility."

"Well, then no doubt you will be relieved to hear that I have no need of your services. I find my own methods to be more...effective. Good day." Barrymore held his arm out to his son. "Come along, Thomas. And Winnie, the binding on my copy of *Paradise Lost* is beginning to look worn. I don't wish it to be neglected."

"Yes, sir, Mr. Joab," Winnie nodded as she gathered up her sewing basket.

Barrymore took Thomas by the arm and led him into the foyer, Winnie following behind. When they reached the front door, he directed his gaze at Heppinstahl who had emerged from the office and was now whispering furiously to Fontaine. "Don't fret, Colonel. It only leads to evildoing."

The instant his colleague left the house, Heppinstahl wagged his finger in Elias' face. "You said you had these people under control. You said this was your town. You said they were your people. You said they care about the Union. Well, I'm saying you better get your people in line, or that madman is going to destroy us all. While I may be amenable to your demise, mine is not part of the plan."

Struggling to hide his anger, Elias remained in the foyer as Heppinstahl retreated to his office. He snarled at Fontaine. "Listen, Major, I could cause a lot of trouble, but I haven't because Colonel Heppinstahl and I had an agreement. Rounding up civilians was not part of that agreement."

"Well, your civilians have been cutting telegraph lines, tearing up railroad tracks, and firing into trains."

Elias glowered at Fontaine. "Have they? Did you witness all these misdeeds with your own eyes or did Barrymore simply hand you a list of names?"

Not expecting the major to answer his accusation, Elias was shocked when Fontaine gave him a piece of paper. "It will do you no good to warn them."

Elias read through the list. Prichard Benefield's name was at the top. Some of the others were relatives of Prichard who still lived in the area. The majority were known secessionists who had no connection to the Benefield gang. They were marked as traitors for other reasons, namely their attendance at "prayer meetings" at odd hours of the night: Johnsey Carroll, Quinn O'Dell, Reverend Land, Bryce Calhoun, Pop Brady, Brandon McKinney, none of whom was a surprise, and none of whom caused Elias inordinate grief. The two names he had dreaded to see were not on the list, and even if they were, Elias had no reason to worry. He handed the list back to Fontaine. Barrymore had a son, and he was all the leverage Elias needed to secure his agenda.

Chapter 11

No Marions in Marlbridge

ALEXANDRA huffed as she sat looking out her bedroom window. Not one Yankee had appeared at the Corbin plantation. Evidently, her enemies didn't think Drake Corbin was important to the Confederate war effort either. Apart from Cass' condition, everything was as it had always been on the Corbin plantation since her father's death. Wilson stayed in his library, Laura Catherine fussed over any appearance of impropriety, and Lellen spent most of the day scolding one or more of the house slaves.

The slave population on the Corbin plantation was small in comparison to most plantations in North America. In truth, the Corbins were a few slaves shy of the planter class, but Laura Catherine refused to acknowledge her demotion to the yeomen ranks. While Alexandra had never thought to count up the number of slaves on the farm, she knew them all and thought of them as a permanent part of her life. She had never given much thought to whether or not they wanted to be there, until recent events had curtailed much of her own freedom.

In any case, she still didn't see what business it was of Yankees, living a long way off, to meddle in affairs that had nothing to do with them any more than it was the business of King George, living a long way off, to tax the colonists without representation, dissolve their legislatures, and send an army to suppress them. She hated meddlers. The nationality, religion, or color of the meddler was of no consequence to her. If God hated slavery as much as the abolitionists said He did, He should have put it in the Bible so there would be no question. Alexandra reprimanded herself for telling God what He should do, but she came by it honest. Neither her mother nor Lellen ever failed to let the Lord know when they didn't agree with what He was doing.

Accepting that she had done her due diligence as a lookout, Alexandra made her way to the library to select a book to read to Cass. Wilson was sitting at his desk, making notes on some Hebrew text by the looks of it. Since he married Laura Catherine, he had tripled the number of books in the library, and despite her frustration with his lack of fighting spirit, Alexandra shared his love for a good tale of adventure and romance.

Wilson looked up when she walked by the desk to retrieve Parson Weems' account of the life of Francis Marion that he had laid out for her. He gestured across the hallway to the parlor where nearly a dozen ball gowns were strewn across the furniture. "It seems there's no escape from the party."

Laura Catherine was out of sight, but anyone within ten yards of the house could hear her fussing at Lellen's daughter, Jenny. "But Miss Laura Catherine," the teenager cried, "There's nothin' nobody can do 'bout the blockade."

Alexandra flopped onto one of the wingbacked chairs. She hated the Founders' Ball, and this year was worst of all—Elias Kelson was hosting. "Surely in light of everything that's happened, we can do without at least one of our traditions."

"Lamentable as it may be to do away with an old tradition, I'm far more concerned that we may have established a new one—I'm told the Yankee officers are invited."

"I will *not* dance with a Yankee!" Alexandra sprang out of her chair and paced in front of Wilson's desk. "You have to talk to Mama," she begged.

"Tell her you have a headache unless you have employed that tactic too many times, in which case I recommend that you invent another ailment. There's the most recent medical tome. Third shelf, next to Newton's *Principia*. It's all rubbish, but might prove useful after all, if one wishes to concoct a conspiracy."

Alexandra scowled at him.

He removed his spectacles and wiped them with his handkerchief. "Beyond that, I cannot aid you in this endeavor, but, on other fronts, you'll be happy to know that your mother has given up on her fanciful notion that I am of any importance to the enemy and has promised to never again force me to wear a petticoat. Furthermore, I now fully support your wearing pants when you go out riding. In truth, and I don't mind saying it, I firmly believe all women should wear pants when riding horses. Why, if a good wind were to catch one of those hoop skirts, I daresay it would lift the poor girl right off the saddle and dump her in the middle of the road."

Her mood unaltered, Alexandra tucked the book under her arm and turned to leave.

"One more thing," Wilson called out as he waved a new book at her. When she reached for it, he held it back. "I will warn you. It's about a governess, but a very interesting one, so don't scoff."

"I won't scoff," Alexandra yielded.

"Personally, I find the first part a bit boring—the plight of a poor orphan and her time at boarding school—so don't be put off by the slow start. Stay with it. You'll be glad you did when you get to the part where the heroine embarks on a new journey and meets," he paused, eyes twinkling with suspense, "Rochester."

Wilson handed her the book. As she flipped through it on her way upstairs to Cass' bedroom, she remembered hearing about the book years ago from the other inmates at Miss Daschle's School for Girls. She vaguely remembered Susan Walden rattling on for hours about Mr. Rochester, but she couldn't recall how to pronounce the heroine's last name nor the author's last name. Not that Cass would mind.

Cass made no acknowledgment of Alexandra's presence as she curled up in the bedside chair and read the preface to Weems' book:

> While memory looks back on the dreadful days of the revolution; when a British despot, not the nation, (for I esteem them most generous,) but a proud, stupid, obstinate, despot, trampling the holy charter and constitution of England's realm, issued against us, (sons of Britons,) that most unrighteous edict, taxation without representation! and then, because in the spirit of our gallant fathers, we bravely opposed him, he broke up the very fountains of his malice, and let loose upon

us every indescribable, unimaginable curse of civil war; when British armies, with their Hessian, and Indian, and Tory allies, overran my afflicted country, swallowing up its fruits and filling every part with consternation; when no thing was to be seen but flying crowds, burning houses, and young men, (alas! too often,) hanging upon the trees like dogs, and old men wringing their withered hands over their murdered boys, and women and children weeping and flying from their ruined plantations into the starving woods! When I think, I say, of these things, oh my God! How can I ever forget Marion, that vigilant, undaunted soldier, whom thine own mercy raised up to scourge such monsters, and avenge his country's wrongs...The fathers, of the years to come, should talk of thy noble deeds; and the youth yet unborn should rise up and call thee blessed. Fired at the charm of thy virtues, they should follow thee in the path of thy glory, and make themselves the future Marions of their country.

Alexandra snapped the book shut. *Future Marions of their country? Well, there are no Marions in Marlbridge*, she concluded. From everything she had heard, the invaders were enjoying their stay. Colonel Heppinstahl spent most of his time feasting on local cuisine, and the Unionists were making fat profits selling their wares and foodstuffs to the enemy who numbered close to a thousand by the latest tally. Not even one Yankee had ventured outside the comforts of Marlbridge to confiscate Alexandra's weapons or her horse.

Disgusted with the men and women of Marlbridge for allowing the enemy to swoop down unopposed, Alexandra tossed Weems in a drawer and reluctantly opened the other book, her chief aim being to disprove Wilson's thesis that a governess could be interesting.

Not wishing to know any more about boarding schools than she had already experienced for herself at Miss Daschle's School for Girls, she skipped the first ten chapters or so, until she got to the part where Jane is walking along a dark, lonely road and meets a stranger. Though the author didn't give the stranger's name at that point in the story, Alexandra knew he had to be Rochester.

When Alexandra raised her head from Charlotte Brontë's novel several hours later, Cass was looking at her. "Well, it's a good thing I'm not a gambling woman, or I would owe Wilson a great deal of money had he offered me a wager," she sighed as she stood and stretched her back and arms. Setting the book on the seat, she decided that she had stayed home long enough to fulfill her duty as a sister. She had to see the invaders for herself.

Alexandra met no one on the road as she made her way toward Marlbridge, not even Virgil Doggett, the peddler, until she reached the outskirts of town. A small group of men in dark blue uniforms were blocking the road, talking and laughing as if they were at a shindig.

"Halt, miss," the least unattractive one ordered as Alexandra approached. Shadow flattened his ears when the soldier took hold of his bridle. "What's your name, little lady?" he asked with a smile.

"Alexandra."

"Just Alexandra, eh? Don't you have a family name, or are you a poor little orphan?" he teased.

"Corbin," she declared. He made her nervous, but she wasn't about to let him know it. Shadow, however, made no such pretense. He tried to sidestep the man, but the man's hold on his bridle kept him in place. Alexandra patted Shadow's neck and scowled at the Yankee. "I answered your questions, so let me pass. I have business in town."

"Business?" He turned to his comrades with an incredulous grin. "What sort of business could a young lady as pretty as you be involved in, Alexandra Corbin?"

One of the other soldiers, the short, tubby one, snickered, and Alexandra must have looked as if she was about to bolt because the tall, redheaded corporal added, "It's all right, ma'am. Bevins means you no harm. However, I regret to inform you that we can't allow you to pass."

"Why not?" Alexandra demanded. "I've done nothing wrong, and I really must get to town right away. I have a family member who is ill and needs medicine." The sentence was partly true, and while she hadn't set out to purchase medical supplies, she had every intention of doing so now.

The redheaded corporal waved Bevins away and took hold of Shadow's bridle. "I'm sorry, ma'am. We have orders. No one in or out."

"Who gave such an order?"

The corporal grimaced. "Colonel Barrymore's orders. Trust me, you don't want to cross him, ma'am. He isn't as understanding toward the ladies as a gentleman ought to be, in my opinion."

Even Bevins spoke in a serious tone. "That's true, miss. Now, I like to have my fun with all the girls. Doesn't matter to me which side of the Mason-Dixie they come from, but Colonel Barrymore—best you stay away from him, miss. I wouldn't want to see any harm come to you."

For a brief moment, Alexandra considered making a run for it. They wouldn't be able to catch her on foot, and in spite of them being Yankees, they didn't seem to be the sort of men that would shoot a woman. Nevertheless, she thought about Cass and what would happen to him if she got killed. So, she complied.

Alexandra spent the entire ride back to the Corbin plantation chiding herself for taking orders from a Yankee. When she rode into the yard, Matthew offered to take Shadow, but Alexandra chose to rub her horse down herself, hoping the activity would keep her from dwelling on her failure to resist the enemy.

She had just finished the job when Cass appeared in the doorway with his out-of-breath manservant, Jasper, close on his heels.

"The minute my back was turned, off he went," Jasper explained. "It won't happen again, Miss Alexandra."

Alexandra smiled at Cass. "I'm just glad to see him up and about."

Jasper glanced over at Cass before he asked, "Is it true the Yankees ain't lettin' nobody in or out of Marlbridge? I was gonna take Mister Cass into town. Thought it might do him some good to see folks."

Cass said nothing as he shuffled over to the first stall. A small black horse with gray hairs scattered across his coat stuck his head over the door. The light in Cass' eyes changed, and he almost smiled when his old childhood friend snuffled his hair. Whether Cass stroked Prince's nose out of muscle memory or a deliberate action, Alexandra took it as a sign of improvement. She took his arm and rested her head on his shoulder. He petted her hair, and she kissed him on the cheek. "I wish you could understand how much I've missed you." When she lifted her head, Cass was watching her with a look of confusion. "It's all right. I'm just being a silly girl. Let's go to the kitchen and see what we can find."

Alexandra, Jasper, and Cass were just making their way to the big house when Bryce Calhoun came galloping into the yard and slid to a stop. "Miss Alexandra, I have terrible news!" He paused to size up Jasper. "Is it safe to talk in front of him?"

"Yes, of course," Alexandra replied, a bit insulted that Bryce would question the loyalty of any person living on the Corbin plantation.

Bryce still seemed uncertain. "Well, I hope I didn't cause offense, but these are strange and difficult times we've found ourselves in. At least one of our people has gone over to the enemy and another made off with a silver candlestick. I never dreamed I'd see the day when one of our own Negroes would turn against us."

Jasper didn't say anything, but the tightness around his mouth indicated he did not appreciate Bryce's speculations.

"But, if you are certain of this one's loyalty," Bryce continued, jerking his thumb at Jasper, "I will take your word for it, Miss Alexandra."

"Please tell us the news, Mr. Calhoun," Alexandra implored.

Bryce wiped his face with his handkerchief and recounted what he had heard about Johnsey and the attempts to round up "rabid secessionists."

"Selling out their own friends and neighbors!" Bryce fumed about their fellow Marlbridgians who supported the Union. "They didn't like it when we gave them a hard time when they came out against secession, but now, they are doing the same thing to us." He stopped to catch his breath. "Miss Alexandra, I don't mean to alarm you, but no one's seen Drake in over a week. If you know where he is, you need to get a message to him. Chance Mullins and myself and whoever's left are meeting over at Storm Chase to see what can be done, and we want Drake with us. We have to save our friends and family from Colonel Barrymore. We can't let the injustice go unanswered."

After Alexandra reassured him that Drake would be at that meeting, Bryce rode off to warn as many people as he could. The moment Bryce was out of sight, Alexandra ordered Jasper to keep Cass in the house and lock him in the cellar if need be. She couldn't risk the Yankees showing up and taking him prisoner.

"Tell Matthew and Clarence to hide the horses in the thicket we discussed the other day. And one more thing…" She waited to make sure she had Jasper's full attention. "Do not under any circumstances mention the name Drake Corbin to anyone."

Jasper nodded. "You have my word, Miss Alexandra. By the way, we all know about Drake. You don't have anything to fear from us. We do our own sneakin' around from time to time, so we know how it is."

Alexandra ran inside the house to get her pants and her gun.

Chapter 12

Captain Alexandra

Bryce, Quinn, and Chance were the only ones left by the time Alexandra rode out to Storm Chase. In her haste, she failed to secure the strands of hair that had fallen from her hat before she entered the house. She kept her head down, but it was too late.

Quinn was the first to approach her. He tilted his head to see up under the brim of her hat. When he saw her face, his big, dumb eyes grew wide and he grinned, the slow, cumbersome, sweet grin that everyone loved and pitied. "Hey there, Alexandra. Whatcha doin' dressed like that for? We thought you was Drake there for a minute. You're prettier than Drake though." Quinn blushed and ducked his head.

Chance punched Quinn in the arm. "Quinn, even somebody dumb as you ought to be able to figure that out. There is no Drake. It was just Alexandra the whole time." He sank into a chair. "Well, no use planning a rescue now."

Alexandra snapped, "What do you mean 'it was just Alexandra the whole time.' Everything you asked Drake to do, that was me."

"Just 'cause you can ride a horse like a man doesn't mean you can fight like one," Chance retorted.

Alexandra marched over to his chair and punched him in the nose. He screamed as blood spurted onto his shirt and hers. Alexandra wanted to scream, too, as pain shot through her knuckles, but she couldn't let Chance and the others think she was weak. She turned to Bryce as she wiped Chance's blood off her hand with a handkerchief. "Whatever action we take, I want a part in it."

Bryce didn't argue with her.

"So what are we going to do? Storm the jail?" Chance moaned.

"We can't be sure that's where the Yankees are holding them. Barrymore's no idiot. He'll be expecting a jailbreak," Bryce replied, adding a curse on that fool, Johnsey Carroll, for causing so much trouble and nothing to show for it except more enemy soldiers.

"Where else would they keep prisoners?" Alexandra asked.

"I don't know, but I have an idea who might. There's a guard post just outside town. It's secluded and manned by four Yankees at the most with no officers."

"Hey, we could kidnap 'em and make 'em tell us where they're keepin' our people," Chance added.

Alexandra slapped her handkerchief into Chance's palm. "A colonel wouldn't share military secrets with enlisted men."

"Well, Alexandra, if you're so friendly with the Yanks, why don't you just go ask 'em yourself." Chance pouted as he held Alexandra's handkerchief to his nose.

"I could if I wanted," she declared.

Chance threw the handkerchief at her. "Prove it then."

* * *

Alexandra could feel the guards watching her as she swam against the mild current of the creek that ran close by the guard post outside town. The rainfall from the day before made the water cooler than usual, but the primary reason for Alexandra's shivering was not the Yankees nor the cold water—it was the cottonmouths. The infernal reptiles would appear as harmless sticks before they shot across the water and sunk their fangs into the flesh of any living thing that entered their domain, man or beast. If it hadn't been for the dire necessity of the mission, Alexandra wouldn't have dared to get in that water.

She struggled to maintain a calm demeanor as she swam closer to the spot where the soldiers were hiding in the bushes. The one they called Kenny, an awkward eighteen-year-old by the look of him, covered his eyes in protest. "We ought not be here. Isn't right standing here gawking at her, Bevins."

Bevins, who was probably less of a rogue than he made out, observed, "A Northern girl would never go swimming stark naked like that. Who's brave enough to go down there and steal her garments?"

He popped the eldest soldier of the group on the arm. "I know you'll do it, Hitch."

When Hitch and Kenny didn't move, Bevins attempted the scandalous deed himself, but scurried back as Alexandra swam toward the bank and grabbed the towel she'd hung on a nearby branch. As unconventional as she was, she was not swimming naked as Bevins had imagined, yet her cut-off chemise and knee-length drawers clung to her body in a way that to uphold the rudiments of modesty, she wrapped herself in the towel before she revealed too much.

Concealing herself behind the old willow where many of her childhood games had taken place, Alexandra listened to make sure the soldiers were not approaching.

Moments later, she came out from behind the tree wearing her shirt and trousers. Bevins hooted, "Sweet Mary! She's wearing pants. I gotta get me a girl like that."

"Hey, isn't that the girl we stopped earlier?" Kenny asked.

Bevins exclaimed, "By golly! It *is* her. What's she doing?"

Hitch bopped Bevins over the head. "Sshh! She'll hear you, you buffoon."

Alexandra whistled and Shadow trotted up. The Yankees scrambled back toward the guard post as Alexandra swung onto Shadow's back and headed straight for them. They piled to a stop when they saw Bryce, Quinn, and Chance were waiting for them.

Chance grinned. "Howdy, boys. You know we don't take it too kindly when outsiders come down here and try to take advantage of our womenfolk."

Kenny shook his head emphatically. "We didn't see anything. I swear."

Bevins pushed Kenny aside. "We saw enough."

Hitch took a menacing step toward Alexandra. "You set us up, you little hussy!"

Quinn shot the man dead. Then he shot Bevins and Kenny as they tried to escape.

"Quinn!" Alexandra screamed, but it was too late. Bevins already lay dead. Kenny writhed for a few seconds, choking on the blood gurgling in his mouth.

Chance yelped in horror, "Quinn! You just shot them boys in cold blood!" Quinn coolly returned his revolver to its holster. Chance bellowed at him, "Do you realize what you've done, Quinn, you half-wit? You just made us all murderers!" He shoved Quinn to the ground.

Quinn looked at him with wide-eyed innocence. "I don't understand. You said we were going to stop the enemy. Doesn't that mean we have to kill them all?"

Chance howled, "Yeah, *on the battlefield*, where they get a chance to shoot back! You shot 'em like they were buck rabbits for the stewpot. And now, we're all gonna catch hell for it, including your little sweetheart over there." He pointed to Alexandra.

Quinn rolled to his feet. "But they threatened her."

"That was the plan. Alexandra lures them into the trap, and we capture them and extract useful information. Information we can't get now that they're dead!"

"They're not all dead. We still have him." Bryce pointed to the redheaded soldier who had remained at his post when Bevins, Hitch, and Kenny had gone off to the creek. In the meantime, Bryce had gagged him and tied him to the nearest tree.

Chance walked over to the soldier and removed the gag. "That crazy colonel has arrested some of our kinfolk. We mean to get 'em back. Where is he keepin' 'em?"

The redheaded soldier kept his mouth shut.

"Is he keeping them at the jail? Come on, Red." Chance patted his head. "There's a good dog. Tell us everything you know, and I promise we won't hurt ya."

Red raised his eyebrows. "Surely you don't mean everything. That would take quite a while. Are you sure you have the time?"

Chance drew his pistol and grasped the soldier's shirt. "Don't give me that lip, Red. You saw what we did to your comrades over there."

Alexandra pushed Chance away from Red. "Leave him alone. He's just a corporal. He doesn't know anything."

Bryce silenced them all when he held up his hand. A distinct, jangling sound was approaching down the road.

Yankees!

Alexandra was the first to make it back to Storm Chase. Chance rode up a few minutes later. It was another half-hour before Bryce returned with Red in tow, mounted on Quinn's horse.

"Where's Quinn?" Alexandra asked.

"I needed his horse for the Yank, so I sent him home on foot," Bryce replied as he pulled Red off the horse and shoved him toward the house.

"What if he's captured?"

"The Yankees will disregard him like everyone else does. Quinn may be a half-wit, but he's a quick half-wit who knows how to play the part when he has to."

"It's a wonder they didn't capture us all. Do you think they saw us?" Chance croaked.

"I don't know," Bryce groaned. "I doubled back to cover our tracks as best I could, but four horses all headed for the same place? Even young Arliss could pick up our trail. One thing's for sure: we won't be safe here for long."

They all sat in the parlor staring at Red who refused to answer any of their questions.

"What are we going to do with him if he doesn't tell us anything?" Chance asked.

Bryce threw up his hands. "What are we going to do with him if he does?"

Chance stormed, "We have to do something! He's going to tell the rest of 'em what happened, and they are going to come after us. Confound that Johnsey Carroll. This is all his fault. If the Yankees don't hang him, I've a good mind to do it myself." He glared at Red. "And kill this one, too, while I'm at it."

Alexandra pointed her finger in Chance's face. "You are not going to hang Johnsey, and you are not going to kill this soldier. I will not allow you to turn us into a bunch of Tarletons."

"What's a Tarleton?" Chance wailed.

Red spoke up. "Banastre Tarleton was a British colonel who didn't follow the rules of gentlemanly warfare to the letter, according to the colonists, that is."

"So we're fighting the British now, too?" Chance moaned.

"Different war, and yet, not so different come to think of it," Red answered with a smile.

Chance stood over the soldier. "I wouldn't be smiling if I were you."

"Why shouldn't I be smiling? It's evident who the commanding officer is around here, and she has already said you can't kill me."

Chance patted the soldier's head. "You know, you may have something there, Red. A fact I had overlooked until this point, though I don't know how I could have." Chance turned to Alexandra and gave her a mock salute. "Captain Alexandra, you're the dead sheriff's daughter. Why don't you give us some orders on what to do with this threat to the Confederacy?" he chirped, pointing to Red. "Or better yet, why don't you give us one of your enlightening speeches on what Captain Ramsey would do?"

To acknowledge his insolence would have only made him worse, so Alexandra took a determined breath. "We'll find Captain Ramsey and hand 'Red' over to him as a prisoner. He'll know what to do with him."

"How do you figure on us knowing where to find ol' Renegade Ramsey?"

"There's a man at Bolivar's Tavern who knows where to find him. If one of you can tell me where Bolivar's Tavern is, I'll go and take Red with me." She gave Red a threatening look. "He won't give me any trouble."

Bryce came over and put his hand on Alexandra's shoulder. "Alexandra Corbin, you are the bravest girl I know, but it falls to us men to set things right, not you. The best thing you can do is to go to the Founders' Ball tonight. If you aren't there, it will look suspicious. Who knows? A little brandy might cause one of the officers to reveal where they're keeping our friends. We need you to be our eyes and ears. It would be an invaluable service and, I hope, a safer one."

The blood drained from Chance's face as the magnitude of the predicament finally caught up with him. "Dear God, they're going to hang us."

Chapter 13

The Informant

THE hill that overlooked the town of Marlbridge from the south had marred the town's scenic view for nearly fifteen years since a whirlwind stripped it bare. It wasn't as vicious a storm as the one that had hit the other side of Marlbridge back in the early part of the century, the same one that Cranston Ramsey had lauded as a sign of divine approval for the construction of his own miniature Zion. The trees that had survived were decapitated and limbless, their shattered bark held in place by the vines that encircled their trunks. The young trees that had begun to grow back were just tall enough to conceal a horse and rider and had become one of the best places to hunt rabbits that took shelter in the briars, too thick in some places for even a small hunting dog to get through.

From his perch on top of the hill, Ramsey watched the enclaves of enemy soldiers that were stationed all over town. Everything appeared as he had expected.

A sergeant stopped a man on horseback. The man reluctantly reached into his pocket and retrieved a piece of paper. The sergeant examined it then waved the man on.

Two ladies in their late forties clutched their bags and hurried away as one of the soldiers hammered a notice to a post.

Further down the street, a young corporal was trying his best to get the attention of a pretty young woman in a yellow day dress. Taking his antics as an affront, the girl whacked him with her parasol. The damsel was rescued by a pack of slingshot-wielding school boys who ambushed the poor fellow. He chased them as she cheered them on.

Ramsey lowered his field glasses to check the time, but something drew his attention back to the town. He raised his glasses again.

A group of Yankees were driving a buckboard into town. Ramsey recognized the young major who ran out to meet them. He had seen his old friend one other time since they ended up on opposite sides of the war. It hadn't gone well. For all his good qualities, Marcus Fontaine was not the forgiving sort.

Fontaine stopped the buckboard and peered in the back. An enlisted man gawked over Fontaine's shoulder and shook his head. At that distance, Ramsey couldn't hear what they were saying, but their general demeanor indicated something had happened to one of their own and someone in Marlbridge was going to pay for it.

A hefty colonel came bustling through the crowd. He peeked into the back and nearly fainted.

Ramsey turned suddenly when he heard someone approaching from the woods. He relaxed when he identified the man as his informant. "I'm surprised you were able to get away."

"It wasn't easy," the informant muttered as he took the field glasses Ramsey offered him. "That's a lot of fuss over three dead Yankees."

Ramsey replied, "Yeah, they'll be out for blood, but at least it won't be ours. Who's commanding the garrison?"

"Colonel Heppin-something. Heppingrass? —stall? That's him leaning against the buckboard."

Ramsey took the field glasses back. He chuckled as Heppinstahl waddled away from the buckboard and struggled to pull himself into his own carriage. The horses turned and looked at him, appalled.

The carriage creaked past Brady's Mercantile where two soldiers were standing guard. "What happened at Pop Brady's?" Ramsey asked.

"The enemy found out too many rebels frequented that establishment."

"Did they close down the churches, too?"

"Not yet, but it won't take them long to realize folks weren't attending Pop Brady's prayer meetings just for the ginger snaps."

"Did they arrest Pop?"

"Yes, but I don't know where they're keeping him or any of the other prisoners."

"Who all have they taken?"

"Besides Pop Brady, there's Brandon McKinney, Virgil Doggett—"

"The peddler? I thought he'd be for the Union."

"He's for whoever he's with at the time. They arrested Lawrence Carroll soon after they caught Johnsey in Huntsville trying to hire a man to assassinate General Mitchel. I don't believe Lawrence was involved. If he'd known, he would have stopped Johnsey from carrying out that foolishness."

"Do you imagine any of them had anything to do with those dead Yankees?"

"I hope not. Barrymore is the one making all the arrests. If Bryce and the others were involved, he'll know, and unless God Himself intervenes, they'll be swinging at the end of a rope in a fortnight."

"You don't appear to be overly distressed at their demise," Ramsey observed.

"I used to care about the people in this town. But after all I've seen, I've only got enough love left for one person, and I'm as good as dead to her."

"She'll be glad to know the truth when the time comes."

"I'm not too sure about that. Alexandra hates liars, and I think I've done more lying in the past week than my whole life, and I wasn't all that committed to the truth to start with. Not if it meant saving my neck."

"Or your sister's neck."

Cass laughed. "Or my sister's neck. Come to think of it, I've done more lying on her behalf than mine." He rubbed his face and grunted in frustration. "I wish I hadn't listened to Elias. This whole charade was his idea to start with. He said if I wanted to live and if I wanted to keep Alexandra out of harm's way, I'd better do what he said."

"You took a risk contacting me. If Elias finds out your playing both sides, he's not gonna be too happy about it."

Cass frowned. "Well, Elias plays sides most people don't even know about."

"That'll be the death of him sooner or later."

When Ramsey and Cass reached the turnoff to the Old North Road, Ramsey paused at the massive gate with the ornate "R" on the front that loomed over the entrance to Storm Chase. He wasn't sure if Cass would want to follow him to the place where Jonas was killed, so he said, "There's something up at the house that I need to go back for, so if you want to go on home…"

"No, sir," Cass answered quickly. "Between Mama, Lellen, and Alexandra, I'm feeling a bit smothered."

Ramsey nodded and led the way up the long winding drive that never seemed to shed its fog completely even on the best of days. At present, it seemed even longer than it had been when he was a boy eager to get home to escape the shame he had endured at school. To be the son of a failed aristocrat was far worse than belonging to a family that had always been poor. Even in the midst of their disastrous financial predicament, the Ramseys still had more than most people. Miles Ramsey could win or lose in one night at the poker table what took most men a full year to accumulate, making the fall all the more tragic.

Ramsey dismounted in front of the house that had once been a haven, a memorial to the honorable parts of his family history. He looked out across the thicket of briars and white ash saplings that used to be a pasture for the estate's champion thoroughbreds. "I imagine Elias has sold all of his horses to the enemy at a big profit."

Cass grinned. "No, he hasn't. In fact, I'm surprised a cunning cavalry officer hasn't stolen them yet."

"That's because cunning cavalry officers generally wait for the opportune moment."

"Such as the Founders' Ball Elias is hosting tonight?"

"They still celebrate that?" Ramsey asked, incredulous.

"Every year," Cass admitted as he followed Ramsey into the house.

Ramsey shook his head. "That's because they never met the Founders. If they had, they wouldn't be commemorating it."

The floorboards creaked under Ramsey's boots as he strode toward the library. When he paused at the library door, Cass ventured, "This Colonel Barrymore, do you know him?"

"I knew him before secessionist guerrillas set his house on fire with his family still in it." Ramsey walked over to the desk and lit the lantern. Then he pulled the rug back to reveal the trap door.

"I reckon there's no forgiveness for that," Cass replied.

Ramsey stared at the blood stain on the floor. "No, I reckon there isn't."

Cass looked at the trap door. "What's down there?"

Ramsey chuckled, "What I came for last time, but I got distracted and took off without it." He opened the trap door and descended the ladder with Cass following behind. Ramsey walked over to the wine cupboard and pulled one of the bottles out. After examining the label, he put it back and reached for another. Just as he was about to reach for a third bottle, he nearly dropped the lantern when he heard a muffled voice. Holding the lantern in the direction of the voice, Ramsey saw a redheaded Union soldier sitting on the floor with his back against one of the support posts. His hands and feet were bound and his torso was tied to the post.

When Ramsey ordered the soldier to identify himself, the man squinted at the light and waited for Ramsey to remove the gag. "Which name shall I give? Lately, I have acquired several. My captors call me Red. You may do likewise if it suits you. Though I would appreciate it if you would cease from shining that light in my eyes. It's rather painful."

Ramsey set the lantern on a barrel. "Your captors?"

"A handful of rebel civilians attacked me and my comrades. Evidently, they thought because we had blue uniforms, we knew where their friends were being held."

"We saw the Federals bringing in three dead soldiers. Are they the comrades you mentioned?"

Red glanced at his fetters. "Obviously, I wasn't in town to identify the bodies, but I can say with certainty that my comrades are dead."

"Who did the killing?"

"The crazy one killed my comrades, and the mouthy one would have killed me if the girl hadn't insisted on keeping me alive."

"What girl?" Cass gripped the front of Red's shirt. "Where is she?"

"I don't know. She and her cabal tied me up and left me down here. They mentioned something about sending me to Captain Ramsey. Would that be you?" Red cocked his head at Ramsey.

"That's what people call me." Ramsey kept his eyes on Cass, who had turned away from them and was leaning against the ladder with his face in his hands. "What were they expecting me to do with you?"

"Well, I certainly don't know," Red declared. "I was not privy to their plans. If they had asked for my input, I would have told them to send me to my father instead."

"Who's your father?"

"General Belgrave," Red answered flippantly.

"Edwin Belgrave?" Ramsey asked, trying to keep his astonishment out of his voice.

"Yes, I am Edwin Belgrave the Fourth."

"What are you doing here, stationed as a corporal?"

"I believe you and I have a mutual friend: Marcus Fontaine. I enlisted under an assumed name. Marcus, of course, discovered me, but nevertheless chose to go along with my wishes. Though, I'm sure by now the secret is out. I hope your friends are far away from here. Heppinstahl will stop at nothing to ingratiate himself to anyone with political power, and Barrymore will punish them simply because he enjoys it. It's funny when those who have lost loved ones to violence turn out to be the bloodiest of tyrants themselves if given the opportunity."

Cass suddenly pulled his revolver and aimed it at Red.

"What are you doing?" Ramsey exclaimed.

"Get out of the way, sir," Cass implored.

"Holster your weapon!"

"I can't," Cass replied, gritting his teeth.

Ramsey had been in enough fights to know when he could talk a man down and when he couldn't. He drew his Colt and pulled back on the hammer.

Cass didn't lower his weapon. "He knows about Alexandra."

Ramsey glanced at Red. "You've met Alexandra? I'm surprised she didn't shoot you."

"On the contrary, she was the most levelheaded of the bunch, and they all did as she commanded." Red eyed Cass' gun. "If I may offer my perspective on the matter, I propose that you let me go to my father. I will testify on behalf of your friends, all except the crazy one who will have to answer for his deeds. Nothing can be done to prevent that, but once I make known to my father how Barrymore has terrorized the populace, he will have him removed. You have my word."

Ramsey waited until Cass lowered his weapon before he responded. "You expect me to believe your father will remove Barrymore simply because you asked?"

"If you knew the history of my father's relationship with Barrymore, you would know that my father has every reason to want him 'removed' and would do so now except he apparently doesn't know Barrymore is here. I was about to abandon my post to go to my father when I was kidnapped."

"You were going to abandon your post to save Marlbridge? I don't believe you," Cass growled.

Red laughed. "Heavens, no. I was doing it to save myself." Then he grew more serious. "The truth is, I was with the men who set Professor Barrymore's house on fire, and I'm sure that he, understandably, wants me dead. Of course, it wasn't until later that my associates and I found out his family was still in the house." He clenched his jaw and swallowed the lump in his throat. "We were told that they were away."

Cass narrowed his eyes. "If you're a secessionist, what are you doing in the Union Army?"

"I'm not a secessionist."

"It was secessionist guerrillas who murdered Barrymore's family," Cass accused.

Red snorted, "They always blame it on guerrillas or renegades or bandits because they correctly assume that no one will question it."

"Who sent you against Barrymore?" Ramsey demanded.

"I think you already know the answer to that question. If you do, then you know they are not very pleased with you at the moment. The only reason you are not dead is because of your name. Only a Ramsey could get away with unwittingly transporting gold that was stolen from the Council. Yet another reason why you should let me go: one word from my father and all of this will be resolved."

Growing impatient, Ramsey rubbed the back of his neck. "What does the Council have against Barrymore? He was a college professor before your actions turned him into something else."

"I'm sure you are knowledgeable regarding the Council's designs for certain parts of the Tennessee Valley. As with all such operations, secrecy is paramount, and when it comes to sniffing out conspirators, there's not a hole deep enough that Joab Barrymore can't find them. The man is a bloodhound."

"You still haven't given me a reason to trust you."

Red sighed. "I see. Well, do as you must, but to let me go would be a show of faith that my father would not ignore, nor would any of the other…powers-that-be."

"Maybe so, but I've always had a strange way of showing my faith." Ramsey cut Red loose then yanked him to his feet.

"Then the girl's faith in you is misplaced. When the rebels were discussing what they should do with me, she said, 'We'll find Captain Ramsey; he'll know what to do.' She must have expected you to do the right thing, but you're not going to do that, are you? Not that I blame you. You're a bullheaded Southerner. Can't tell you people anything." Red's smile was more good-natured than his words sounded.

"Why don't you try telling me something I want to hear? For instance, where is Barrymore keeping the civilians he arrested?"

Red rubbed his chaffed wrists. "If I tell you, will you release me to go to my father so he can come down here and straighten out this mess?"

Ramsey glanced at Cass before he responded. "You said the girl had faith in me to do the right thing. Then I can't release the only person who can clear her name, can I?"

"So, it comes down to a choice between saving the town and saving the girl. It doesn't have to be that way. I like the girl. What did you say her name was? Alexandra? I like Alexandra. She's misguided to be sure, but I want to help her. If it's a show of good faith that you need, then I'll tell you that there's a decommissioned boxcar at the train station in Marlbridge. I don't know what's in it, but it must be something of value since they doubled the guard this morning."

Ramsey turned to Cass, "Can you find out what's in that car?"

"I've already been gone too long. I'll have to wait until Mama and Alexandra leave for the ball. I can slip out then. If not, I can send Jasper. He's a slave, but I trust him. Besides, he already knows the truth."

"You're in enough danger already. No sense dragging anybody else into it." Ramsey paused to consider a brash idea. "Go to the ball. You might learn something, and you're gonna need an alibi."

"For what?"

Ramsey looked at the stain on the cellar floor where Jonas Corbin's blood had dripped down through the floorboards above. "It's time I settled things with Elias."

Chapter 14

Drastic Measures

ONCE Alexandra was safely inside the confines of her bedroom, she began stripping off her clothes. She had just stepped out of her pants when Lellen caught her. The older woman's placid nature had been tested more than once in the years she had served the Corbin family. She pursed her lips and shook her head as she looked Alexandra up and down.

"Where's Cass?" Alexandra asked, genuinely concerned at her brother's absence and also desperate to avoid any questions about her afternoon activities.

"Jasper took him walkin' in the woods. You know he always liked that," Lellen replied as she reached down to scoop up Alexandra's clothes.

Both women jumped when the door flew open.

Laura Catherine stood in the doorway. Lellen stepped on Alexandra's pants and slid them under her skirt, but Laura Catherine did not miss the intended cover-up and pronounced in her haughtiest voice, "Don't bother, Lellen. Alexandra insists on making a spectacle of herself. It's no use trying to conceal it." She turned to her daughter. "Do you have nothing to say for yourself? No excuse? No lies? Come, Alexandra, you must at least devise a good story, so let's have it."

Alexandra had no defense for what had taken place that afternoon. She was beyond lies and even farther beyond the truth, so she said nothing.

Laura Catherine insisted that her daughter give an account of her whereabouts.

Still, Alexandra said nothing.

Laura Catherine shook her. "We are in the middle of a war! We are held captive by an invading army, and you gallivant as if there is nothing to fear."

Alexandra shoved her away. "There is nothing to fear! What can those Yankee yellow bellies do to me?" She stretched to her full height, several inches above Laura Catherine's head. Truth be told, she was terrified of what might happen if anyone discovered her role in the deaths of those Yankees, but she couldn't let anyone see her fear, and she really wanted to believe her own declaration.

Laura Catherine rose to her tiptoes. "They are not schoolboys, Alexandra. They are grown men, devoid of Southern sensibility."

"If you are concerned about my attire, I would think they'd have a harder time getting my pants off than lifting my skirt."

Laura Catherine didn't blink. "Lellen, gather up Alexandra's inappropriate clothing and burn them."

As Lellen scooped up the clothes, Alexandra flung open her hope chest, yanked out a wad of lace and linens, and tossed the whole pile at Lellen as she roared, "Burn this, too!"

Laura Catherine lifted her chin and snipped, "You want to destroy everything for which I have worked so hard? You do it yourself." She retrieved the bundle from Lellen and shoved it into Alexandra's hands. "Lellen is too respectable for such ungrateful, thoughtless rebellion."

Still clutching the wad of lace and linens, Alexandra flopped onto the bed as her mother whirled out of the room. Lellen scolded her with her eyes and jerked a nod at the trunk. Alexandra tossed the billowing heap into the trunk.

A little while later, Alexandra emerged from somewhere within the trappings of a green dress and petticoat. Her transformation from Drake, the brilliant war hero, to Alexandra, the lackluster wallflower, was almost complete. She fluffed the dress, and with a pout as good as any Meredith Kilroy herself could have given, she remarked to Lellen, "Well, whatever my imperfections, nobody could find them in all this fluff."

Lellen fastened the buttons in the back. "Reckon that's why that fluff is so expensive."

Alexandra struggled with her hair as she grumbled, "Where is Captain Ramsey? It's bad enough the Yankees made it this far. Now we have to eat with them and dance with them and pretend to like them." If only she had been born a man and a few generations earlier. The war between the Americans and the British seemed so much simpler than this new war.

With her dress and hair finally situated, Alexandra sat at the window and stared out across the dirt field to see Prudence, Lellen's youngest daughter, struggling to carry a yoke of water buckets to some field hands. When she tripped and spilled some, her father, Clarence, a powerfully-built black man, left the row he was tilling and trotted over to her. He bent down to help her up. She looked like she was about to cry as she dusted her skirt. Clarence smiled, patted her arm, and placed the yoke on his own shoulders. He handed her the dipper and started them off in a song as she followed him into the field.

From her vantage point, Alexandra couldn't hear the words, but she figured it was probably "Wade in the Water." It was one of Clarence's favorites and he always got a kick out of selecting a song to fit whatever situation in which he found himself. Suddenly, father and daughter stopped singing and looked toward the road.

A cloud of dust emerged at the end of the drive. Yankees! Nearly tripping over her dress, she scrambled to her hope chest and tossed the linens and laces aside to get her pistol. She paused at the door and ran back to get her handbag. After stuffing the pistol in the bag, she cracked open the door and crept into the hallway.

When she reached the bottom of the staircase, Lellen spotted her and waved her back. Alexandra ignored the warning, Lellen scowled, and both women flinched at the banging on the door.

Laura Catherine entered from the parlor and nodded for Lellen to open the door.

If the Yankee officer standing on the other side of it was expecting to meet a docile female, Lellen did not oblige. She had put on her angry mama bear expression and was now glaring Major Fontaine down right through the floor boards.

Fontaine gave Lellen a slight nod of deference. "Pardon the intrusion, ma'am."

Lellen gave no indication that she was at all impressed by his manners except that she opened the door wide enough for him to step in. Standing in the foyer, he kept the door wide open, leaving his band of Union cavalry in full view.

Fontaine glanced at Alexandra before he addressed Laura Catherine. "Is your husband home, ma'am?"

Laura Catherine stalked to the library and knocked on the door. Wilson peeked out, his nose still partially concealed behind a book as his wife called to him. "Wilson, dear, we have company."

Turning her back to Fontaine, Laura Catherine gave Wilson a ferocious expression that compelled him into the foyer.

Wilson cleared his throat as he introduced himself. "Wilson Metcalf. What can I do for you, sir?"

Fontaine furrowed his brow. "Metcalf? I was told this was the Corbin residence."

Laura Catherine chimed in, "Jonas Corbin was my first husband. He passed away. Then I married him." She nodded toward Wilson.

"Ma'am, I'll get right to the point. There was an incident earlier today not too far from here, and my superiors think your son might have been invloved."

Until that moment, Laura Catherine had denied anything was wrong with Cass, but if she said as much to Fontaine, she would put Cass in danger. As she fumbled for the right words, she peeped over Fontaine's shoulder to see Elias riding into the yard.

When Fontaine saw Elias, he pinched the bridge of his nose as if to stall the onset of a headache.

As Elias dismounted and led his horse to the hitching post, Laura Catherine took a deep breath and told the truth. "It deeply saddens me to say that my son, Cass, is an invalid. He couldn't—" She paused to regain her composure.

"I'll need to see for myself," Fontaine pressed.

Wilson spoke up, "Oh, I'm afraid Cass isn't here. I had one of the slaves take him for a walk. In his condition, a leisurely walk is about the only activity he's able to enjoy."

Elias stepped onto the porch and leaned against the railing. "It's true. I've seen the boy with my own eyes. He couldn't have been involved in…well, whatever incident to which you are referring," he drawled to Fontaine as he removed his hat and dusted the rim.

"Mr. Kelson, we have an eye witness," Fontaine continued.

"Maybe your eye witness didn't really see Cass Corbin. Perhaps he only saw someone who looked like him. Alexandra—"

Alexandra's grip tightened on her handbag. She was surrounded by her enemies, too many to kill before they killed her, but she was prepared to shoot Elias first.

As if he'd heard her thoughts, Elias narrowed his eyes, daring her to open that handbag. "Where's Cousin Drake?"

When Elias shifted his gaze to Alexandra's mother, Laura Catherine seamlessly adjusted her performance accordingly. She gave Elias and Fontaine the saddest smile in her arsenal. Then she waited for a single tear to materialize.

"I'm afraid Drake Corbin is gone forever," she sniffled. "He has abandoned his family and run off to God knows where. I am ashamed that he ever set foot in this house. Please believe me when I tell you he has gone from here and will never return. If he does, I will bring him to you myself."

Alexandra preferred to face her enemies head on, but decided, just this once, she should follow her mother's lead. Shrugging away from Elias, she reached into her handbag and pulled out a handkerchief instead of her revolver and gave the handkerchief to Laura Catherine.

"Oh, thank you, dear. You know how bitterly disappointed I am. What a scoundrel that Drake turned out to be," Laura Catherine cried. When she noticed Fontaine watching her closely, she sniffled a few more times to make sure he heard her distress. "My apologies, Major. I know how it must upset a gentleman such as yourself to see a lady give in to such an outpouring of emotion. I am thoroughly ashamed of myself."

Fontaine looked away from Laura Catherine's tears as if he was afraid he would either be compelled to do whatever she commanded or be turned to stone. "I am sorry to upset you, ma'am. If Drake does happen to return, it would be better to hand him over to me than to anyone else who might come looking for him." He ended the visit with a curt nod.

Elias waited until Fontaine and his men left before he announced, "Mrs. Metcalf, I believe you have a horse for sale."

Laura Catherine stared at him in confusion then her eyes brightened. One side of her mouth curled upward. "Of course, with all that's happened I'm afraid I completely forgot our arrangement. Lellen, go tell Matthew that Mr. Kelson is here to take Alexandra's horse."

Alexandra gasped, "What? No! You can't sell my horse!"

Wilson tried to smooth things over. "Alexandra, I'm sure your mother—"

"My mother needs her husband to restrain her!" Alexandra barked at him.

Wilson raised his eyebrows. "I might do that if I didn't agree with her. Mr. Kelson, if you will come into the library, we will draw up the papers."

Alexandra started to chase after Wilson and Elias, but Laura Catherine caught her by the arm, allowing the men to escape into the library. "Shadow was the only happiness I had left in this place," Alexandra declared.

Laura Catherine pressed her lips to Alexandra's ear as she snarled, "The little charade you call Drake is finished. We will never hear of that name again. Do you understand me?" She released her daughter and marched up the stairs to Alexandra's bedroom. She scooped up Alexandra's pants and threw them into the cold fireplace.

Alexandra lunged to retrieve them before Laura Catherine struck the match, but as the two women scuffled, Laura Catherine fell against the vanity. Alexandra reached to steady her. "Mama, I'm sorry—"

Laura Catherine held up her hand and righted herself. After checking her appearance in the mirror, she lit a match and set Alexandra's clothing on fire. "Lellen, Alexandra is not to leave this room until I send for her." She flounced out of the room.

Lellen followed Laura Catherine into the hallway and closed the door behind her. As Alexandra crossed the room to escape, she heard the lock.

* * *

Elias waited for Laura Catherine at the bottom of the stairs. When she came down, Elias ushered her into the library and closed the door.

Wilson had finished drawing up the bill of sale for the horse but remained at his desk. "Well, Laura Catherine, my dear, what's to be done about Alexandra? Selling her horse won't be enough to keep her away from danger, I'm afraid."

Ignoring Wilson, Laura Catherine spun around to face Elias and slapped him. "How dare you risk my daughter's life!"

Elias was about to seize Laura Catherine by her soft, ivory neck and say all the hateful things he'd been holding back for the past twenty years, but when Wilson cleared his throat and peered at him over the rim of his glasses, he restrained himself. "Laura Catherine, you and your family need to leave Marlbridge. I don't know what incident Cass was involved in, but if Colonel Barrymore catches him, he'll hang him as a spy."

"A spy!" Laura Catherine exploded. "That's ridiculous. Anyone can see that he's—" She gasped. Cass was standing in the doorway.

When Laura Catherine sank into the nearest chair, Cass closed the library door and came to kneel at her feet. "I'm sorry, Mama. I know I've hurt you, but I didn't know what else to do," he confessed, glancing at Elias, "given the circumstances."

Laura Catherine glared at Elias. "What have you done?"

"I promised Jonas—"

Laura Catherine cut Elias off. "Don't tell me about how Jonas was your friend and how you promised him to look after his poor widow and orphans. Your promises mean nothing, but I am interested to know what is so important that you would dare risk the lives of my children!"

"They aren't children." Elias wasn't yelling, but he was close to it. "As for your son, I didn't twist his arm. I even offered to help him escape. He was going to desert anyway."

When Laura Catherine gaped at her son, Cass stood and walked to the window. "I didn't desert. Captain Ramsey granted me leave."

"You failed to mention that part earlier," Elias said.

"Would you have believed me? You hate the Ramseys," Cass replied.

"Why would Captain Ramsey do that?" Laura Catherine asked.

"He said it was only a matter of time before the Confederates issued a draft. He couldn't do anything about that, but he could give me some time to get things settled in my mind."

"What things?" Laura Catherine stood and began pacing the room. "You have a duty! I can't imagine that you would even consider—Do you mean, after all my efforts, I have borne a coward?"

Cass gripped her shoulders. "I have to know that I haven't abandoned my family for nothing, that I haven't left my loved ones behind to chase after the wind. Did Papa run off to fight the war with Mexico without settling it in his mind first? You, yourself, told me how he agonized over leaving us behind to serve a country that wasn't half as noble as the blood the men in Washington were willing to shed for the sake of some unproven 'manifest destiny.' "

When Laura Catherine composed herself, Elias stepped in. "There's no use dwelling on decisions already made. What has to be done now is that you all have to leave. Join the other secessionists who have already fled."

Wilson took off his glasses, folded them, and put them in his pocket. "What good is there in deciding to escape when there is nowhere to go? The enemy has effectively split the Confederacy in two. They control the telegraph and the railroad. The blockade prevents any escape to Europe or South America. We might yet escape to Bridgeport and from there to Chattanooga, but already the enemy plans to lay siege to that city as they will do to Corinth and eventually Atlanta and Charleston and on and on until there is no place left. If we go to Canada they will find us there. If we go to Mexico they will find us there. So, I say, if we are to be surrounded by the enemy no matter where we go, we might as well stay here. Besides, like Jefferson, I cannot live without my books." He swept his hand at the bulging bookshelves.

Elias felt a smidgeon of satisfaction when he imagined an artillery shell striking the house, burying Wilson under a pile of literary rubble. He raised his eyebrows at Laura Catherine to see what she had to say.

"Well, I don't see how we can leave now," she snapped. "We are already under suspicion thanks to your meddling. No, Mr. Kelson, we will stay and weather this storm without your assistance as we have always done. Now, if you will excuse me, I have to prepare for the ball." Laura Catherine glowered at Cass. "I will deal with you later, but for now, you will keep things as they are. Your performance thus far has been impeccable, so you will attend the ball to keep up appearances. If you are caught and hanged as a spy, it will be your own fault. Furthermore, you will not tell your sister of anything that has transpired. Do you understand?"

Cass nodded. "Yes, Mama."

Laura Catherine left the room and slammed the door so hard that one of the overburdened shelves broke, spilling a dozen books onto the floor.

Elias studied Cass. "Can you keep up the act for one more night? Because if you can't—"

"I know. I'll be dead."

"I was going to say, if you can't, you leave for Chattanooga right now and take your sister with you."

"Why do you care what happens to us?"

Elias cleared his throat. "I already have Corbin blood on my hands. I don't wish to accumulate more of it, that's all."

"If you think blaming yourself for what happened to Papa is some form of atonement, it's not. How many people have to die before you'll repent of your constant scheming?"

Elias remained silent. It wasn't a question to which he wanted to know the answer.

Wilson intervened, "Cass, may I suggest you somehow let your sister know that you have returned from your 'walk in the woods' safely. She has been worried for you. That Fontaine fellow's visit has no doubt escalated her concern."

Cass nodded his assent and left Wilson to deal with Elias.

"So, Drake is to be the scapegoat," Wilson observed.

"Do you have a better idea?" Elias growled.

"I wish I knew the details of the incident in which 'Drake' was supposedly involved, but I'm certain we will find out soon enough," Wilson sighed. "In the meantime, I agree with Laura Catherine that to flee would only invite more suspicion, and rather than solving the problem, we would only succeed in transporting it to Chattanooga. However, I do know a ship captain who may be of assistance, but I will need a few days to make arrangements. I have no doubt that Cass will play his part admirably. The question is what to do with Alexandra. I'm appalled that the safest course of action I've yet devised is to lock her in the cellar until all of this has blown over."

Elias tugged at the strips of black silk adorning his neck. "No, not the cellar. Make sure she attends the ball tonight. After everyone leaves, I'll lock her in my attic. What heroine doesn't secretly wish to be locked in an attic by the villain of her story?"

"Elias, I was joking," Wilson protested. "I could never lock her in the cellar or the attic or anywhere else."

"It's better than a coffin."

Chapter 15

Fraternizing with the Enemy

ARM-IN-ARM with Cass, Alexandra strolled through the spacious foyer of the Kelson mansion, hoping to avoid the group of women who were huddled near the staircase, gabbing amidst a flurry of fans and peacock feathers. Ignoring their stares and whispers, Alexandra focused her attention on the design of the room.

Taking in the quatrefoil-patterned molding and the red-and-gold Medici damask wallpaper, she was surprised by how much she remembered from the times Laura Catherine had taken her to the Kelson plantation as a child and bored her to death with lectures on Gothic architecture.

She had just noticed that the portrait of Montague Kelson was missing when the front door opened, and Mr. and Mrs. Hanson Rainier entered, followed by Garrett. Alexandra moved toward him, but stopped when a strange young woman entered the house. She was tall and slender with long arms, one of which was wrapped around Garrett's arm. The girl stiffened in disgust and tightened her shawl around her as Raulston Porter, who'd had a little too much to drink, bumped into her, nearly pouring brandy all over her dress.

Garrett leaned over and whispered in Alexandra's ear, "Gwyneth is my father's idea, not mine."

Alexandra's back stiffened as she glowered at him. "Of course it was. I would be shocked if you actually thought of it on your own."

When Alexandra turned her back to the couple, Elias was standing in front of her. He spoke so near to her face that she jumped. "I don't know what he sees in that Yankee girl."

Before she had a chance to reply, Elias took her arm and escorted her to the dance floor.

The more sophisticated ladies always considered it a pleasure to dance with Elias Kelson. He was as smooth on the dance floor as he was in business and politics. Alexandra wasn't a bad dancer herself when she paid attention. She went through the motions, occasionally stepping on her dress, as she watched Garrett dancing with Gwyneth.

"I see you are still upset about your horse," Elias observed.

Instead of pleasing him with a show of anger, she stated reasonably, "Shadow doesn't belong to Wilson or to my mother, so they have no right to sell him."

Elias led her into another well-crafted turn. "You must leave these matters to the men, my dear. It is our duty to establish such arrangements for the security of our women, children, and property."

"As I am *not* your woman, your child, or your property, I will thank you to refrain from making any more arrangements on my behalf," she snapped. "Besides, I raised that horse. I broke him in."

"You may have done the work, but true ownership is always a question of property rights, outlined in appropriate documentation, which, in this case, you don't have."

"I will get my horse back. You can bet on that." Alexandra pushed away from him and left him in the middle of the dance without a partner. If it was documentation that was required, her best chance of finding it would be in the library unless Elias kept all his records in a separate office. When she entered the house earlier, she had noticed the library door was closed. At a gathering of this size, the men almost always congregated in the library. Whatever Elias was hiding in there, it must be important enough to warrant breaking custom.

Alexandra weaved through the crowded room only to discover that her exit was blocked by Major Fontaine and Colonel Heppinstahl, who had somehow squeezed himself into a comparatively small chair and was guzzling brandy, though he didn't appear to be drunk. The colonel glared up at Fontaine. "There will be hell to pay for this, let me assure you. None can escape the coming wrath. Even now, that madman Barrymore is out hunting the rebels down. God help them if he finds them, and God help us if General Belgrave comes down here and finds all this merriment while his son's murderer goes free." He consumed the last drop of his brandy and waved the glass. Whit, one of the house slaves, took the empty glass as Heppinstahl reached for another. "I don't know why Elias insists on such displays at the most inappropriate times."

Alexandra held her breath and wrestled with her nerves as she tried to ease past the two officers, but her skirt bumped hard against a table, pitching her right into Fontaine's arms. He smiled politely as he righted her. "I'm surprised to see you here, Miss Corbin. May I?" He offered her his hand.

Fontaine appeared to be a gentleman of the highest order. If she refused him, he would not cause a scene, but she couldn't risk arousing more suspicion. Nor could she pass up an opportunity to show the invaders that she was not afraid of them. She took his hand.

Out of all the dance partners she'd had, Marcus Fontaine surpassed them all, even Garrett. He led her so skillfully in the waltz that she didn't even step on her dress once. She almost forgot he was the enemy.

"I'm not your enemy, Miss Corbin. You may not believe me, but I love the South. It's my home and I would die for it, as I'm sure you would also if it came to that. I don't want it to come to that." He stopped dancing. "If Colonel Barrymore suspects that you are harboring Drake Corbin, he will not care that you are a woman. Please, you must turn your cousin in before a worse tragedy befalls you."

"You'll never see Drake Corbin again. Whatever his deeds were, he isn't coming back." Alexandra stepped away from him. "Please excuse me."

Ignoring Fontaine's curt bow, she hurried out of the room and into the foyer. She glanced around. Satisfied that no one was watching, she snuck into the library. The stacks of ledgers and the safe in the corner confirmed that Elias conducted his business affairs in that room. As she turned to close the door, Cass appeared in the doorway. She tried to shoo him away, but he didn't seem to notice her efforts as he shuffled past her to look at the collection of rapiers, sabers, and daggers that decorated the walls. Alexandra caught his hand when he reached out to touch one of the blades. She steered him away from the wall and led him to a chair. He sat without a fuss and stared at the dark fireplace while Alexandra rummaged through all the papers on top of the desk, none of which looked like a bill of sale for her horse.

The office was not as tidy as she would have expected from a man of Elias' tastes. She didn't see how he could keep track of anything in that mess. The desk was cluttered with newspapers, ledgers, charts, and maps. The ledgers were hastily stacked with loose papers stuffed between some of the pages. Judging by the dust on the furniture, the overflowing wastebasket, and the general disorderliness of the room, Elias even forbade his house slaves to clean it.

She lifted one of the ledgers and several papers fell out. One of them was a list of dates and times, half of which had already passed. She quickly dismissed it when she spotted a set of documents buried under the papers on the desk. When she opened the leather binding, her eyes widened at the treachery scrawled on the paper. It was a record of detailed assessments of every estate in the county including the Corbin plantation. Every building, animal, and human belonging to each estate was assigned a market price and a corresponding purchase price, which was a pittance in comparison.

Suddenly, the library door opened. Alexandra jerked back from the desk, almost scattering the papers on the floor.

"What are you doing?" Garrett demanded in a harsh whisper.

"Elias and that Yankee colonel are going to take all of our land!"

She handed him the documents. He glanced at them then tossed them on the desk. "Alexandra, this is a misunderstanding."

"A big misunderstanding," she declared as she picked up a letter opener and paced the room.

He moved to stand in front of her. "For your own good, let it go."

"My own good? The enemy is about to take everything my father worked for! So no, I'm not letting this go, and you wouldn't let it go either if you weren't a—" She stopped herself from saying "coward."

Garrett wrestled the letter opener away from her. "This is a dangerous game. Stay away from it."

Alexandra began to tremble with anger. Her display was cut short when a low rumble emerged from outside. She ran to the window.

Confederate cavalrymen were thundering toward the house.

When Garrett cracked open the library door and peered into the foyer, Alexandra snatched the land deal documents and used the leather strap to tie them to the inside of her leg. Once the documents were secure, she tried to slip past Garrett, but he caught her before she escaped into the foyer. "Wait."

From her vantage point just inside the library doorway, Alexandra saw the Yankees scrambling for their guns and hats.

"Stay here," Garrett ordered.

Alexandra poked her head out into the foyer and watched as Garrett worked his way across the room to Gwyneth. He halted abruptly when Confederates poured in from the back of the house. While some of the civilian guests yelped in horror, others cheered.

The front door swung open. Alexandra, partially concealed behind the library door, watched in awe as Captain Ramsey strode into the room.

Several Confederates emerged from the dining room with Heppinstahl in tow.

"What's the meaning of this?" the colonel demanded.

Ignoring Heppinstahl, Garrett pushed Gwyneth behind him with a protective arm and moved to stand between Ramsey and the rest of the party. "There are women here, sir."

Ramsey looked at Garrett for a moment. "I can see that for myself." He shifted his attention to Gwyneth. "My apologies, ma'am, if I frightened you. I forget not all women are accustomed to sabers and guns and manly things." He glanced at Garrett.

Gwyneth stiffened and raised her chin as she snipped with a sharp, nasal accent, "If I had a gun right now, I'd shoot you dead, you rebel trash."

Ramsey drew his Colt. When Gwyneth stepped back, he turned away from her to address the rest of the crowd. "I want you all to put your weapons down, if you even have any, and move back against the wall."

As the crowd obeyed, Elias made his stand at the foot of the staircase. Ramsey greeted Elias with a cold smile. "It looks like the war between the Kelsons and the Ramseys isn't going to end until one of us is dead."

When Elias opened his mouth to speak, Ramsey cocked his revolver and leveled it at his face. Alexandra caught her breath. As enraged as she was at Elias, she didn't relish the sight of his head exploding.

After a lengthy silence, Ramsey released the hammer and holstered the gun. "I didn't come here to kill you. Not tonight. I only came for the horses."

A Confederate approached Ramsey. "Cap'n, you want us to take 'em all?"

"Surely not the carriage horses! How will we get home?" Mrs. Porter protested.

"No offense, ma'am, but next time you get an invitation to fraternize with the enemy, stay home." Ramsey turned to answer the Confederate's question. "Confiscate every horse on the premises."

Alexandra stifled a gasp. She had to escape and save Shadow before he was carried off with the rest of the horses. The front door was blocked. Besides, she would never get through the crowd undetected, so she stepped back from the library doorway and retreated further into the library.

She froze. Cass was gone. She ran over to the open window and looked out, but she couldn't find her brother in all the commotion. Confederate cavalrymen were rounding up horses and cattle and chasing the flock of terror-stricken hens that were flapping about the yard. Even in all that chaos it seemed impossible that Alexandra and her ball gown could squeeze through the front window without being seen, so she moved to one of the side windows.

When she realized the window was too narrow for her gown to fit through, she pulled her skirt up and clawed at the strings that were holding her caged hoop in place. After removing the hoop slip, she ripped the skirt of her dress so that the jagged hem came up above her ankles. Once she was free, she climbed through the window.

With as much stealth as a girl in a green ball gown could hope for, Alexandra evaded the Confederates as she scrambled toward the stable. When she slid the heavy doors open, Shadow stuck his head over the stall door.

Alexandra reached for a bridle. She jumped as Luke stepped up behind her and put the bridle back on the hook. He looked down at her short skirt. "There has never been a Kelson for at least three generations back who couldn't hold his liquor," Luke smirked as he steadied himself, "but the combination of spirits and your fiery disposition is making me feel a little more intoxicated than I actually am."

Alexandra rolled her eyes and scolded him. "Captain Ramsey and his men are here, and they are going to take all your horses. Are you going to do anything about it?"

"They aren't *my* horses," Luke leered as he reached across her to pat Shadow's neck. When Alexandra tried to duck away from him, he slipped his arms around her. She struggled against him, but he wouldn't let her go. Finally, after he'd already kissed her, she broke free of his embrace and shoved him back. He waited for a slap, but she punched him in the nose instead.

To her surprise, he didn't yelp as loudly as she would have thought. With a muffled groan, Luke pulled a handkerchief out of his pocket. As he dabbed his bloody nose, Alexandra slipped the bridle over Shadow's head and leapt onto his back. She ordered Luke to open the door.

Still holding his nose, Luke trudged to the door. Just as he opened it, gunfire broke out on the other side of the yard. He ducked back into the barn.

Ignoring the danger, Alexandra remained mounted. "Let me out!"

"You can't go out there!" Luke yelled. When he took hold of Shadow's bridle, Alexandra kicked at him. He dodged the kick but didn't let go of the bridle. "I'm trying to save you, you stupid girl!"

Suddenly, two Union soldiers burst into the stables and aimed their rifles at Luke and Alexandra. Luke raised his hands and said, "Easy there, gentlemen. We're on your side."

"I am not!" Alexandra blurted out as she kicked at Luke again. This time he caught her ankle and squeezed hard enough to make her wince.

"Outside!" the shorter of the two Yankees ordered as he forced Alexandra to dismount.

The other soldier kept his gun on Luke.

As Alexandra stumbled through the door, Barrymore's men were pouring into the yard close on the heels of the fleeing Confederates. Smoke was billowing from the burning cotton barn. Alexandra blinked at the stinging sensation in her eyes. The Yankee who was holding her arm began to cough. Seeing an opportunity, Alexandra shoved him into Elias' overseer who was standing in the middle of the yard barking orders to the slaves who were trying to put out the fire. She might have escaped if she hadn't paused to look for her brother. That's when she saw Bryce Calhoun, Chance Mullins, and Quinn O'Dell tied to the back of a wagon, their faces so bloodied and bruised she almost didn't recognize them. She rushed toward them, hoping she might be able to free them in all the commotion, but she hadn't made it five yards when someone caught her from behind and dragged her to the ground. As she fell, she thought she heard her mother screaming.

Chapter 16

Judgment

Sᴡᴇᴀᴛ and dirt clung to Elias' face as he pressed his knee into Alexandra's back. Keeping her down was no easy task, but he couldn't let her up. The girl had no sense. If she saw the Yankees leading her brother into the yard with a rope around his neck, there was no telling what she would do.

The yard had become a mass of shawls and petticoats, top hats and canes as the party guests clattered en masse through the front door and converged on their horseless carriages. The exodus ceased immediately when Barrymore raised his gun and fired into the air. "The next person who attempts to leave these premises will be shot," he stated calmly. To convince them further he pointed the gun at Raulston Porter.

Mr. Porter's already pale skin turned whiter, then burst into several escalating shades of red as he stepped down from his carriage. If there was any doubt that Elias was the king of Marlbridge, it was laid to rest by the look that Mr. Porter gave him for his evident failure to contain the "Yankee problem."

When Laura Catherine saw Cass, she collapsed onto the ground, shrieking as Wilson tried to console her.

Barrymore remained unmoved. He waved his hand, and two of his men brought out Virgil Doggett, the peddler. "I want you to explain to all these people why this young man, Cass Corbin, is going to hang."

It took all of Elias' strength to keep Alexandra still. She had managed to turn her head just enough to see that it was Elias holding her down. "No!" she screamed. "Let me go!"

Elias covered her mouth as he leaned close to her ear and growled,

"The best thing you can do for your brother right now is to keep quiet."

Virgil glanced around the crowd. When he saw Laura Catherine, he looked away and stammered, "Well, it all happened so fast and they were wearing hats, so I didn't get a good look at their faces."

Barrymore pushed the barrel of his revolver against Virgil's cheek. "That is not what you said previously. You identified these three and you said the fourth was the Corbin boy. Tell the people what you witnessed."

Virgil sputtered, "I was pulling my wagon down the road when I heard gunfire. Then I saw four young men standing over the dead, but I don't see how Cass Corbin coulda been one of 'em. He's just a halfwit. Everybody knows he was injured in the war. Anybody can see he ain't right in the head."

Virgil paused and looked to Elias for confirmation. When Elias gave him a slight nod, he continued. "If I said it was the Corbin boy, then I reckon it coulda been that other Corbin boy, Drake. I've heard he's back in these parts."

Barrymore said nothing at first. Then he addressed the crowd. "Three Union soldiers were murdered today and a fourth is missing, kidnapped by these men and at least one of the Corbin boys." He pointed to Bryce, Quinn, and Chance as he threatened the citizens. "I know that every one of you have betrayed your country in some way either by rebellion or by your failure to suppress the rebellion in your midst. These young men before you have given themselves over to the evils of secession and resistance to federal authority, deceived by unscrupulous men who have rejected the bonds of liberty that are found only in the States as they were united by blood and sacrifice by our forefathers. To spurn such a gift is a transgression against mankind. There are only two actions that will save you from the disaster you have brought upon your own heads. Bring me Drake Corbin and return the kidnapped soldier unharmed, or I will hang these young men and anyone else who participated in this evil deed."

Laura Catherine cried, "Drake Corbin is gone! He's as good as dead!" She spun around wildly, searching for her daughter. "Tell them, Alexandra. Tell them it was Drake."

Alexandra wriggled under Elias' knee, but he kept his hand over her mouth. He couldn't risk letting her go. In service to her misguided sense of duty, the girl would ruin everything he had been working toward since the war began, and worse than that, if she said the wrong thing, she would get them all killed. What Elias hadn't anticipated was that Cass was just as stupid as his sister.

The crowd gasped in surprise when Cass turned to face Barrymore and declared, "Drake didn't kill anyone. Neither did I, but if you must hang someone, hang me, not Drake. Though, I expect a fair trial first."

Alexandra bit Elias' hand. When he jerked his hand away from her mouth, she shouted, "No! It was Drake! It was all Drake's fault. Spare my brother, and I will tell you where Drake is."

"Where?" Barrymore demanded.

Elias clamped his hand back over Alexandra's mouth, enduring the pain as her teeth dug into his fingers. "Drake is with Ramsey," he answered. Alexandra stopped squirming. "I saw him when they came for the horses." He glared at Heppinstahl. "Speaking of which, I want my horses back."

"Good heavens, man!" Mrs. Porter hissed. "These young men, Marlbridge men, are about to die, and you are worried about your horses? The Devil take your horses!" Several onlookers agreed with her.

Barrymore turned to Heppinstahl who had said nothing during the whole ordeal. "Colonel Heppinstahl, I am detaining the three suspects for further questioning along with Reverend Land and the other secessionists in our custody. At least until the missing soldier is safely returned and *all* those responsible are brought to justice." He pointed to Cass. "As for this man, he has already declared himself guilty of duplicity and treason. So that others will be deterred from following his ways, Cass Corbin will hang by the neck until dead."

Struggling to wrestle out from under Elias' knee, Alexandra thundered at Barrymore, "No! You said to tell you where Drake is and you would spare my brother!"

Barrymore replied coolly, "I never said that."

The crowd burst into protests—nothing along the scale of a full-fledged riot, but a decent show of outrage for the populace of Marlbridge. Furthermore, it was enough of a disturbance to rouse Heppinstahl himself to protest the hanging. And it might have all turned out differently if Heppinstahl had taken charge of the situation, but his vehemence shriveled when Barrymore leaned over and whispered in his ear. His face blistered and drew up as if someone had shoved a persimmon in his mouth.

Finally, with his hands behind his back, Heppinstahl announced, "I want it stated for the record that I do not condone Colonel Barrymore's handling of this situation. Occupation of a state that was once a sister to the Northern states has proven difficult for both sides of this bloody conflict. All of you know that I have pursued a conciliatory policy as required by my superiors. This man," he pointed to Barrymore, "takes it upon himself to judge you, and I cannot dissuade him. Nor can I forbid him, for he is not under my authority. Let it also be recorded that I do not defend the actions of this rebel who has confessed to treachery, nor do I defend the actions of his accusers. All have transgressed against the Union in one form or another; therefore, I wash my hands of this entire affair."

Barrymore took the reins of a Confederate horse that had been left behind. Sensing trouble, the tall strawberry roan laid his ears back and danced away from Barrymore. When Barrymore jerked the reins, he shook his head and reared. Only when Cass put a hand on his thick neck did the horse settle down.

Elias covered Alexandra's eyes, but she begged him, "No, please, let me go. Let me go to him. I can stop it. I can stop it. Let me go."

Barrymore compelled Cass to mount, the rope still around his neck. Cass leaned forward as far as the rope would allow and spoke into the horse's ear, "Easy there, Jack." With Cass firmly in the saddle, Jack did what he was trained to do. He barely flinched when Barrymore struck him on the rump. Even when the colonel fired his gun into the air, Jack still didn't budge.

Cass beamed with reckless pride. "Jack is the toughest old war horse who ever lived," he taunted the colonel. "It's going to take more than a smack on the rump to scare him."

Barrymore shot Jack in the head. The onlookers screamed as the horse collapsed. Cass kicked the air, struggling to find a foothold.

Laura Catherine ran to her son, but he was already dead by the time she tore through the Yankees blocking her path.

"Bring me Drake Corbin and the missing soldier," Barrymore declared, "or I will start hanging the secessionists in my custody, one by one. If these measures seem harsh to you, bear in mind that it was your people, your army who practiced them first—capturing Union soldiers and holding them for ransom, firing into trains and killing innocent men who were doing nothing more than fighting for their country, setting a family's home on fire because the man of the house didn't agree with your politics."

As Barrymore and his men departed, Elias pulled Alexandra to her feet, gripping her shoulders so she wouldn't fall, but she kicked him in the shin and ran toward the barn. He limped after her and barely got out of the way as the girl and her horse plunged through the door.

Still reeling from the pain in his leg, Elias grimaced when Luke approached him. "Father, what have you done? I saw you nod to Virgil Doggett." Luke's eyes widened. "Cass Corbin was your informant, wasn't he? You trusted him over me?"

"Trust has nothing to do with it," Elias groaned. "I saw an opportunity, and I took it because I thought it would be the path with the least damage to all parties concerned." He watched as Raulston Porter and Garrett Rainier cut Cass down from the tree. "If you're expecting me to apologize to you and say that I regret choosing Cass over you, fine. You have my apology and my regret."

"Well, I sure don't want to see what happens to Drake Corbin when that mad colonel gets a-hold of him. He has you to thank for that," Luke popped Elias on the shoulder and sauntered toward the house.

Elias remained in the yard until Garrett and Mr. Porter wrapped Cass' body in a blanket and laid it in the back of a wagon.

"What a shame," Mrs. Porter sighed. "I always liked Cass Corbin." She folded her arms and rested them on her bosom, settling back onto her heels. She curled her lip at Heppinstahl who was sitting on the front porch, fanning himself as he argued with Major Fontaine. "We cannot allow this to go on, Mr. Kelson. Something must be done." She lowered her voice. "Perhaps the organization to which you and my husband belong should be called in to set things right since no one else seems able to do it."

Elias stiffened. "I have no idea what you're talking about, Mrs. Porter."

"You know perfectly well what I'm talking about." She snapped her fan against his chest. "In your arrogance, you men think you've kept all your activities hidden from us women, but you are mistaken, sir. We know all of your secrets. So, here's no secret for you: if you men don't do something about that rabid colonel, we will. Let us hope castration will not be involved." She gave him a haughty smile and commenced her march down the drive.

"Lavinia!" Mr. Porter called. "Where are you going?"

"Captain Ramsey has ungraciously stolen my horses," Mrs. Porter shouted over her shoulder. "So, I will walk home as I don't intend to stay here. You may accompany me if you like."

As Mr. Porter waddled after his wife, Elias turned to go into the house when Laura Catherine stopped him. "This is your fault! It should have been you hanging from that tree just like it should have been you that Miles Ramsey killed instead of Jonas. How can you live with what you've done?"

Elias extinguished the tiny bit of sympathy he had for Laura Catherine over the death of her son. "I live with it the same way you do, my dear: I blame someone else." He left Laura Catherine crying in the yard and retreated to his library only to discover that someone had gone through his desk. His heart jumped into his throat. The land deal agreement he had made with Heppinstahl was gone. "Luke!"

A moment later, Luke stumbled into the doorway with a near-empty glass of brandy. "At your service, Father." He bowed. "What is it that you need me to do this time?"

"Go fetch Prichard," Elias seethed as he looked out the window at the charred ruins of his cotton barn. "I may need his services."

With an exasperated grunt, Luke stomped off, hollering for one of the slaves to saddle his horse.

Chapter 17

No Tears

ALEXANDRA remembered nothing of the ride to Storm Chase. She only came to her senses when she tripped over the rug in the foyer. The fall brought to mind the image of Cass' hanging that she had fought off only by throwing herself into her next mission.

As she lay on the floor, her anger began to overtake her. Why had Cass lied to her? If he had told her the truth, she could have saved him. Hatred welled up in her for Elias. If only he had let her go, she could have saved her brother. She knew she could have, but what did Elias care? His only concern was keeping the peace, so he could conspire with the invaders to steal their land.

Her father had told her never to pursue vengeance, that vengeance belonged to God, but it seemed to her that God hadn't done anything. No one had done anything. Not Elias. Not Wilson. Not Garrett. If her father had been here, he would have done something. He would've stopped the Yankees. He would've made Cana Ramsey stay and fight.

She pushed herself to her knees and looked up to see Cranston Ramsey's portrait mocking her from the stairwell. She nearly fell on the landing when she jerked the portrait off the wall and let it crash down the stairs, breaking the gilded frame into several pieces. Alexandra had never met Cranston Ramsey, but it was time someone in that house paid for all the trouble that had been born here.

She wished she had obeyed her mother and never set foot on this land. What she had done to save her town from the Yankees had brought nothing but more trouble. Nevertheless, if she gave up Red and turned herself in, she had a chance to prevent more deaths.

She yanked open the trap door and descended into the cellar. Several strands of rope lay on the floor. Red was gone.

* * *

Alexandra left Shadow to roam the front yard as she forced herself to walk toward the Corbin house dreading what would soon take place. They would bring the body home in the back of a wagon and Laura Catherine would cry and they would lay his body out in the parlor, dressed in his church clothes. Then all the neighbors would descend on the house, bringing food and questions. She had promised on the day her father died she would never endure all that again, and no one could make her.

She marched onto the porch where Garrett was waiting for her. He caught her by the shoulders when she started to walk past him. "I know you are angry about Cass and Elias and the Yankees," he acknowledged in his most soothing tone. "I know you want revenge, and I do not condemn you for it. But, there are things going on here that you do not understand, things in which your brother and father would not have wanted you to get involved. So, please, honor them and stay out of harm's way."

Alexandra stared at Garrett as if he were a stranger. "Do you not know me at all?"

When she pushed his hands off her shoulders and moved to enter the house, Garrett grasped her hand, but not too tightly. "I am sorry about Cass. If there was anything I could do to bring him back, I would."

Alexandra stood quietly for a moment, refusing to look at Garrett. If he had felt anything for her, if he truly understood the anguish she felt at the loss of her brother and her town, she thought he would have seen that she was right, that he would do whatever it took to save their town, even if it meant going against his family. Regardless of her feelings or his, Garrett had made his position clear enough—Alexandra was on her own.

Leaving Garrett on the porch, Alexandra entered the house and closed the front door. On her way to the stairs, she paused at the parlor entrance. Her mother was sitting in a chair, staring at the wall. When Laura Catherine saw her, she rose to her feet, forgetting that Cass' framed portrait was cradled in her lap. It clattered to the floor. She picked it up and handed it to Alexandra. "Put this above the mantel next to your father's." When Alexandra took the miniature, Laura Catherine returned to her post.

After placing her brother's portrait on the mantel, Alexandra reached past it to wipe a smudge from the framed glass through which her father's image stared back at her. She saw nothing of herself in his dark brown eyes or his thin, tightly drawn lips, and anyone who had witnessed her actions of late might find it hard to believe that she was his daughter at all. She set the frame down and pushed it back, away from the edge of the mantel. Regardless of whatever else she had not inherited from Jonas Corbin, she hoped she still had his spirit.

* * *

Alexandra stood in her bedroom, looking into the vanity mirror. There was only one thing she could do now. Finding Ramsey and convincing him to come back to Marlbridge was not a mission she wanted to take on by herself, but it was her only hope of rescuing her friends and herself from the gallows. Knowing she would have no help from the people of Marlbridge, she had lost faith in her town, but her father died in its service and now Cass. It had to be worth more than she could see. Otherwise, they had died for nothing. If saving the town was the only way to redeem their sacrifice, then it must be saved at all costs.

Yet, there was another part of her that wanted nothing more than to sit down and have a good cry. Nobody would blame her, nobody except Drake. Drake was unforgiving and inescapable. It was Drake's face she was looking at in the mirror. Drake's deep-set hazel eyes. Drake's full lips. And Drake's long, thick, honey-colored hair.

No tears, she swore to herself. Drake Corbin had a job to do, a town to save, a brother to avenge, and blood to shed if it came down to it. She would not allow Alexandra, the girl her father and brother had left behind, to stand in the way. Gathering her hair in one hand, Alexandra picked up a pair of shears in the other, and cut her hair off at the nape of her neck.

Within moments, she had ripped the fabric of her dress and let it crumple to the floor. She clawed at the strings of her corset until it gave way, replacing it with a wide strip of cotton cloth to conceal her breasts. Emptying the sack of candy sticks and paper cartridges she had gotten from Pop Brady before the Yankees came, she picked out the strawberry stick and twisted it in her mouth as she loaded her brother's Colt Army. The .44-caliber revolver was larger and heavier than the pocket pistol Cass had given her before he went off to war, but it wasn't nearly as unwieldy as her father's Walker that Laura Catherine had forbidden her children to even touch lest the infernal thing explode in their faces. When Alexandra finished loading the gun, she took one last suck on the candy stick and threw it away.

She retrieved Cass' hunting knife and uniform hidden in the false bottom of her wardrobe and laid them on the pink-and-gray quilt that covered her bed. The sleeves of Cass' shirt and double-breasted shell jacket were a little too long, and his boots were a little too big, but she put them on anyway. Once her transformation was complete, she tucked what was left of her hair behind her ears and covered it with Cass' hat. She reached into the back of her wardrobe, past all the dresses that blocked her way, and took hold of her father's saber. Cass had carried it to war. Now, it was her turn to take up the mantle.

Alexandra opened her bedroom door and froze. Wilson was sitting in the chair across the hall, waiting for her. He stood, clasping his hands behind his back. "I'm not here to stop you. There's no use pretending it wouldn't be a futile attempt, but before you go, there's something I want to give you for your journey." He moved toward the stairs and waited for her to follow.

She followed him downstairs to the library. He walked over to one of the bookcases and began removing several books. He had told her many times over the years that a book could solve any problem, but if he thought she was going to carry a stack of books with her to war, he was mistaken. She was about to object when the bookcase swung out to reveal a hidden gun cabinet containing a collection of smoothbore and rifled muskets, two carbines, an assortment of revolvers that included her father's Colt Walker and a Baby Dragoon, a pair of matching daggers, and a battle ax.

Wilson smiled at her astonishment. "I discovered this cabinet one day when I was rearranging my books," he explained. "Must have been a decade ago now. Anyway, while I am not a courageous man by nature, I have a great appreciation for the courage I see in others, hence my love for tales of adventure. I also wanted you to know that of all the men of my acquaintance over the years, Jonas Corbin was the one I most respected. So when God saw fit to entrust his family to a lowly servant such as myself, I endeavored to honor Jonas by adding to what he had begun and to keep it safe for times such as these."

Wilson reached into the back of the cabinet. "Now, this is for you," he announced as he retrieved a new Henry repeating rifle and handed it to her. Seeing her shocked expression, he added, "I acquired it on my last business trip. I gave its twin to Cass, but a rifle can't safeguard against every calamity it seems."

Alexandra leaned the rifle against the desk. "I know that what I have to do is dangerous, but if I don't do it, Cass will have died in vain."

Wilson looked at her over the rim of his glasses with as stern an expression as he was capable. "No death is ever more in vain than that which is incurred by way of revenge, but, if your motives are pure, then you go with my blessing, for what it's worth."

"Tell Mama I couldn't bear another funeral in this house, so I went to stay with Aunt Charlotte in Chattanooga like she wanted me to."

Wilson kissed her hand. "May your enemies say of you what Banastre Tarleton said of Swamp Fox: 'Let us go back...as for this damned old fox, the Devil himself could not catch him.' "

* * *

Alexandra was relieved to find Matthew sleeping soundly in his quarters on the opposite end of the barn. Shadow snorted his displeasure when Alexandra reached for the saddle blanket instead of the brush. His mood improved when she shook the treat bag and pulled out one of the apple-and-oat treats that Matthew had Jenny bake for the horses. After Alexandra finished saddling Shadow, she stuffed the treat bag in her knapsack and led Shadow out of the barn.

Alexandra jumped. On the other side of the barn door, a large black man was blocking the way.

His sudden presence frightened her at first until she saw who the man was. "Clarence, you scared me."

"I mean to," he replied as he took hold of Shadow's bridle. "D'you think you could run off without Lellen knowin' it?"

Alexandra blinked at his forcefulness. Clarence had never been disrespectful, but he wasn't docile either. If you weren't straight forward with him, he didn't respect you. "I have a duty, and it's not your place to stand in my way," Alexandra stated, her gaze unwavering, her back and shoulders rigid.

Clarence did not budge. "My place is where the Lord say my place is, and the Lord got His reasons. Jonas Corbin was a good man, and I showed him respect like I do all good men, but I ain't here cause he gave some slave trader money. Look at me. You really think there's a man or woman on this earth that could stop me from doing anything I had a mind to do?"

Alexandra was about to say "Lellen," but the man's posture told her she better not give an answer even if she had one.

"I tell ya," Clarence shook his head. "The Lord puts folks in some strange places, but I know fo' sho' the army ain't no place fo' a woman. Lord ain't called no daughter o' His to do somethin' like that, and Miss Alexandra, you knows it."

"There's no place for me here, either."

"Just cause you don't like a place don't make it any less of where you 'spose to be and what you 'spose to be doin' while you there. When I'm out in that field and they's crops to be brung in and that sun's beatin' down, shoot, I don't like my place neither, but I don't run off. I stay and do what needs doin'. An' if we all let go our pride, we'd all see that they's levels 'tween folks. They's a level where we all slaves to somethin' or other. And they's a level where I'm a slave and you free. Then they's this other level, God's level—and e'er body on God's level is free to do whatever it is that God called 'em up outta Egyp' to do. On that level, I'm a father who cares fo' all God's daughters like they my own, cause Jesus make it so we all blood kin. An' it always gonna be my place to look out fo' my kin folk. You ain't got no say in that. Never."

When Alexandra saw that there would be no convincing him she was in the right, she played the only card she had. Clarence was a good man and a good father. His two girls, Jenny and Prudence, adored him, and he was the only person on the earth who could sweet talk Lellen into anything. Alexandra appreciated his concern for her, but if she wanted to win this battle, she would have to hurt him, and nothing hurt Clarence more than for someone he cared about to reject his concern for them. "Well, Clarence, you're probably right, but the only way you're gonna stop me is to manhandle me. Are you willing to do that?"

Clarence looked at her as if she had run him through with a cavalry saber. "No, Miss Alexandra, I ain't gonna do that."

"Then step aside."

After a moment, Clarence lifted his chin and looked down at her. "I'm glad yo' daddy ain't here to see this. He be 'shamed of ya."

Unprepared for his counter blow, Alexandra would have crumpled into a dejected pile at his feet, but just as a tear began to fight its way to her eye lid, she gritted her teeth. "I'm through trying to be what dead people expect me to be." She pulled herself into the saddle and kicked Shadow into an agitated canter. Alexandra held on and didn't look back.

Chapter 18

Bolivar's Tavern

IT was the darkest part of the night when Alexandra came upon Bolivar's Tavern. A small band of Confederates were perched on the front porch of the tavern, laughing and drinking as if there wasn't a war at all. As Alexandra approached and dismounted, a skinny runt of a man, who must have been Bolivar judging by the way he was boot-licking and jawing with the patrons, leaned back until the front legs of his cane-bottom chair came off the floor.

"Zeke! Get out here!" Bolivar hollered.

A little black boy no older than eight scooted out from behind a barrel and scampered onto the porch. Bolivar snatched him up by the suspenders. "What devilment you been into, boy? You s'posed be out here takin' keer of these good folk's hosses."

Zeke's eyes grew wider with every word. "Ain't no debilment, Bolivar, I git right to it."

Bolivar turned Zeke loose and laughed, looking around the group of Confederates with a smugness unique to uppity mulattos like himself. "Ain't nothin' in the world better for sport than a docile nigger."

Alexandra tied Shadow to the hitching post. She had witnessed masters abusing their slaves before, and like every other well-trained, little Southern girl, she had kept her thoughts to herself as she had been taught by most of her elders not to interfere with how a man chose to treat his property. Well, maybe she didn't have the right to chastise a man for mistreating a slave, but surely she had a right to chastise a grown man for mistreating a child. She marched up to Bolivar and kicked his chair over.

"What'd you do that 'fore?" he yelped.

Before Alexandra answered Bolivar, a massive black man with one eye missing loomed in the doorway. "I reckon he done it fo' sport like you said. Ain't much sport 'round here, is they, Bolivar?"

Bolivar glanced up at the man who towered over him. "What do you know about it, Mose? Sport is for white men."

Mose laughed, a deep, jarring laugh and went back inside. Bolivar wallowed on the floor, his light-skinned face turning a deeper shade of red with every passing moment of silence from the other patrons who were gawking at Alexandra. She thought she saw Bolivar reach for the pocket pistol stuffed in his waistband, but Zeke slipped in between her and his master. "I kin do it, suh. I may be little, but I knows my way 'round hosses. An' you kin count on me doin' a good job, too, 'cause Mose gimme a good beatin' if I don't."

The relief on Zeke's face was evident when Alexandra relented. "My horse is winded from a hard ride, so mind you don't let him drink too fast," she replied in a commanding tone to keep up appearances.

"Yessuh." Zeke scurried off the porch and led Shadow to the water trough.

Alexandra had just stepped past Bolivar when a Confederate cavalryman and a brawny civilian burst through the tavern door, locked in a fist fight. The Confederates sprang to their feet, cheering for their comrade. Two more civilians came out onto the porch, chanting their man's name, Big Squire.

"Woo-ee, sic him, Cap'n." one of the onlookers hooted as "Cap'n" pounded Squire with his fists. The damage he inflicted wasn't enough. Squire regained his balance and landed a fierce blow to the soldier's chest. "Cap'n" stumbled backwards and careened into Alexandra, knocking her off the porch. She fell on her back, and had no time to roll away before "Cap'n" landed on top of her.

When Alexandra opened her eyes, Captain Ramsey was staring back at her. "Where did you come from?" he demanded as he staggered to his feet.

Alexandra stared up at him, trying to collect herself. Ramsey gave her boot an impatient kick. "Hurry up and answer me before Big Squire rips my ears off."

She stood up and announced, "I've come from Marlbridge."

Ramsey sidestepped Squire who had bounded off the porch to meet Ramsey in the yard, and the brawl resumed. Ramsey pummeled Squire until the big man head-butted him. He staggered backwards and collapsed.

Alexandra pushed past Big Squire to stand over Ramsey. "Captain Ramsey, you must return to Marlbridge. Colonel Barrymore has taken civilians prisoner." Ramsey rubbed his forehead as she went on, "Did you hear me?"

"I heard you." Ramsey kicked her feet out from under her. He picked himself up off the ground. When Alexandra started to get up, he shoved her back down with his boot. "I think you need to stay down there a while, boy, until you learn to show some respect."

She tried to push his boot off her chest. When that didn't work, she punched the side of his leg.

"You're gonna have to hit harder than that." Ramsey glanced over his shoulder at Squire. "Squire, you mind if we finish this later? I need to teach this pup a lesson."

Squire grinned. "Reckon I wouldn't mind someone else taking your punches for a bit, Ramsey."

The Confederates joined Squire's men in heckling Alexandra as she squirmed beneath Ramsey's boot. "Whew! That one's mean as a snake. You can tell by lookin' at him. Put him in his place, Cap'n!"

Alexandra pulled out Cass' knife, but Ramsey caught her and wrenched the knife out of her hand. "Time for you to settle down." He jerked her up and flung her into the water trough. "You ready to do this the easy way now?"

She coughed and sputtered, "The Yankees—"

Ramsey shoved her back down in the trough and held her for a few seconds until he jerked her back up. "Answer the question."

"Yes," she spat.

He dunked her again. "Yes, what?"

"Yes, sir."

Ramsey relented, "What's your name, boy?"

Alexandra recovered in time to avoid her real name. "Drake! Drake Corbin! Don't you remember me?"

Ramsey released his grip on her jacket and stood back as she climbed out of the trough and wrung the water out of her hat.

"What are you doing here?"

Alexandra yanked the water-logged documents out of her pocket. "The enemy has taken over Marlbridge, Elias Kelson is going to take all the land, and Cass…" She fought the stinging sensation in her eyes and nose and forced the words out of her mouth. "Cass is dead. Sir." The last word came out more like a growl.

Ramsey's expression softened when he glanced at the patch on her sleeve. "Is that his jacket?"

"Yes." She slapped the documents against his chest, her insolence raising a few eyebrows amongst the spectators.

Ramsey took the documents and exhaled a deep breath as he examined them. "I'm sorry to hear about Cass." He turned on his heel and disappeared into the tavern. Confederates filed past Alexandra and resumed their card games that had evidently been interrupted by Ramsey's altercation with Big Squire.

Alexandra started to follow them inside, but Bolivar blocked her at the door, no doubt relishing the outcome of her encounter with Captain Ramsey.

The rat smirked as he sized her up. "Well, I guess e'erybody needs to be reminded of their place e'ery now and then." He stepped aside and granted her permission to enter his domain.

She shoved past him and marched into the tavern.

Ramsey was laying the documents out to dry on the bar. He bristled as Alexandra reminded him of his duty. Again. "Captain Ramsey, you have to do something."

"About what?"

"About our enemies. You can't just abandon your people."

"*My* people? Is that what they're calling themselves now?"

Alexandra choked back a little shame. "A few of us tried to stand up to the enemy, but we failed."

Ramsey faced her squarely. "No, to stand up to your enemy is to face him on the battlefield. Trapping and killing poor, unsuspecting Yankees in cold blood—that's cowardice. From what I've heard, it only made things worse."

Alexandra couldn't hold back any longer. "At least we did something besides ride around stealing horses."

"Do you know what the casualty rate is for horses? We go through horses quicker than Stonewall Jackson's foot cavalry goes through shoes. I understand you thinking that's all we do. I feel the same way."

Alexandra pressed on. "I didn't mean for those Yankees to get killed, but Colonel Barrymore has arrested innocent people. He will hang them if we don't do something."

"We?"

"Well, I can't liberate a whole town by myself. I need an army."

Ramsey howled with bitter laughter as he glanced around at his ragtag following. "What I wouldn't give for one of those. Well, I'll tell you, if I had an army, and if I didn't have more pressing matters to attend, I still wouldn't go on a fool's errand." He turned back to the bar.

Alexandra stood there for a moment, marveling at her own naiveté. She had been avoiding the truth all this time, in spite of the evidence. There wasn't a man left in her world upon whom she could depend. All the men she had looked up to, back when she was just a girl, were all gone. It had fallen to her to rescue her friends, and stop Elias Kelson from taking their land. There was no one else.

She didn't make two good strides toward the door before Ramsey grabbed her collar from behind and pulled her back. "Where do you think you're going?"

She whirled around and snapped, "To rescue my people! Since there's no one *else* to do it."

"You're not going anywhere dressed like that."

"Cass wore this uniform. No reason why I can't."

Ramsey leaned into her face. "There are a good number of reasons. For one, Cass wasn't stupid enough to ride around in the middle of the night with enemy patrols all about. It's a wonder they didn't catch you before you got here."

Before she could protest, a Confederate stuck his head through the door and hollered, "Cap'n! It's Langley come back!"

Ramsey strode onto the porch. Alexandra followed him and almost choked when he lit a cigar and took a long drag as he leaned against a post.

A Confederate scout came tearing into the yard, and jumped off his horse before he came to a complete stop. "Captain Ramsey! Yankees! A small party. I would say no more than a hundred."

Ramsey frowned. "A hundred? That's not a small party up against our thirty, Langley. Where is St. Clair? He should have been here by now."

"I don't know what's keeping him, sir. He sent me on ahead to warn you. We hit the train on schedule, but whatever was supposed to be on it wasn't. You want me to ride back and see what the holdup is?"

"No, I need you here."

"Yes, sir," Langley saluted and led his horse to the other side of the tavern where the rest of the horses were tethered.

Ramsey nodded at a tall soldier with a bushy, red beard who began shouting orders in a booming Scottish accent. If the Yankees had been uncertain of the Confederate position before, they were certain now. The Confederates sprang into action. Cards and shot glasses flew everywhere as they flipped the tables over, carried them outside, and set them as barricades stretching across the yard to the other side of the road.

Alexandra stood in the midst of the operation, watching the faces of the Confederates as they flurried all around her and took up their positions behind the barricade, guns ready. Ramsey gave no orders. He didn't have to. As he leaned against that post, smoking his cigar, whatever he wanted to happen happened as if everyone around him knew what to do and did it without hesitation, without question, without fear, and all they needed from him was just to be there.

It wasn't until the Confederates finished their work and knelt silently behind the barricade that Alexandra heard what had triggered all the activity. The tinny clatter was faint but unmistakable. Metal canteens. Scabbard rings clanging. An indecipherable number of horseshoes striking every rock that dotted the road between the Confederates and their approaching enemy.

Alexandra looked at Ramsey. "You knew they were coming."

Ramsey took a long drag on his cigar.

"This is a trap," she accused.

He exhaled a cloud of smoke.

"You said traps were cowardly."

He extinguished the cigar. "No, I said trapping and killing poor, *unsuspecting* Yankees was cowardly. The Yankees coming down that road know full well what they're about to get."

Alexandra didn't wait for him to give her an order. She marched to where Zeke had tied Shadow. She pulled out her Henry rifle and moved to a position behind the table closest to the porch. If Ramsey thought Drake Corbin was a coward, he wouldn't think so after she showed him she could be just as good a soldier as all the others under his command.

The soldier next to her was a small man with sharp eyes. When he saw her rifle, he exclaimed to his comrade, "Gosh-a-mighty! Looky here what this young feller has got. Bradford, d'ye ever see the like?"

Bradford's eye bulged. "Lawd, son, what Yankee did you murder in his sleep to get a-hold of that thang? Lemme have a look-see." He scooted closer to her.

Alexandra handed him the rifle. Several other soldiers began to crowd around asking all at once, "Whar d'you get that thar piece? Hey, Cap'n, looka here what this new feller has got."

The growing crowd parted to let Ramsey through. He took the rifle from Alexandra and examined it closely. "A Henry repeater. A weapon like this could do some real damage to the enemy—if it was loaded." He handed it back to Alexandra and returned to his post.

She blushed as the men laughed. *A fancy gun with no cartridges.*

Bradford whacked her on the shoulder. "Don't pay these yahoos no mind, Drake. Sal, here, forgets to load his gun all the time. At's why you keep your cartridge box on your belt."

Sal, the small soldier with sharp eyes, grumbled, "I've had about enough of yer talk, Bradford. I only forgot to load my gun once, and yer the one who runned off and left yer cattridge box in yer tent."

Alexandra looked down at the black leather box on Cass' belt. She hadn't even noticed it. She opened the box to find that Cass had left it nearly full.

"Here, gimme that thang," Bradford coaxed her. She handed him the rifle and a handful of cartridges. "I hear these Henries'll far sixteen rounds. That true?"

"I've never fired it before," Alexandra admitted.

When Bradford finished loading the rifle, he handed it back to Alexandra then motioned for her to keep quiet.

The dark road fell silent for a moment until a lone rider appeared. Alexandra peered through a knothole in the tabletop. The rider stopped right in front of her. She clamped her hand over her mouth to catch the sound of her gasp. The man was Major Fontaine.

Fontaine pushed his hat back and let out a tired sigh as Ramsey stood in front of him. "What are we gonna do now, Ramsey?"

Ramsey removed his hat and dropped it onto the last barricade as he stretched and yawned. "Well, Marcus, being that it's getting pretty close to dawn and we've been up all night reveling, we'd just as soon let y'all go in peace, but if you insist, Madcap Charlie is waiting for you down the road."

Fontaine smirked. "I don't know where Charlie Whisenhunt is—nobody on my side or yours can keep track of that man—but I do know where he *isn't*."

Ramsey drew his gun and examined the chamber. "Then I guess we could go ahead and settle things right here. You can take a little time to consult with your officers if you want. I'm in no hurry."

Fontaine adopted a more serious tone. "You should be, especially since you're outnumbered three to one. If Barrymore catches you, he won't take prisoners, and you know it."

"I find it difficult to believe he'd be that upset over a herd of horses," Ramsey answered.

"He isn't after the horses. He's after Drake Corbin for killing three Union soldiers and kidnapping a fourth. Everybody who has ever heard the name Drake Corbin seems to think he rides with you."

Bradford and Sal looked at Alexandra from behind the barricade. "So, you did kill you some Yankees," Bradford whispered.

Alexandra pulled her knife out and held it under his nose. "Keep quiet." Bradford put his hands up.

Ramsey replied to Fontaine. "I don't claim Drake, but Cass Corbin was one of mine, so you go back and tell your Yankee overlords they shouldn't have killed him because one of these days I'm gonna collect on my vengeance."

Fontaine took a deep breath. "Well, then, there's nothing left to say." He turned his horse around and started to ride off, but just when Alexandra let herself breathe again, Fontaine came back. "Ramsey, who told you Cass Corbin was dead?"

Alexandra peeked through the hole. She gripped her rifle even though she knew it couldn't save her. To shoot Fontaine would start a fight the Confederates might not win. If she didn't die in battle, she would be taken prisoner and then carried off to Marlbridge for her hanging. To shoot Ramsey would condemn her to death at the hands of the Confederates, not to mention that without Ramsey the South might lose the war. To give up and turn herself in without Red as a witness...

Ramsey made the choice for her. "Bradford! Get out here!"

"No," Alexandra whispered harshly at Bradford, moving her knife close to his nose.

Bradford whispered back, "I'm sorry, but I'm more skeered of the Cap'n than I am of you." He leaned away from Alexandra and stood. "Here, sir," he squeaked.

Alexandra was about to run when Ramsey said, "Bradford, why did you tell me Cass Corbin was dead?"

"Sir?" Bradford stood dumbfounded for only a second before he seamlessly launched into a yarn. "Was I the one that told you that? That Cass Corbin was dead? Shoot, I reckon if I said it then it must be true. See, it all started when we was leavin' that plantation with all them horses. In the midst of that firefight betwixt us true Americans and you all, well, I seen the murderous look of the Devil hisself in that one colonel, the tall, pale one, you know the one that looks a whole lot like what I think Death would look like if Death was to take on flesh and walk around in a Yankee outfit. That's the colonel I'm a-talking about, not the other 'un. All I seen in the other 'un's eyes was figgy puddin', and that's the color his eyes are too, color of figs, but I digress. Anyhow, I seen the murderous look—"

Fontaine smacked the pommel of his saddle with his fist. "Enough! Ramsey, if you don't hand Drake Corbin over to me, and put an end to this right now, you and your men will answer for it."

Ramsey flipped his pocket watch open. "Oh, I think our chances are pretty good. You were right, though. Madcap Charlie isn't waiting for you up ahead. It's what's behind you that you ought to be worried about."

Fontaine's eyes grew wide when he heard the sound of gunfire in the distance, accompanied by the fierce scream by which the Rebels typically announced their presence on the battlefield. The Confederates outside Bolivar's Tavern remained silent as they aimed their rifles at the road, but held their fire. Alexandra peered over the barricade, but saw nothing.

"What you want us to do with this 'un, Cap'n?" one of the Confederates asked, jerking his head at Fontaine.

"Let him go back to his men," Ramsey ordered. "Sounds like Thaddeus St. Clair is tearing them to pieces."

Fontaine wheeled his horse around and dashed back down the road in the direction of the battle noise. He had scarcely been gone ten seconds when Sal sniffed the air and struck a dramatic pose in front of the barricade for everyone to see. "Prepare yer ears, gentlemen. In the midst of all this thunderous racket with the aroma of gunpowder I feel a poem comin' on." He cleared his throat.

The Yankees did dare run into a bear.
His name was St. Clair.
He'll cut off their hair to take to his lair.
Blue devils beware.

Bradford and several others rolled their eyes as they took hold of Sal and dragged him back behind the barrier. "Save it for *The Atlantic*, Longfeller."

Sal curled his nose. "*The Atlantic!* Pshaw, I ain't savin' nothin' for them ab'litionists. None of us'd be in this predicament if it wharn't fer them and that Stowe woman stirrin' the pot. They ought left well 'nough alone. Whatever strife they is betwixt white folk and the Negroes, we kin sort it out fer ourselves. Them two-faced, industrializin' scoundrels is always callin' fer us to let the Negroes go, but when we call fer them to let us go, they send an army to kill us. Now, I want to know what sort of justice is that?"

Once everyone else was secure, Ramsey took his position behind the barricade next to Alexandra. "If you're gonna wear that uniform, you're gonna stay and fight, Corbin, and if you play the coward and try to run, I'll shoot you."

Alexandra drove her knife into the barricade, near Ramsey's hand. "Nobody calls me a coward." The words sprang up of their own volition, but there was no going back on them now.

Unwavering, she stared back at Ramsey, bracing herself for the consequences of her unsanctioned boldness. To her surprise, Ramsey didn't strike her. Instead he replied calmly, "Well, Corbin, if you gotta cut something off to prove your manhood, at least have the decency to spare me my trigger finger." He yanked the knife out of the wood and tossed it in her lap.

Bradford and Sal released a nervous chuckle. When Ramsey turned back toward the road, Sal smacked Alexandra on the arm. "Ye sure have got a mouth on ye. Be the death of ye like as not if ye don't get a-hold of it. And I don't know ye well enough to recite a poem upon yer demise, so don't be expectin' it."

Alexandra sheathed her knife and glanced up at Ramsey. If he was angry with her, his face gave no indication. She had just spoken with such force, and now she wanted to sit down and cry. No one wanted to do the right thing more than she did, and yet, everything she did was wrong. She wondered what was keeping the Yankees. Of course, she wanted St. Clair to win the battle, but it might make her feel better if she got a chance to shoot somebody.

Suddenly, the gunfire in the distance ceased. The Confederates waited on edge as the jangling of cavalry accoutrements grew louder. The first of the victors to appear was a striking lieutenant who exuded a gallantry so pure it was downright inhuman. Alexandra had never been given over to excessive speculations on any man's gallantry, but there was no other way to describe him. Equally statuesque was the palomino charger upon which the lieutenant was mounted.

Alexandra joined the men as they cheered for their gallant St. Clair. If Ramsey wouldn't save her town, maybe this man would. As she came out from behind the barricade, she stopped when the lieutenant dismounted and saluted Ramsey. "We have dispatched tha enemy with vera few losses ta our side," he announced in the unhurried, stately lilt typical of the Southern gentry, the white plume in his hat bobbing. The rest of the company filed in behind him with several wounded and one dead body.

While the healthy soldiers were bringing the wounded into the tavern, Alexandra sought an opportunity to approach St. Clair, but he and Ramsey were inseparable. They retreated to a backroom of the tavern and remained there for nearly half an hour when Ramsey came out alone and gave the order to move out. St. Clair was nowhere to be found. When Alexandra asked Bradford where she could find St. Clair, he informed her that he reckoned St. Clair was off doing whatever Captain Ramsey ordered him to do, as was his custom.

Alexandra stood in the middle of the tavern as the men came and went, tending their wounded, breaking down their barricades, draining their glasses, stuffing away their playing cards, and doing nothing to help Alexandra save her town. In the bustle of it all, Alexandra made her escape.

Chapter 19

The Long Ride

HIDING in the woods near the Marlbridge jail, Alexandra tied Shadow to a tree and waited for her chance to strike. Despite her best efforts, she had returned to her people with no army, no Red, and no one to stand between her and her enemies. A girl with a horse and a rifle would have to be enough.

Fortunately, it was Sunday morning, and folks wouldn't be coming to town for church for at least another hour. Still in her Confederate uniform, she stole up to the back door of the jail. She peeked in the barred window to see Bryce lying on a cot. Quinn was sitting against the wall, and Chance was sprawled on his back on the floor. She didn't see anyone else in the jail.

She also didn't see Captain Ramsey standing right behind her until she turned away from the door and almost bumped into him. She bit her lips and drew in a sharp breath to contain an involuntary scream.

"What do you think you're doing?" he asked.

"Rescuing my men," she answered.

Brows knit and teeth clenched, Ramsey and Alexandra stared at each other.

Ramsey blinked. "How many?"

"Three."

He started to walk away.

She caught up to him. "I'm not leaving my friends behind."

"You'll be leaving them behind if we don't get some horses. Or, were you expecting your men to outrun the Yankees on foot?"

If Alexandra had hoped to show Ramsey she wasn't an idiot, she doubted any of her recent endeavors had convinced him otherwise. Ashamed of her lack of foresight, Alexandra threw up her hands. "How are we gonna get more horses?"

"Steal 'em."

* * *

Stealing horses out from under the noses of a thousand Yankees on a Sunday morning turned out to be a much easier task than Alexandra had anticipated, even though it might be the worst sin she had ever committed on a Sunday. Instead of going to the corral at the end of town where the Yankees were camped, Ramsey led Alexandra to the back of the Rainier mansion.

"I thought we were going to steal horses from the Yankees."

"We only need three. No sense in disturbing a nest of Yankees when we can take what we need from the Rainiers."

Ramsey and Alexandra stopped short when a black man carrying a bucket of oats caught them entering the stables. Ramsey pulled his Colt, but the man only stared at him, unimpressed. "Y'all aimin' to steal Marse Hanson's hosses?"

"You aimin' to stop us, old man?" Ramsey answered with a little more playful sass than Alexandra would have expected.

The old man raised his eyebrows. "Shoot, naw. I help you saddle 'em. 'Course, now, soon as y'all out de do,' I'm gwone run tell Marse Hanson how two Johnny Rebs snuck up and held me at gunpoint and run off wid de hosses."

"Won't he still give you a beating?" Alexandra asked, somewhat preoccupied as she wondered which horses belonged to Garrett and if he would ever forgive her for stealing them.

He chuckled. "Marse Hanson ain't gwone lay a hand on de keeper of his prize possessions." He set the bucket of oats in front of a handsome, chestnut thoroughbred. "Even if he did, it be worf it to see de look on his face when I tells him which hosses y'all run off wid."

Ramsey grinned. "We'd be happy to take your recommendations."

* * *

Once they secured the three Rainier horses with Shadow and Solomon, Alexandra and Ramsey snaked their way to the back door of the jail. Not wishing to display any more incompetence, Alexandra did not attempt to kick the door in but waited to see what Ramsey would do. He didn't attempt to kick the door in either. When he tried the doorknob, it turned.

Ramsey hesitated in the doorway. "Something's not right."

Alexandra shoved past him and ran to the cell where Chance, Bryce, and Quinn were locked up. "Where are the rest of the prisoners?"

Bryce mumbled through swollen lips, "I don't know where he's keeping them—if they're still alive."

"I'm sure these three were left here as bait," Ramsey growled as he reached through the bars, snatched Bryce's water cup, and banged on the cell bars.

A moment later, the door to the sheriff's office flung open, and a guard appeared. Ramsey jerked him through the doorway, and Alexandra closed the door.

Holding his knife to the guard's throat, Ramsey ordered him to open the cell.

The guard obeyed, and Alexandra took his gun.

Leaving Alexandra to hold the guard at gunpoint, Ramsey sheathed his knife and entered the cell to examine Chance. "This one's too far gone. If we take him, he'll die and slow us down, but if we leave him, they'll let him lay here 'til he dies. You want me to put him down?" He looked up at Alexandra as Quinn and Bryce stared at both of them in horror.

The guard inched closer to the cell as he addressed Ramsey. "I been praying somebody would put that poor boy out of his misery. At least give him some laudanum. Major Fontaine wanted to, but Colonel Barrymore wouldn't let him. Said his moans would be useful to pierce the hearts of the unrepentant."

When Alexandra nodded, Ramsey took Chance's head in his hands.

"Ramsey?" The dying boy opened his eyes and mustered a smile until he choked. A trickle of blood streamed from his mouth as he stammered, "I didn't believe you'd come back."

"It's all right. I didn't believe it either." Ramsey covered Chance's eyes and with a swift, subtle move, snapped his neck.

As Alexandra and Quinn helped Bryce to his feet, they heard the sound of another guard approaching the door to the sheriff's office.

"Higgins! What's going on in there?"

Ramsey cracked Higgins on the head with his gun.

When the second guard came through the door and saw what was happening, he reached for his sidearm but froze when Ramsey leveled the Dragoon at his face. "It won't do you any good to kill me, Reb."

"Give me your gun," Ramsey ordered.

The instant the guard handed over his gun, Ramsey jerked him into the cell and slammed his head against the bars. The guard stumbled backwards and fell unconscious next to Chance's body. Ramsey dragged Higgins into the cell and closed the door.

As the rebels ran for the horses, a pack of Federal soldiers swarmed the jail. One of them shot Bryce in the chest. Alexandra started to go back for him, but Ramsey ordered her to leave him. Ramsey shot two Yankees as Alexandra and Quinn mounted their horses. When Alexandra turned, she saw Ramsey trapped behind a tree. Alexandra pulled Solomon to the tree and tried not to yelp like a girl when a minié ball shattered the bark. Ramsey sprang into the saddle, and they escaped into the woods, taking three of Hanson Rainier's champion thoroughbreds with them.

Failing to launch an organized pursuit, the Yankees didn't chase them very far, and they ran a good, long distance before Quinn, who had taken a bullet during their flight, fell off his horse. Ramsey scouted the perimeter to make sure the Yankees had given up before he dismounted and dragged Quinn to a fallen log. Alexandra tended to Quinn who was grasping at the hole in his stomach. After Ramsey examined the wound, he pulled out a flask of whiskey and handed it to Alexandra before he went back to the horses.

Quinn took a sip. "Y'all go on without me."

Alexandra placed her hand on his shoulder. "We aren't leaving you behind, Quinn."

"It's all right." He took her hand. "I'm not sorry for what I done." He hesitated before he asked, "I know it wouldn't mean nothing, but if you wouldn't take offense to my asking…" He couldn't get the words out, but Alexandra knew what he meant. She glanced over her shoulder to make sure Ramsey wasn't looking then leaned over and kissed Quinn gently on the lips. Afterward, she saw the corners of his mouth turn up in a faint smile as he exhaled for the last time.

During the chase, Alexandra had not allowed herself to feel anything that would hinder her performance as Drake. The swiftness of the day's events aided her in shoving aside any bothersome emotions, but as she looked at Quinn, she began to feel the weight of all the deaths that had resulted from her failure to talk Chance and Bryce out of kidnapping those Yankees. Furthermore, it was her involvement that had escalated the violence. "Quinn killed those Yankees because they threatened Alexandra. I think he was in love with her."

Ramsey chuckled. "In love with Alexandra?"

His amusement irritated her. "What's wrong with that?" she demanded, her melancholy over the deaths of her friends temporarily vanquished by her frustration with Ramsey.

Ramsey retrieved a worn letter from the lining of his jacket. "She must have been seven or eight when she sent me this letter. I left Marlbridge after Sheriff Corbin died, but she was convinced I was supposed to come back and be the next sheriff." He laughed. "I really hated her for that." When Alexandra reached over to take the letter away from him, he secured it in his pocket.

Alexandra had forgotten about the letter she had written back when she was a stupid little girl. "Well, if her letter was so offensive, why'd you keep it?"

"Why, I might forget about all the duties of Southern manhood I've failed to live up to if I didn't have Alexandra to remind me."

One moment she was ready to punch him in the face, and the next moment, she didn't have the wherewithal to lift her arm. She had been raised to think that reminding a man of his duty was a woman's most important job. How could she have ever thought Cana Ramsey would appreciate her sense of duty when he evidently got along fine with unfulfilled duties looming over his head?

Ramsey unfurled a blanket from his bedroll. "Are you going to help or not?"

Alexandra remained silent as they wrapped Quinn's body in the blanket and hoisted him onto the back of his horse.

"Mount up. We got a long way to go yet," he ordered.

Ramsey took the reins of Quinn's horse, but Alexandra snatched them away from him. Without bothering to reprimand her, he mounted his horse and rode off with the two extra horses in tow.

She didn't follow him. Instead, she stood there holding Shadow's reins and the reins of the horse carrying the dead body of the boy whose face had lit up every time he saw her. No matter what she was wearing. What would she tell Quinn's mother?

"You can't go back."

Alexandra jumped. She hadn't noticed that Ramsey had come back for her. She turned away from him. "I have to find Red."

"Red?"

"The soldier we kidnapped. We called him Red. I went back to the place where we were keeping him, and he was gone. Barrymore said he would start hanging civilians if I didn't turn myself in and bring Red back unharmed."

"And you believed him?"

She whirled around to face him. "Yes!"

"If you believe he'll go away because you gave in to his demands, you're more naïve than I thought."

"My people are in danger, and I can't walk away, like *you* did."

Ramsey clenched his jaw and pulled back, taking a deep breath before he responded. "Listen, whatever happens to Marlbridge from now on, it's out of your hands. You did what you had to do, and you failed. That's it. There's nothing more to be done. Now get on that horse and obey orders like a real soldier."

Alexandra did as she was told. Not because she recognized Ramsey as a legitimate authority over her, but because she knew he was right—there was nothing else she could do—for the time being. Even if she escaped Ramsey, the likelihood of her finding Red at this juncture was about the same as returning home and finding Cass alive. She could no longer deny her situation. All her plans had come to naught. Returning to Marlbridge without an army would only lead to more failure. If Ramsey meant to carry her off and make a soldier out of her, what difference was it to her if she was held captive in Marlbridge or held captive in the army? At least in the army she might get to shoot somebody.

Chapter 20

Cade's Mill

ALEXANDRA and Ramsey hadn't gone very far when it started to rain, hard, and it kept raining for several hours. Around four o'clock, it ended. They had just crossed a rising creek when Ramsey suddenly reined his horse in and held up his hand. Alexandra jumped when gunfire erupted in the distance. They spurred their horses into a fast gallop until they reached the outskirts of the small town where the citizens were locked in a firefight with an assortment of deserters, scoundrels, drifters, and other lawless persons of various shapes, sizes, and colors.

Alexandra pulled her saber, ready to charge, but Ramsey grabbed Shadow's bridle and shouted, "What are you doing? Put that away and dismount!" Alexandra dismounted and pulled her rifle from the saddle holster. Ramsey shooed the horses out of harm's way and yanked Alexandra behind one of the buildings.

While Ramsey opened fire on the attackers across the street, Alexandra hesitated and pulled her hat further down on her head. One of the scoundrels was Prichard Benefield.

"Corbin, if you ever intend to put that Henry to use, now would be a good time," Ramsey hollered over the gunfire.

Alexandra threw the rifle to her shoulder. This was no time to melt into a silly girl worried that someone from back home might recognize her. She fired a couple of rounds that hit nowhere near where she thought she was aiming. Fortunately, Ramsey was too preoccupied to pay any attention to her poor marksmanship. He emptied his revolver, killing at least two of Prichard's men who were hiding in the livery across the street.

When Ramsey stopped to reload, Alexandra made a snap decision. As much as she hated to admit her shortcomings, she couldn't let her pride get in the way of her duty. She handed Ramsey her rifle in exchange for his empty Colt. "You're a better shot. I'll reload."

Moments later, the rest of Ramsey's men appeared with Lieutenant St. Clair leading the charge down the middle of the street. The renegades lit out like scalded dogs.

Fortunately, Shadow, Solomon, and Quinn's horse had not strayed too far. When Ramsey whistled, Solomon trotted up immediately, followed by the other two.

As Ramsey and Alexandra remounted and made their way into the street, St. Clair rode up to meet them, his face flushed with anger, his green-gold eyes blazing. Ramsey smiled when the finicky lieutenant yanked the tattered remnant of a muddy white plume out of his hat and shook it at him.

"Survived Donelson, Shiloh, and Fallen Timbers only ta be butchered by a gaggle of low-life derelicts!" St. Clair stormed, throwing the feather on the ground with a disgusted huff.

"Sorry about the feather. Now, do you wanna tell me what the Benefield gang was doing in Cade's Mill?" Ramsey redirected.

St. Clair resumed the graceful air with which he normally conducted himself and postponed his report just long enough to brush a speck of dirt off his sleeve. "If you are wondering how it is that we have come so late ta tha party, you should know we arrived hours ago and made camp about five miles yonda. As to why Benefield and his gang of miscreants set upon the town I cannot fathom, but they had ta have known we were in the area, and they attacked anyway. Can you believe tha audacity? It's an outrage!"

"We're low on ammunition and men, and they know it. Did you get the horses to safety?"

"Indeed. And they are of tha highest quality."

"Corbin and I came by three more, if you can catch 'em." Ramsey grimaced as one of Hanson's prized beasts dashed wildly up and down the street.

"I have no doubt that Colonel Whisenhunt will be pleased when he arrives," St. Clair ventured.

Ramsey scowled. "What's Madcap Charlie got to do with it? They're our horses, not his."

St. Clair raised an eyebrow. "You do know our battalion has been reorganized?"

Ramsey gave St. Clair a wary look. "No."

"Madcap is now tha regimental commander. We, along with Stark and Peterson, now comprise a new battalion under Kinkaid."

"D. H. Kinkaid?"

The corner of St. Clair's mouth twitched at Ramsey's surprised expression.

"Kinkaid's a good man, but don't you think he's too…" Ramsey hesitated.

"Too old?" St. Clair finished. "Perhaps, but Whisenhunt trusts his judgment, which means, if Madcap goes all madcap, it might be that tha old man can talk him out of it. In any case, Stark and Peterson should be comin' in any time now. Whisenhunt is ta arrive tha day after tomorrow with tha rest of tha regiment. I imagine we'll be sent ta aid in tha defense of Bridgeport." St. Clair halted in the middle of his speculation to point at Quinn. "Whose dead body is that?"

Ramsey handed St. Clair the reins. "Quinn. Have him buried with the rest of the dead. I'll see about getting word to his family. If they want him, they can come dig him up."

Both men turned as a small, cat-like soldier perched atop a good-sized horse, rode up and handed him a note. "From Captain Stark," the scout announced, talking around the cigar in his mouth.

Ramsey read the note and gave it back to the scout. "Tell Captain Stark to proceed."

The scout took the note, but instead of riding off he continued, "I know it ain't my place to say, sir, but if you're lookin' for more men, a term I use loosely to define people of military age who ain't women, I know where some's been hidin' themselves."

Ramsey replied, "If you got names, give 'em to Lieutenant St. Clair. Dismissed."

The scout saluted, but before he rode off, he paused to size up Drake Corbin. Alexandra ignored him and followed Ramsey to the house across the street next to the church. Ramsey dismounted at the back of the house and tossed Solomon's reins over the hitching post, but before he even set foot on the porch, the back door opened.

Ramsey grinned. "Afternoon, Ms. Evelyn."

"Evening, more like," replied an attractive duchess of a gal in her early fifties.

At first, Alexandra thought Evelyn was about to scold Ramsey, but the woman smiled and hugged him tight.

Not sure what to do, Alexandra dismounted but stayed by her horse until Evelyn motioned to her and asked, "Who's this young man?"

Ramsey frowned when he saw Alexandra standing in the yard. "My shadow, evidently."

Alexandra blushed. "I'm sorry. I didn't mean to intrude. I didn't know where—"

"For some reason, new recruits follow me around like a dog. Then, they annoy me further by apologizing for it."

Evelyn popped Ramsey on the shoulder as she studied Alexandra with the air of a benevolent matriarch. "What's your name, son?"

"Drake Corbin."

"Well, Drake Corbin. Welcome to Cade's Mill."

Ramsey interjected, "You know, when a man rides up and saves a person's whole town, you would think that person would be so grateful, she might fix him something to eat."

Evelyn returned his roguish grin. "It's already on the table."

Alexandra stammered, "I'll see to the horses."

"You will not," Evelyn ordered. "My boy, Bud, can do that. Don't you pay attention to Cana Ramsey, young man. When you're in this house you listen to me. If I say you are invited to supper, that means you're invited. Doesn't matter what anybody else has to say about it." Evelyn looked out toward the barn and called for Bud. A teenage mulatto emerged from the barn and shuffled over. "Bud, take care of these horses." The boy nodded. "Thank you, dear."

When Evelyn caught Alexandra staring at her in amazement, she explained, "That's my boy, Bud. His mother was a white woman from up North who took up with a free black. They were killed, and Bud was left for dead. Then the Lord brought him to me. I say he is my slave so no one will bother him, but my husband and I had no children, so we took Bud as our own. Of course, there are some who don't approve, but I say if they don't like it, they can take it up with the Lord. Now, let's eat."

Ramsey started to walk through the door when a large black woman carrying two blankets appeared and planted her broom in front of him. "Naw, suh, Cap'n Ramsey. You ain't 'bout to set foot in dis house wid de smell a deaf on you. And soakin' wet, too. Mmphm. Comin' in here stankin' like a wet dog. Take it off."

Alexandra was stunned when Ramsey said, "Yes, Miss Henrietta," and promptly stripped down to his ankle-length drawers when the buxom housekeeper turned her back. Alexandra stared at Ramsey's bare chest until Henrietta ordered her to undress, too. When she balked, Henrietta made the same grunt Lellen made when she meant Alexandra better do what she said. Alexandra carefully removed everything but her undergarments, hoping Henrietta wouldn't notice that her undershirt was a modified chemise. She placed her clothes on the bench next to Ramsey's and folded her arms over her chest.

Wrapped in the blankets, Ramsey and Alexandra sat down at the table. Alexandra had forgotten that she hadn't eaten since the day before. Yet, starvation aside, out of habit, she ate small bites slowly as her mother had taught her.

Evelyn gave Ramsey a hopeful look. "So, you all will be staying for a while this time, I hope."

Ramsey gave her a weak smile. "I imagine Madcap Charlie will be calling us up before the week is out, but we'll stay until then."

"Colonel Whisenhunt is such an agreeable man," Evelyn mused. "I don't see where he got the name Madcap." She glanced at Alexandra who was still picking at her food. "Private Corbin, you don't eat much for a young man. Don't be shy. There's plenty for everyone."

Pleased with her new freedom, Alexandra tore into her food like a man.

Ramsey remarked, "Corbin here tried to liberate Marlbridge, single-handed."

Evelyn raised her brows. "That was a brave act. Did you succeed?"

Alexandra forced down the food in her mouth. Bravery aside, none of her actions so far had saved anyone. "No, ma'am."

"I would think Marlbridge to be a strategic location," Evelyn observed. "Is it not?"

Ramsey scowled. "We can't save every town from Union occupation, and believe it or not, I do have superiors whom I answer to. If Colonel Whisenhunt intended to save Marlbridge, he would have done so." He took his coffee cup and got up from the table.

* * *

On their way back to camp, the Confederates split up into foraging parties. Bradford, Sal, Langley, Alexandra, and the big-boned Scot they called McCabe stayed with Ramsey. For over an hour they rode from house to house collecting any food, livestock, and manpower that the civilians could spare. Some were more willing than others, but not even the most stubborn could refuse Captain Ramsey in the end. Whatever he couldn't accomplish by appealing to the Cause, he accomplished with his Colt Dragoon.

With each interaction, Alexandra felt more ashamed. She hoped her father couldn't see what she was doing. She had a feeling that he would not approve of any of her actions of late, and in taking from her enemies she felt justified, but taking from her own people was a line she had not been prepared to cross. The last light of the day was retreating behind the mountains when they made their last stop.

They waited silently in the yard of the Taylor farm as Mama Taylor, a thin, tough woman in her forties, made her last stand on the porch with a Kentucky long rifle. Two elderly slaves, a man and woman, stood helpless at the far end of the porch as Mama Taylor told Ramsey, "You ain't takin' my boys. I'll be cold in the grave before I'll see you take 'em."

Ramsey ordered McCabe to get a shovel. Alexandra hoped it was a bluff, but Mama Taylor must have believed him. She broke down into tears as she wailed, "But I seen a vision. They's all three laying dead right next to one 'nother as if God had struck 'em down with the same bolt of lightnin'."

Alexandra cringed. If there was any man who was wholly immune to a woman's tears, it was Captain Ramsey. Nevertheless, Ramsey dismounted and removed his hat as he addressed Mama Taylor with a gentleness Alexandra had not thought him capable. "Mrs. Taylor, the government in Richmond will issue a draft if they haven't done so already. That means sooner or later some other officer is gonna come for those boys, and they'll sell their men a lot cheaper than I will. I can promise I'll look out for them, and I'll teach them how to fight. It's not me who's taking your boys away from you. It's bankers and businessmen up North who sent an army down here to make a profit. You've done what was yours to do, fighting to keep this place and raising those boys right. Now let your boys go, so they can fight for you. It's their right and their duty. It'd been wrong to keep them from it."

Mama Taylor wiped the tears out of her eyes and hollered into the house. "Boys! Y'all git yer things and git out here. Come on now. Don't make Captain Ramsey have to wait on ya."

The Taylor boys, ranging in age from eighteen to twenty-two, stepped out of the house. They each kissed their mama on the cheek and joined Ramsey in the yard. The youngest Taylor tried to control his trembling as his brothers placed strong hands on his shoulders.

Ramsey watched them for a moment before he let out a heavy sigh. "Ma'am, you got any slaves?"

Mama Taylor nodded her head to the two elderly slaves. "Just them two."

Ramsey looked at the man and woman who were gripping each other's gnarled hands. He grabbed hold of the youngest Taylor, barking the order so as to detract from the mercy of it, "You stay here. There ought to be a man around in case there's an uprising." The two slaves stared at him in astonishment before they finally gave him a pair of toothless smiles.

Alexandra released her breath. The rest of Ramsey's cohort must have known all along how this game worked, so they maintained their stern expressions as Mama Taylor sank to her knees and clutched her chest. The two elder Taylor boys nearly collapsed with relief as their little brother returned to their mother.

The eldest saluted Ramsey. "Thank you, Cap'n. We'll do our duty. We swear it. You won't ever see us run."

Ramsey glared at him. "Good. I don't wanna have to steal God's thunder."

The exhausted Confederates had scarcely made it to their camp, when Bradford commenced with supper. As Ramsey approached a few minutes later, Sal and Bradford were perched on a log devouring some beans. Alexandra was struggling to stay awake as she picked at the beans. Bradford offered some to the captain. Ramsey grinned as he accepted the plate. "You don't waste time, do you, Bradford?"

"Naw sir, I'm the youngest of nine. I had to fight for ever meal I et. Then, darned if I didn't have to fight my brother for puttin' pepper in my peas." Bradford chuckled. "Course, then Momma whooped us both for fightin' at the table."

Ramsey took one more bite and handed the plate back to Bradford. He kicked Alexandra's boot. "Get up," he ordered.

Alexandra set her plate aside, but before she stood, she stretched slowly. Too slowly. Ramsey pulled her up by her collar. "Quartermaster. Go." Alexandra picked up her gun belt and scabbard and trudged toward the quartermaster's wagon way down at the other end of camp. When she thought she was out of sight, she ducked into a wooded area and squatted behind some bushes to relieve herself.

Ramsey appeared on the other side of the bushes. Alexandra jumped up, holding her gun belt in front of her as Ramsey barked yet another order, "And get a pair of boots that fit."

As her commanding officer strode away, Alexandra wanted to scream. *Can't I go anywhere without somebody fussing about what I'm wearing?* She straightened her jacket and marched toward the supply wagon.

Alexandra stood motionless as an immaculate little sergeant circled her. Bouchard smoothed his pencil-thin mustache with his index finger. He shuffled through the back of the wagon and reemerged with a pair of boots that he dangled in front of her. When she reached for them, he pulled them back. "These are not your run-of-the-mill clodhoppers. These are the finest cavalry boots manufactured in Europe. You will take care of them as they cannot be replaced. It is not every day, you know, that you happen upon a pair of legs that used to belong to a very wealthy Yankee general with small feet."

Alexandra tried to block out the accompanying images that flooded her mind and took the boots as Bouchard adjusted the sleeves of her jacket, crinkling his fingers away from the dirt stains and the patch on the sleeve. "Well, it is obvious this jacket was not tailored for you. It will have to be taken up on both sides, and the sleeves are too long," he huffed. "I assume you know nothing of laundry or textile repair."

Happy to disavow her womanhood without penalty, Alexandra smiled and handed him the jacket.

Bouchard shook it out and held it away from his own impeccable uniform. "I will do what I can to make it presentable." He dropped the jacket into a mending basket as he promenaded to the back of the wagon.

He returned a moment later with a plain, single-breasted shell jacket and an armful of supplies that he promptly dumped into Alexandra's arms. "This jacket is on loan until yours can be repaired. Do not damage it. It is a matter of pride for me and for the captain that the men of this company are well-dressed. You will not tarnish my reputation nor the captain's by going about in a filthy uniform." He clapped his hands at her. "Off you go."

Alexandra scooted away. As she traipsed down a row of tents hunting a spot, she came across a shallow, freshly dug ditch at the end of the row where several men were standing along the edge. She gave them a curious look. The only one she recognized was McCabe. When McCabe turned around to face her, she quickly ducked her head and hurried away from the latrine.

McCabe hollered out in his thick Scottish accent as he buttoned his britches, "Weel, I never woulda mistaken ye for the modest type, Corbin, with that breech-loading, sixteen-shooter ye been waving around in our faces, ye wee mad dog."

If she hadn't been so embarrassed, Alexandra would have scolded them all for such indecency, but nevertheless, with her cheeks flaming, Alexandra kept on walking as McCabe and his compatriots guffawed. One of them followed her—the scout from Stark's company who had come to Cade's Mill earlier that day.

Alexandra turned when the scout called out, "You can set your tent over this way if you like."

Alexandra walked over to the spot the scout indicated but kept her supplies bundled in her arms. She wasn't sure that sleeping next to any man was a good idea, especially one who put her at so much unease, even if they were in separate tents.

The scout extended his hand. "Joss Larkin, Stark's company."

With her hands full, Alexandra nodded. "Drake Corbin, Ramsey's company."

"Yeah, I seen you at Cade's Mill. Set your load down."

"I have a spot over there," Alexandra lied.

"No, you ain't. I been watching you wander around like a lost kitten. One thing you gotta learn about soldierin' is to do as you're told. Now, set your load down."

Alexandra did as she was told.

Joss snatched Alexandra's hand and examined it. Whatever Joss was looking for, he evidently didn't find it. He shrugged as he dropped her hand and remarked good-naturedly, "Thought maybe you were some rich planter the way you walk around here like you own the place, but your hands are too rough. Planters don't work, and they don't ride without gloves."

Alexandra struggled to keep the high-pitched, annoyed female tone out of her voice as she retorted, "I don't walk around here like I own the place. I don't own anything but my gun and my horse."

"Well, I reckon that's all you need." Joss winked and sauntered over to a group of soldiers who were playing cards.

Something about Joss unnerved Alexandra. She thought perhaps she better stay away from him, but it was too late to move her tent. That would invite even more suspicion. And, it was rude. At least, she assumed it would be rude to move one's tent just because you didn't like the person next to you. Maybe things worked differently in the army.

Alexandra sighed. Again she found herself in a world where she didn't know the rules, but she figured if she kept to herself and mimicked the other soldiers, she would get by well enough. She hoped she could figure out what to do before she made any mistakes that would expose her. The punishment for violating societal rules amounted to ridicule and shunning, neither of which caused Alexandra any significant distress, but she had no knowledge of what the punishment would be for violating army rules. She decided that whatever it may be, it was not worth agonizing over. She would probably die in the battle to save Marlbridge anyway, if she ever got back there.

It took well over an hour for Alexandra to cobble together a decent shelter out of the pile of stakes and canvas Bouchard had given her. The tent was not tall enough for her to stand up except in the middle, but the space was adequate for anyone of normal size as long as they were wearing men's clothing. Not one of the skirts she had left behind would have fit in her new quarters. Having secured the flaps from the inside, she unfurled her bedroll and collapsed with her boots still on.

Chapter 21

Preparing for Victory

April 21

IT seemed as if only seconds had passed in between the time Alexandra closed her eyes and when she felt something wet streak across her face. When she opened her eyes, it was morning, and she was staring down the black-and-white muzzle of Corporal Carter's birddog, Boone. Alexandra groaned and rolled over. As the company mascot, Boone was not one to be deterred. He jumped on top of her and stuck his nose under her blanket to get at her face. A half-dozen licks later, Alexandra finally disentangled herself from dog and blanket and sat up.

Groggy as she was, it took her a few moments to remember her whereabouts. Outside her tent somewhere, someone was trying to find "Rose of Alabamy" on a harmonica. How she could have slept through that she couldn't imagine. After shooing Boone away, she snatched up her weapons and scrambled out of the tent, ready for war.

What she thought was early morning fog turned out to be smoke from the campfire across the way. As she peered through the cloud, her enthusiasm dissipated. For as far as she could see, men were sitting around outside their tents playing cards, smoking pipes, spitting tobacco juice, and sewing buttons on their shirts, muttering oaths whenever they stabbed themselves with the needle.

Sal and Bradford were in the middle of cooking some kind of meat. Boone trotted up to take a sniff then whined and crept away. Sal handed Bradford a slice of a dried peach he had procured on a foraging excursion. "Try ye some of that right there."

Bradford took a bite then spat it out in a dramatic fashion.

Sal swatted him. "What d'ye do that for? Didn't yer gran-maw teach ye nuthin'? It's the sire ones makes the best pie."

"Well, fix me a pie, and I'll et that sour peach," Bradford sputtered.

Corporal Carter, a middle-aged fatherly type, was sitting nearby with his nose stuck in a book. He looked up when Boone came over and licked his hand. Spotting Alexandra, he greeted her. "Morning, Drake."

Alexandra marched over and demanded, "What are y'all doing?"

"I believe Sal and Bradford are frying up shoe leather. I, on the other hand, am preparing for victory." Carter handed her a weathered collection of Jefferson's writings that included the *Kentucky Resolves*.

Alexandra handed the book back to him. "I don't see how victory comes from sitting around reading books. Or playing harmonicas." The harmonica player two tents down had given up on "Rose of Alabamy" to butcher "Dixie" instead.

Carter eyed her thoughtfully. "Wars get started when idle folks start dwelling on how somebody did them wrong, and they can't think of anything else to fill their time. A good book will cure that."

"It might surprise you to know I do enjoy a good book, every now and then, Corporal, but not when the people of my town are being held hostage by a hostile foreign power!"

She was about to storm off, when Sal caught her by the arm. He chomped on a peach and smacked, "Hold yer horses, Drake. There'll be plenty of fightin' soon enough. Now, set down and have some breakfast."

At Sal's behest, Bradford slapped a burnt piece of meat on a plate. Alexandra grimaced at the thought of putting anything that disgusting in her mouth, but she couldn't let the men think she had a weak stomach. She was just about to take a bite when Ramsey appeared and took the plate out of her hand. "It'll take an hour to chew that. Get up and come with me."

As Ramsey gave the plate back to Bradford, Alexandra sprang to her feet and grabbed her rifle, ready for whatever perilous deeds awaited her. Ramsey handed her a biscuit he had gotten from Miss Evelyn's the day before. It was hard and dry, but it was edible.

Alexandra followed Ramsey to an open field where several men were already standing. There weren't enough of them to form a battle line, but they were armed and facing a line of blue coats stuffed with straw, hanging on posts.

Ramsey shoved her towards the field. "Get to it."

St. Clair was pacing in front of the line of new recruits, waving his saber and shouting orders. When he saw Alexandra, he glowered. "Do not think you are entitled ta special privilege on account of your relation ta Cass Corbin, who was, by all standards of measurement, a fine soldier whose boots you are not wuthy ta fill. You will not be late again. Is that understood, Private Corbin?"

Alexandra had come to expect unprovoked rudeness from Ramsey, but coming from St. Clair, the very image of a Southern gentleman, it was irredeemably disheartening. "Yes, sir," she muttered.

As she moved to stand with the other recruits, Ramsey grabbed the barrel of her rifle and pulled it out of her hand. He replaced it with a Springfield rifled musket and a box of paper cartridges. "Rimfire cartridges for these Henries are hard to come by. You aren't going to waste them. You can have your Henry back when you learn how to shoot."

Alexandra swallowed the huff that would have exhibited her disdain for following orders, took the musket, and joined the Taylor boys and a passel of green troops as they stood shoulder to shoulder, their guns correctly poised.

Ramsey stood by and watched as St. Clair drilled them mercilessly. "Men, I trust you will quickly master tha art of warfare as have your more seasoned brethren."

The "more seasoned brethren" lounged nearby, spitting tobacco juice and commenting on the new volunteers and conscripts.

The barrel of Alexandra's musket began to bob as St. Clair went on, "Tha enemy is determined that he should come down here and lord over us in our own fields. Private Corbin, keep that musket steady." Alexandra readjusted her stance and steadied the gun.

McCabe held up a Confederate dollar and waved it as he pointed his thumb at Alexandra. "I say that one ends up on his arse." Alexandra glared at him.

By this time, St. Clair was completely caught up in the moment. "But I say ta you, tha enemy shall not prevail! What say you, gentlemen?"

They shouted in unison, "The enemy shall not prevail, sir!"

"Fire!"

Alexandra forgot to brace for the kickback, and she almost fell. McCabe and the others laughed, so she turned up her nose, stuck her chin out, and marched over to McCabe. She snatched the bill out of his hand. "Well, I didn't end up on my 'arse,' did I?" McCabe chortled and slapped her on the back so hard that she almost fell on her face. As she stumbled, she caught Ramsey laughing with the rest of the men.

She turned her back to all of them and took out another cartridge. Biting off the end of the paper tube, she wrinkled her nose at the taste of the black powder. She rammed the powder and ball down the barrel easily enough, but she dropped the percussion cap on her first try. When she stooped to look for it in the grass, St. Clair yelled, "Corbin! What in tarnation are you doin'? Do you think tha enemy will stand there waitin' politely for you ta reload? If you drop tha percussion cap, leave it and get another! Gawd-a-mighty, you are the wust parlor soldier I've ever seen!"

Despite the obvious "greenness" of her soldiering skills, Alexandra survived the rest of the grueling drill and performed at least as well as the Taylor boys who were only farmers. The most disappointing confirmation of the day was that she was no great marksman. She fared a little better with the musket than the revolver, but not enough to make her feel any better. Back in Marlbridge, she had carried that Colt around assuming if anyone attacked her, she could just shoot them. It had never occurred to her that she might not be good at it.

Her performance with the saber was passable, but nothing to brag about. She knew the basic movements Cass had taught her, but they had always played with wooden swords. She struggled to hold the unwieldy, two-and-a-half-pound blade in the proper position as St. Clair, who was even more relentless with the saber than he had been with the revolver, barked instructions. She locked blades with her opponent. The veteran showed no mercy, and it only took Alexandra a few swings to figure out why men referred to the heavy cavalry saber as "Old

Wristbreaker." It wasn't until later that Sal and Bradford informed her that sabers were mostly just for looks, and she'd probably never have occasion to use it.

"We don't need them when we charge the enemy?" she asked.

"Charge the enemy? With sabers?" Sal pulled her to the side. "Uh, Drake, I don't know whar ye been gittin' yer idears on modern cav'ry tactics and maneuvers, but this ain't gonna be no 'Charge of the Light Brigade.' The glory days of cav'ry is over. It's them gol-dang rifled muskets. See, used to…" Sal continued his lecture until he concluded, "So, ye see, the main difference 'tween infantry and cav'ry is them poor devils in the infantry's gotta walk all them miles to the battlefield, and we git to ride." He grinned and whacked Bradford on the arm. "Say, Bradford, what'd ye give to see ol' Drake here try to load and shoot that Henry at a dead gallop."

Bradford added, "Chargin' 'cross a half mile of open field with a whole brigade of Yankees all lined up blazin' away with their Sprang-fields."

Alexandra ignored their snickers.

Finally, towards the end of the day, the recruits trained with their horses. Ramsey joined them for that exercise. On horseback, Alexandra balanced perfectly to stay in the saddle while blocking heavy blows as they charged their horses across the field. In one mock altercation, Ramsey brought the flat side of his blade down on Alexandra's fore-arm. The blow caused her to drop her revolver. She turned Shadow around and galloped back to the place where she had lost the gun. In a swift, graceful move she swung down and picked it up then resumed the fracas.

Out of the corner of her eye, she caught Ramsey looking in her direction. She turned her chin up and rode harder. It didn't seem to matter where she was or what she was wearing, there was always going to be someone around to assess her every move. Had she not been so accustomed to Laura Catherine's scrutiny, her performance might have faltered under Ramsey's inspection, but Alexandra must have played Drake well enough. When she ventured to look in the captain's direction, he didn't look displeased. In the midst of one of the exercises, Alexandra overheard St. Clair observe to Ramsey that Drake was the best rider of the lot, despite his tendency to let his saber clank against everything within a three-foot radius.

At the end of the day, after the recruits had tended to their horses and trudged back to their tents, Sal stole up to Alexandra and glanced around to make sure no one else was listening. With a mischievous gleam in his eye, Sal announced in as serious a tone as he possessed, "Come on Drake, we done got ourselves a special assignment." Alexandra's eyes lit up as she followed Sal.

The longer they walked the more excited she became, anticipating an attack on a Union supply line or train robbery or...Sal led her right to the creek where men were splashing in a swimming hole.

Sal hooted as he jumped in. His head popped out of the water, and he sputtered, "Come on in, Drake."

Not amused, Alexandra simply waved, "Y'all go ahead."

Bradford snorted, "What's the matter, Drake? Water too cold for you?"

Alexandra scowled, "Too occupied." She didn't dare tell them she was scared of snakes for fear a harmless variety would end up in her bedroll that night.

Coming from the opposite bank, Joss stepped across the dry rocks protruding out of the rushing water to stand in front of Alexandra. Joss lit a cigar and inquired, "You killed a man yet?" Alexandra shook her head. "Well, you better git to it. That's what you came for, ain't it?"

Alexandra growled, "I came to do my duty like every other man here."

Joss smirked, "That's how they talk anyway. You almost had me fooled. At first, I thought you followed some man here, but it's obvious you ain't got one."

Alexandra tried not to sound nervous. "I don't know what you're talking about."

Joss circled her. "I know what you are, and I know what you're after."

Alexandra broke the circle and leaned into Joss' face. "Listen, if you know what's good for you, you'll get away from me."

"Relax, honey, I ain't no traitor to my own kind." Joss glanced around then unbuttoned her shirt.

Alexandra gasped when she saw the cloth binding Joss's breasts. "Are you mad?"

Joss smirked again as she buttoned her shirt. "Just as much as you."

Alexandra straightened her own clothes and looked at the men splashing in the creek. "What do you mean, exposing yourself like that?"

Joss chuckled. "They ain't payin' no attention." She took the cigar out of her mouth as a thought occurred to her. "That's why you're here, ain't it? Somebody hasn't been payin' attention. Somebody hasn't been doin' their duty?"

Alexandra loomed over her. "I joined the army because they wouldn't let me shoot Yankees in a dress."

Bradford, sporting a ridiculous grin, lumbered over to them. "Hey, Drake, me and the boys decided to go down to Johnny Knowles' later tonight. Get us some whiskey and women." He begrudgingly acknowledged Joss. "You can come, too, I reckon."

Joss held her hand up and laughed, winking at Alexandra before she sauntered away.

Alexandra could take no more. It was enough that Ramsey and St. Clair had treated her horribly, but to cut her hair, dress like a man, join the army, endure all their jibes and their buffoonery, and then, for her motives to be questioned and sneered at by another woman? Intolerable. She excused herself and headed off into the woods to be alone.

Once she was out of eyesight and earshot, she threw a hissy fit, a stomping, pouting, hair-pulling hissy fit. Never before in her life had she done such a thing. Only girls like Meredith engaged in that sort of ridiculous behavior. She even dragged God into it. If only He had made her a man, none of this would have ever happened. She wouldn't have let it happen. The Yankees, Barrymore, Elias, Garrett, Ramsey, her mother—Alexandra had tried to right all of their wrongs, but all her efforts only ended up creating more wrongs. Since she had become Drake Corbin, it had been one disaster after another. She was a woman trying to do a man's job, and she had proven herself unequal to the task.

As all her mistakes piled up in her mind, she began to wish she could go back to being a girl. Ramsey and St. Clair wouldn't be so mean and rude to a girl. If she were a girl again, she could think of countless ways to shame them for their ungracious behavior toward her. No one would have taken her rifle away if she were a girl. No one expected a girl to be a great marksman. No one expected a girl to stand out in a field all day shooting at straw.

When she had finally worn herself out bombarding the Lord with all her woes, she sat down against an oak tree, and, strangely enough, a wave of peace came over her. Furthermore, she didn't feel the least bit guilty when she realized she suddenly didn't care about anything. The oppression of duty lifted. She had tried to get Ramsey to come back and save her people, but he abandoned them. She had tried to save her people without him, but they didn't lift a finger to save themselves. She had tried to be more of a lady for Garrett's sake, but he chose a Northern girl over her.

Alexandra got up and dusted herself off. All the men she had spent her life trying to live up to were dead: her father, her brother, Swamp Fox, and all the other war heroes who had come before her. As she made her way back to the creek, she saw Bradford and Sal wrestling with the Taylor boys and getting the worst of it.

"Drake! Get in the water. We need you!" Bradford shouted.

Alexandra hollered back, "Nope, you boys got yourselves into that fix. I reckon you can get yourselves out."

Up to that point, she had not let herself care too much about the men in her company. They were Ramsey's men, not hers. As much as Alexandra wanted to go back to being a girl, she resolved to face her circumstances like a man. There was no place left in the world for Alexandra. The only thing in Marlbridge awaiting her return was the gallows. The only other place for Alexandra was in Chattanooga with Aunt Charlotte where hiding away in an endless stream of dinner parties seemed like another form of death. At least a hanging would be quicker and more heroic. The conclusion of it all was that no matter what she did, Alexandra was as good as dead, but Drake still had a place. All she had to do was play the part right, and eventually, she might get to go home, wherever that was.

On her way back to camp, Alexandra walked past the corral and caught a glimpse of a flaxen chestnut Arabian snorting and prancing along the back fence. A crowd of Confederates were placing bets as Ramsey, laid out in a cloud of dust, picked himself up and stepped over the broken rails into the corral.

"Go get him, Captain," Carter slapped Ramsey on the back and handed him his hat.

When Alexandra made her way to the fence, Carter scooted over to make room. He jerked his thumb at the Arabian and said, "That's Red Sticks. He's been in this war longer than I have. Every man in the company has tried to break him, but so far, he's been the one doing all the breaking. I don't know why Ramsey keeps him. He must see something in him I don't."

Ramsey waited for the horse to calm down, but when he tried to remount, Red Sticks backed up and slung his head around trying to bite him. Ramsey finally let go of the reins and left the horse to prance around the corral.

As Alexandra rested her chin on the top rail of the corral, the unruly horse trotted over to her and shook his head with as much defiance as Alexandra's first pony, Muffin. When Muffin had thrown her during her first riding lesson, her father had said, "Don't let him get away with that. You gotta show him who's in charge. God created horses for a purpose—to help with the work He created us to do. They forget that sometimes, so you have to remind them."

Jonas Corbin had taught his daughter many things that turned out to be just what she needed for the course her life had taken. Few of the lessons were meant for girls, but her father must have known that the world she would inherit would be no place for a girl. All of the years spent at Miss Daschle's School for Girls were of little use. Laura Catherine Corbin had insisted that her daughter learn to sew and cook and run a household, all in order to catch a man and manipulate him into doing what he ought to do. After all, what man could find the right path without a woman?

Alexandra wished Adam hadn't listened to Eve, and that Eve hadn't listened to the snake. Everything was upside down. With the good people acting like the Devil and the bad people playing God, Alexandra could no longer tell friend from foe. All the voices ran together. If God was trying to tell her something, she wasn't sure it would be possible for her to hear Him. The words that had always guided her were those of Jonas Corbin, not the words she'd heard from Reverend Land about God, and not what God had to say about Himself in the Scriptures. Back then, she had relied on her father's nod of approval to reassure her of her actions.

Red Sticks tossed his head and kicked at the fence when Carter yelled, "Hey, Captain, isn't it regulation that all new recruits have to face Red Sticks to prove they belong in this outfit?"

"It is," Ramsey replied with a glint of mischief in his eyes.

"I say we give Drake a go." Carter smacked Alexandra on the back. Stunned, Alexandra took a step back.

"You aren't a coward, are you?" Carter grinned wickedly.

"I'm not a coward."

"Then prove it. Go ride that horse."

Ramsey jerked his head toward Red Sticks. "Go on, Corbin. Break him."

The onlookers cheered and hollered her name—it didn't matter that it wasn't her real name. With them all watching her and her place among them at stake, she had to do as they commanded her. She set her jaw. If she was going to do it, she was going to do it her way. Instead of yelling out her demands to the whole group, she addressed Ramsey. "I need one minute to prepare."

"What's that, Drake? Ye need to say ye prayers?" McCabe guffawed.

Ramsey pulled out his timepiece. "One minute."

Alexandra ran to her tent and grabbed her knapsack.

As she made her way back to the corral, Sal and Bradford caught up to her. "Whar ye off to in sech a hurry, Drake?"

"To fight Red Sticks," Alexandra hollered over her shoulder. Sal and Bradford scurried after her.

By the time Alexandra reached the corral, Red Sticks had worked himself into a frenzy. Foam dripped from his mouth as he champed the bit. He was hot, tired, and thirsty. Alexandra opened her knapsack and pulled out a handful of the apple-and-oat treats she had stolen from Matthew. She slipped through the rails and walked along the boundary of the corral as she took a bite out of one of the treats.

Red Sticks pricked his ears when he heard the crunch. He nosed his way to the treats, but Alexandra held them away from him and turned her back. The horse put his head over her shoulder, sniffing for the treats. She walked away. When Red Sticks followed, Alexandra eased around and took another bite right in front of him. As the horse reached for the treats, Alexandra hid them behind her back. Red Sticks followed her to the back corner of the corral.

Distracted by the treats, he let her maneuver him until his backside was up against the rail. Alexandra lined the treats up on the top rail. As Red Sticks busied himself snatching the treats, Alexandra slipped into the saddle and gripped a wad of mane. Red Sticks jerked his head up. Unable to back up, he lunged forward. Alexandra pulled his head to the side so that every time he bucked he went sideways. After smacking his head into the fence a few times, Red Sticks finally stopped and groaned with exhaustion. He let Alexandra stay in the saddle as she guided him toward the back of the corral. Alexandra dismounted and stroked the horse's neck as she gave him the rest of the treats.

All the men stared in silence as Red Sticks stood quietly and consumed his treats as happily as any other horse. Carter removed his hat as did McCabe and Bradford. Sal was the first to blurt out, "Aw, ye call that breakin' a horse? We all know Red Sticks cain't be broke. He's just foolin' ye, Drake. Give him a minute, and he'll be back at it."

When Red Sticks finished his treats, Alexandra led him out the gate and offered Ramsey the reins. "He's ready to be broken now if that's what you really want."

Ramsey took the reins, but made no effort to mount as he rested his arm on the saddle. He glanced at St. Clair.

With the toe of his boot, St. Clair unearthed a small stone. He picked it up and rolled it around in his hand. "This world doesn't have much use for an unbroken horse."

Ramsey looked Red Sticks in the eye for a moment then handed the reins back to Alexandra. "Rub him down, Corbin. When you're done, you can have your rifle back."

Chapter 22

No End of Devils

FOR him to think of himself as the man in charge of Marlbridge, Elias spent a lot of time being summoned. James K. Polk had summoned him to Mexico to start a war. Jonas Corbin had summoned him to Storm Chase to end a war. Now, Manfred P. Heppinstahl had summoned him to Union headquarters to keep the present war from getting out of hand.

"That madman must not succeed," Heppinstahl vented in between mouthfuls of peas and roasted chicken. "He has done more to stir up these people than if the Republicans had resurrected King George to rule over them. You have to stop him."

Elias nudged his boot at a fallen pea under the table. "How am I to accomplish that?"

"If I knew the answer to that question, I would stop him myself."

"Colonel, while I am touched by your confidence in me, of the two of us, you are the one with an army and the weight of authority behind you." Elias smiled as Heppinstahl dislodged a piece of chicken that was stuck between his teeth. "Barrymore has three hundred men. You have closer to a thousand. He cannot order you to give him command of your regiment, so if you really want to prevent more bloodshed, refuse him. He cannot defeat the Rebels on his own, especially if the rumors are true that Madcap Charlie is about."

"Whisenhunt? Is there no end of devils?" Heppinstahl wailed.

"Not at present, so I suggest we make good use of them while the opportunity remains. By now, Ramsey will have met up with Kinkaid's battalion at Cade's Mill which puts him at about three hundred men.

I say let Barrymore and Ramsey come to blows before Whisenhunt shows up with the rest of the regiment. Perhaps they will kill each other and save you the trouble. You will have two fewer devils and the people will console themselves with the pride of knowing their loved ones died in service to the Cause. They can bravely—and peacefully—endure legitimate acts of war, but if you subject them to any more of these absurd tribunals and executions, they will revolt. They will ransack your headquarters, truss you like a turkey, and roast you on a spit in the middle of the street, and I won't lift a finger to stop them." From the table beyond Heppinstahl's plate, Elias trapped a runaway pea and popped it in his mouth.

Heppinstahl set his fork down. "Well, I certainly do not want to be roasted. Let Barrymore's death be upon his own head. I abhor the man, but I don't wish to disturb my conscience by killing him myself. I'll send Fontaine with three companies to ensure the deed is done."

"The madman's death will be secured with a stroke of your pen," Elias grinned as he stood and gave Heppinstahl an exaggerated bow.

The colonel grimaced, "Elias, you will henceforth dispense with dramatics. I hate poetry and all poets. I can't stomach it. Why, I couldn't eat for two days because of that wretched Poe fellow. I hope he is enjoying his time in the Abyss from which he conjured up all his frightful imagery."

"Speaking of the Abyss," Elias said as if it was an afterthought, "I wonder what will become of you if Edwin Belgrave doesn't get his son back in one piece. He is a member of the Council, you know."

"What council?"

"The Council who founded Marlbridge along with several other 'fiefdoms' in the Tennessee Valley. They didn't tell you about the Council before they sent you to this part of the country?"

"Well, of course, I had heard rumors of such an organization, but few in Washington know of it." Heppinstahl's face turned whiter than the tablecloth. "Do you mean to say the Council actually exists?"

Elias put his index finger to his lips.

Heppinstahl spoke very quietly. "I knew General Belgrave was an important man, but the Council? That's...very bad indeed. Tell me, Elias, you've had dealings with the Council?"

Elias shrugged. "Friends of friends."

"Hmm. Are they really as...dedicated to their mission as one might conclude if one believed all the rumors?"

"Oh, I would say so."

Having lost his appetite, Heppinstahl waved at the door, and a Union private came in and removed his plate. The moment the lad was out of the room, Heppinstahl leaned forward. "Elias, I would be most grateful, indeed, I would be indebted to you if you were able to find the Belgrave boy and return him to me safely."

"Well, I'm sure I could make inquiries. One of my associates will have seen the boy at some point. *If* he's still alive. Of course, if he's not alive, it will be a waste of time that could be spent on more profitable ventures."

"For Heaven's sake, man," Heppinstahl bellowed as he banged his fist on the table. "I told you I would be indebted, so none of your hem hawing. State plainly what you want in exchange for your services!"

Elias straightened a case knife that wasn't set quite right on the table. "If I agree to help you in this endeavor, the hangings in Marlbridge will cease immediately, you will release every one of my people whom Barrymore has taken prisoner, and you will stop looking for Drake Corbin. Those are my terms, and they are not negotiable."

Heppinstahl waited long enough for Elias to wonder whether he would accept the arrangement. "You puzzle me, Elias. I tell you I am indebted. You could have asked me for anything, and this is what you choose? Why? If all goes according to plan, Barrymore will hopefully die in battle, and the arrests will stop anyway. So, I'm curious. What game are you playing?"

A pea had rolled off the table and onto the floor. Elias squashed it under his boot. "A very dangerous one."

Chapter 23

Drake the Dragon

ABOUT early evening, Alexandra, Sal, Bradford, McCabe, and several others moseyed over to the tavern that was a little ways outside of Cade's Mill. As they went, Sal reassured them all once more, "Ol' Red Sticks cain't ne'er be broke. I seen it in a vision. The Arabian has no rider. Weren't no bullet could put him down, just like the Cap'n."

They were nearly halfway to the tavern when Bradford strode up beside Alexandra and talked in a low voice. "Drake, I been meaning to warn you 'bout hangin' 'round that Joss feller. Now, I ain't tryin' to tell you what to do or nothin'. I don't like to butt-in on other folk's business, but I think you oughtta know that Joss feller ain't well-liked 'round here, and I'd jest hate for you to git yourself mixed up with the likes of him. Now, I ain't seen no evidence per se, but I got pretty good instincts when it comes to horses and people. And I jest cain't help but think Joss is a bad apple. 'Course, me and you's friends no matter what, but, well, I see it as my duty to let my friends know when they's a-headin' down the wrong path. That's all I's wantin' to say." Bradford slapped her on the back and trotted over to Sal.

Alexandra wondered if Bradford knew Joss was a woman and that was why he thought she was a bad apple. Maybe he thought any woman who would disguise herself as a man and join the army was a bad apple no matter what she was really like underneath it all. One thing was certain: it wasn't her place to tell Joss' secret, so she kept her mouth shut and walked on to the tavern with the rest of the men.

Johnny Knowles' Watering Hole was much smaller than Bolivar's tavern, but its size only accentuated the general rowdiness of the place.

As they came into the yard, McCabe suddenly charged toward an enclave of ill-clad roustabouts who were terrorizing one of the barmaids and hollered, "Get out of here, ye filthy deserters! Ye got no right fraternizing with us real men! And leave the lass be. Pick up your own skirts and be gone before I tell Captain Ramsey where ye rotten curs been hiding out! He'll put a bullet in ye sure, if I dinna shoot ye myself." The deserters scattered as McCabe kicked at the stragglers and hurled one last insult. "And take ye fleas with ye!"

As the men tromped into the tavern, Alexandra stopped to get a closer look at one of the horses standing at the far end of the hitching post. She had seen him before, a bulky champagne with one blue eye and one brown. He pinned his ears back and snorted, ready for a fight, but not with her.

Out of the darkness, a meaty paw reached out and clamped down over Alexandra's mouth. She fought to free herself as someone dragged her into the woods at the back of Johnny Knowles' Tavern and pressed her up against a tree.

Prichard Benefield sneered. "D'you think I wouldn't recognize you?" Alexandra broke loose, but Prichard jerked her to the ground and held her down. "Now you stay put. I'm tired of chasin' you all over creation. Good thing you're worth a lot of money. Otherwise, I might be tempted to take my pay out of your hide."

Alexandra managed to free one arm and punched him in the face. As she tried to get away, Prichard grabbed her shirt, tearing it down to her navel. She plunged her knife into his gut. He roared and sank to his knees, gripping his belly. Alexandra didn't wait around to watch him die.

She hadn't run ten yards when Joss caught her. "Well, you do mean business."

Alexandra shoved Joss away. Sweat began to drip from her brow, so she wiped her eyes.

Joss scolded her, "Oh, Lord, don't cry about it. Killing a man ain't worth that."

"I'm not crying. How many men have you killed?"

Joss' mood darkened. "All that matters is I haven't killed the one I'm hunting." She stepped closer and tilted her head back to look up at

Alexandra who was a good six inches taller than her. "You remember one thing: if you got the power of life and death over them, they got no power over you." Joss took Alexandra's arm and pulled her toward the tavern. "Come on, and I'll buy you a drink. You ain't never had a drink, have you?"

"I can hold my own," Alexandra growled as she buttoned her jacket to cover the tear in her shirt.

"We'll see about that," Joss chuckled.

The two women left Prichard writhing in the woods and made their way back to the tavern. Joss shoved through the swinging door and strolled into the bar, slamming her hand down on the smooth, dark wood. "Whiskey. For the both of us."

The barkeep set two half-full shot glasses in front of the concealed women. Alexandra stared down at her glass. Though she was sure her assailant was dead, the image of his bear-like face penetrated her mind.

Joss slung her drink back and motioned for the barkeep to leave the bottle. "My husband never could hold his liquor as good as me," she muttered when the barkeep was out of earshot.

Alexandra looked up from her glass, her mind temporarily freed from Prichard's lingering grasp. "You're married?"

"That surprise you?"

"I never heard of a married woman doing a man's work like you."

"Well, you're doing a man's work."

"I'm not married."

"What's married got to do with it? I always done what I pleased. Why, it was my fiery, independent disposition that set Franklin to thinkin' he was gonna marry me," Joss snorted. "That skinny laggard thought he was gonna tame me, too. At first I was of a mind to let him. Funny thing, there was a time I thought I loved him, but he turned out to be a sorry rascal, a cheat, a thief, and a liar."

"Does he know you're in the army?"

"Oh, he knows. He also knows that one day I'm gonna catch up to him and make him regret all his despicable ways."

"You don't know where he is?"

"I wouldn't be here if I didn't know he was headed this way, against his will most like. Must be the Good Lord aims to grant me my request, seeing as how it's a miracle Franklin hasn't already got hisself shot for desertion. Madcap Charlie wouldn't lose a wink of sleep over putting that coward in the ground. Neither would your Captain Ramsey, come to think of it."

Alexandra still had not taken a drink. She swirled the glass, pondering how a woman could end up despising the man she'd married of her own freewill.

"Well, drink up." Joss slapped her on the back.

Alexandra slung her drink back the way she'd seen Joss do it. Immediately, she wished she hadn't. She choked and sputtered, and the patrons who were clustered at the bar erupted in laughter.

Bradford came up beside her. "Aw, come on, Drake. Anybody totin' a sixteen-shooter's gotta be able to hold his liquor better'n that."

It wasn't long before Sal and McCabe joined in. "Aye, Corbin, ye drink like a wee lassie."

Alexandra hadn't been prepared to have her manhood tested in this way. Evidently, it wasn't enough to prove oneself on the battlefield. The men who surrounded her seemed determined to test her in every way possible. She took another drink. This time she braced herself, and it did go down a little easier. By the time the whiskey hit her stomach, she began to feel a little wobbly—and a little bolder. Prichard Benefield deserved what he got, and she was glad to be the one who did it to him.

She barely got her third drink to her lips before she started declaring her revenge on Barrymore and Elias, but then she couldn't help but think that Jonas Corbin, the war hero who got himself killed in the war between the Kelsons and the Ramseys, the most meaningless "war" ever fought in human history, would be mighty disappointed to hear her vengeful, and slurred, speech. At least she didn't use profanity. She remembered that lecture. It was the last one Jonas Corbin ever gave her. He didn't want to hear any more coarse language outta her mouth. Wasn't ladylike. Which meant that lecture wasn't intended for her because there wasn't supposed to be anything ladylike about Drake Corbin because Drake Corbin was a boy. No, Drake Corbin was a man. Drake the Dragon, like Sir Francis Drake. That's what her enemies would call her once she exacted her revenge on their hides.

Chapter 24

Trouble

BOUND as surely by their actions as their words, Ramsey and St. Clair rode toward Johnny Knowles' Watering Hole in silence. Their horses jerked to a stop when they heard the sound of something large crashing through the woods. Expecting a bear or a mountain lion, they drew their weapons. Prichard Benefield stumbled out of the trees and collapsed on the side of the road.

Ramsey dismounted, keeping his gun on Prichard who rolled onto his back and panted, "You won't be needin' that gun, Ramsey. Even the wicked knows when their part in this life is over with. You been after me all this time and looka here if the Lord ain't brung me to ya as I draw my last breath. Reckon it's fittin'."

"Shut your mouth and save all that melodrama for the Devil when you see him," Ramsey snapped.

"Which devil you talkin' about? The one in hell or the one in Marlbridge?"

"If all goes to my liking, you'll see them both before the week is out."

Prichard sneered. "You know they're comin' for you. And for her."

Ramsey poked Prichard's leg with his boot. "What do you mean they're coming for 'her'?"

"If you ain't figured it out yet, I ain't gonna ruin the surprise," Prichard gurgled.

"What is this reprobate babblin' about?" St. Clair interrupted, keeping his attention on his captain. "Surely, he cannot mean tha Yankees are comin'. For what purpose would they stray this far from Mahl-bridge? Not ta recover Elias Kelson's horses, that's for certain."

Ramsey shifted his gaze to St. Clair. "At Bolivar's Tavern, did you fight Marcus face-to-face?"

St. Clair shook his head. "I avoided him. Why? Do you think him a changed man?"

"I think he is a conflicted man," Ramsey mused. "That will be to our advantage."

"If he is here ta do battle, he will not back down. We know that."

"If he is here at all, it is under orders, but Marcus Fontaine only fights when he decides. Otherwise, his heart will not be in it, and he can be made to fall back."

Prichard grumbled, "Enough talk of Major Fontaine. I'm the one's dyin' here."

Ramsey waved his gun in the direction of Prichard's face. "Lieu-tenant St. Clair, take this jackdaw to the big house. See what you can get out of him."

"My pleasure, Captain," St. Clair replied with a cold smile. "Get up, you."

Prichard struggled to his knees, but the pain was evidently too much for him. He groaned and passed out.

"I'll head on to the tavern and send McCabe with Johnny's wag-on," Ramsey volunteered as he holstered his gun.

"Be sure it's tha same wagon I saw Johnny haulin' this afternoon. A bed of manure will be much more comf'table for ol' Prichard here than wood planks." St. Clair scratched his chin as he tilted his head to the stars. "When Prichard said 'her', do you think he was referrin' ta Evelyn? Shall I send guards?"

"I don't think he was referring to Evelyn, but take whatever pre-cautions you deem necessary."

"Vera well, I'll send Langley and Hutcheson to scout the enemy's location. Let's see if Prichard was tellin' the truth."

Ramsey raised an eyebrow. "Isn't Hutcheson the man you saved from a lynching last week?"

"He is."

"The man's a horse thief."

"He's a really good horse thief whose talents have proven ta be an asset of late."

"What's to stop him from killing Langley and running off?"

"It's unlikely that Hutcheson would harm Langley. I've taken every opportunity ta encourage friendship between the two, believing Langley ta be a good influence, and indeed they have become friends. However, as auxiliary precautions, I don't allow Hutcheson ta carry a weapon, and I've given Langley strict orders ta shoot him at tha fust sign of trouble. Do you have any other objections ta tha man beyond your belief that I distrust him?"

"No, you know I trust your judgment. Send Langley and Hutcheson, and if Prichard's telling the truth, we'll inform Colonel Kinkaid. No sense in getting the old man riled up unless we're certain."

Once he secured Johnny's wagon and sent McCabe back to assist St. Clair, Ramsey eased into one of the rocking chairs on the front porch of the tavern. He sat quietly for several minutes, identifying the distinct voices of his men like a hunter listening to his coon dogs.

He had just rested his eyes for a moment when he heard the sound of breaking glass and cracking wood. He got up and looked inside the tavern to see his men ducked behind overturned tables. The barkeep, barely poking his head above the bar, motioned for him to stay out. That's when Ramsey spotted the source of trouble.

Drake Corbin was staggering at the far end of the bar, yelling and waving his gun around. Joss Larkin was sitting on the counter, observing the scene with a satisfied smirk.

Ramsey stalked into the tavern and stopped in the middle of the room. Resting his hands on his hips, he gave a shrill whistle. The commotion ceased. He raised his eyebrows at Bradford who was peeping out from behind a table.

"What are y'all hiding for?"

"We's afraid Drake was gonna start to firin' any minit and shoot up the place," Bradford answered.

"Why didn't y'all take his gun?"

"Law, Cap'n," Bradford declared, "I'll fight Yankees to Kingdom come, but I ain't about to git myself kilt by a pup that cain't hold his tar water."

Ramsey rolled his eyes and strode to the bar. Drake threw a shot glass at him. He caught it and set it back on the counter. When Ramsey took the gun out of his hand, Drake glowered at him for a second then took a swing. Ramsey ducked, and Drake reeled against the bar.

When Drake wagged his head and steadied himself, poised for another strike, Ramsey said, "Son, you're about to find yourself in front of a firing squad if you don't simmer down."

Whatever it was that had set Drake off initially, the fury in his eyes subsided, giving way to wounded astonishment. "You'd really shoot me?" he asked in a heavy slur.

"If you don't believe that, you got no business in the army."

Ramsey tucked Drake's gun in his belt and addressed the rest of his men. "Speaking of firing squads, y'all better shed your yellow streaks. Tomorrow, we got Yankees to deal with."

At that, the Confederates hopped out from behind the tables and began setting the place in order. "Now, Cap'n," Sal whined, "ye knowed we warn't really skeered of Drake. We's just bein' cautious-like. Ye know how ye always tellin' us not to take unnecessary risks. That's all we's doin'. Ye ain't gotta worry 'bout us runnin' from the enemy nohow, but Drake is one of us. Didn't figure ye'd want us to shoot him."

Ramsey glared at Drake. "I don't think shooting him would do any good. A thrashing might."

In response, Drake removed his gun belt and extended it to Ramsey as he mumbled, "Do what you want with me. I'm not even s'posed to be here."

As Drake wobbled out the door, Joss Larkin stepped forward and hollered, "Hold up, Drake. I'll go with you."

Instinct compelled Ramsey to catch Joss mid-stride and steer him away from Drake. "You get on back to your company and stay away from mine."

The corner of Joss' mouth twitched. His cat-eyes glowed with defiance. And amusement. Ramsey leaned into the smaller man's face. If the rascal meant to toy with him, Ramsey meant to snap him in two.

Joss didn't back away. "Feeling a little protective, aren't you, Captain?" he accused in a low voice. "A little possessive, too, I'd wager, and you don't even know why."

Ramsey blinked. That was exactly how he was feeling, and he sure enough didn't know why.

"Relax, Captain," Joss whispered. "It ain't sodomy I'm accusing you of."

"What, then?" Ramsey growled.

The grin on Joss' face faded, and a hint of sadness flickered in his eyes as he continued in a barely audible voice, "I'm accusing you, sir, of the worst sin there is: being a man."

When Joss turned back to the bar and motioned for another drink, Ramsey didn't press the matter, for at some point during the exchange, Captain Stark had entered the tavern with his second lieutenant.

"Ramsey," Stark nodded a greeting as his dark, hooded eyes swept the room. "Is there some kind of trouble here?"

Ramsey noticed that Joss stiffened when he heard Stark's voice, and Stark's gaze in Joss' direction was none too friendly. Whatever storm might be brewing between those two, Ramsey wasn't about to get in the middle of it. He flashed a cocky smile. "Nothing I can't handle."

Stark laughed and slapped Ramsey on the back. "You always say that, and damned if you ain't right, most of the time. Sid, serve this man a drink."

Ramsey waved the barkeep off. "I'm done. If any more of my men come in here, Sid, you send 'em back to camp. I'm not spending the rest of the night rounding 'em up."

"Whatever you say, Ramsey," Sid replied, resting his massive fists on the counter.

Without further interruption, Ramsey walked out of the tavern looking forward to a few hours of sleep. He had decided not to waste another minute looking out for Drake Corbin when he spotted him, passed out in one of the chairs on the tavern porch. Ramsey groaned. The ungrateful whelp had already proven to be a considerable bother. Yet, he couldn't bring himself to abandon the lad. He roused him to a half-standing position, but when Drake almost fell back into the chair, Ramsey hoisted him over his shoulder and carried him to his horse. Solomon turned his head to sniff at Drake as Ramsey laid him across the saddle on his stomach.

Back at camp, Ramsey trudged to his tent where St. Clair was waiting for him. The lieutenant raised his eyebrows when he saw Drake slung over the back of Ramsey's horse. "What happened ta him?"

"Drunk."

"I didn't think he was tha type,"

Ramsey scowled. "Bradford informed me earlier today that Corbin's come to be friends with Joss Larkin."

St. Clair snorted his disdain. "There's somethin' amiss with that Larkin fella. Can't quite put my finger on it, though."

He tapped his lips for a moment then gave up and continued with his report, "Prichard Benefield is still alive and kickin'. It took four of us ta haul him up ta tha big house and tuck him in. Whoever stabbed him got him good. He was bleedin' like a stuck pig. Speakin' of which…"

St. Clair stepped over to Solomon for a closer look at the blood on Drake's collar. He whistled as he pulled Drake's knife from its scabbard and examined the long, wide blade. "Well, it isn't quite long enough ta qualify for an Arkansas tooth pick, but I reckon it'll get tha job done. Tha blade's been cleaned, but there's a thin line here. I can't tell if it's blood or rust."

"What on earth would possess Drake Corbin to pick a fight with Prichard?"

"I don't know. Drake is a mite prickly. Whatever tha fight was about, Prichard caught tha wust of it. Doc said tha fiend was lucky." St. Clair wrinkled his long, slender nose as he glanced down at his uniform. "I cannot say tha same for myself. Tha man is putrid, and it shall be at least another whole day 'til Mrs. Bouchard will see ta my laundry. Do you know she's raised tha price of ironin' ta five cents a shirt? Highway robbery."

"She only charges me three." Ramsey grinned at St. Clair's outraged expression. "Could be because I don't fuss over every wrinkle and bully her into ironing my shirts twice."

"I have never done such!" St. Clair's absolute faith in his chivalry waned somewhat when Ramsey folded his arms across his chest, waiting for a more truthful response. "Well, I wouldn't call it bullyin' exactly," he huffed, straightening his jacket as he changed the subject.

"I'll have one of tha men carry Drake back ta his tent. Or perhaps, tha guardhouse might be more suitable?"

"No, let him sleep it off here where I can keep an eye on him. Besides, if there's a fight tomorrow and Madcap Charlie doesn't get here soon with the rest of the regiment, we're gonna need every man we can get," Ramsey grumbled with a shake of his head. "I knew Corbin would be trouble—I just hope he's not more trouble than he's worth."

"Like Red Sticks?" St. Clair rolled his eyes the way he usually did at the mention of that wicked beast.

"That horse is gonna be the death of me," Ramsey muttered.

"Well, you're stuck with both of 'em, and I do not envy you, suh," St. Clair proclaimed with a renewed sense of superiority. "I see now it was wrong for me ta complain about a measly five cents when others are so much less fortunate. I repent and bid you good evenin', and may I recommend you get some sleep, *Captain*." With a smart salute to match his turned-up nose, he whirled on his heel and marched off, his back straight as a ramrod.

After the brief amusement St. Clair had generously provided, Ramsey turned his focus to the less amusing figure draped over his horse. He pulled Drake down from the saddle, carried him inside the tent, and flopped his limp body onto the cot.

"What have you gotten yourself into, Corbin?" He unbuttoned Drake's jacket to see more blood on his shirt. He observed that the buttons at the top were gone and the front of the shirt was torn right down the middle, exposing the taut binding on Drake's chest. What was underneath the binding was small but unmistakable.

Ramsey froze, scarcely breathing as he gaped at her. The jaw was a little more squared than what he remembered, and the short, unwashed hair that fanned out across the pillow only faintly resembled the honey-colored mane that had been Alexandra Corbin's defining feature, but he didn't need to examine her face very closely to know it was her. Even as she slept, the peaceful expression on her face could not hide the fighting spirit that covered her like chainmail.

So, that was the surprise Prichard had been referring to when he said the Yankees were coming for "her." Ramsey's chest began to tighten. If Prichard knew that Alexandra was Drake, who else knew?

He didn't realize his hand was resting on her breast until he heard Carter call his name. He jerked his hand away from her and stepped back. As he did, he knocked the lantern off the table, and a small fire broke out.

"Captain Ramsey? Sir?" Carter called out again.

"Hold, Carter, I'm coming," Ramsey yelled as he stamped out the flames. After throwing a blanket over Alexandra's half-naked torso, Ramsey slipped outside, keeping the tent flap closed behind him.

"Captain, there's a civilian here to see you," Carter announced. "Are you all right, sir?"

Ramsey nodded as he rubbed his forehead. "What does he want? Or she? Please, tell me it's not another woman."

"It's a man." Carter scrunched his brow and lowered his voice. "Are you sure you're all right, sir?"

"Leave it, Carter," he grunted. "What does the civilian want?"

"Says he's a friend of the Corbin family and has urgent business."

The exhaustion that had been steadily piling up on Ramsey's shoulders fell away as he snapped to attention. "Corbin? Did he give his name?"

"No, sir, and whatever his 'urgent business' is, he didn't look too happy about it."

"Go fetch him then."

Ramsey paced outside his tent, running through a mental list of who this friend of the Corbin family might be. At first, he hoped it was Alexandra's stepfather coming to take her home, but then it occurred to him that Marlbridge was the last place she needed to be. A knot began to form in his stomach. He couldn't send her home, but he couldn't let her stay either. An army encampment was no place for a woman. Unless…

Ramsey had just begun to formulate a plan when Carter returned with the prince of Marlbridge himself—the last person Ramsey wanted to see at that moment. He gave Garrett Rainier no greeting, just looked at him, daring him to give words to the contempt that was shining in his dark brown eyes.

Garrett gritted his teeth. "Against my better judgment and at great risk to my life, I came to warn you. Barrymore has already hanged two civilians whom he falsely accused of aiding Drake Corbin's escape. He has vowed to hang more if Drake Corbin is not brought to justice."

"What does that have to do with me?"

"I know Drake Corbin is here in this camp. If you care anything for the people of Marlbridge, hand Drake over to me. I will make sure he gets a fair trial."

"Like you did for Cass?"

Sidestepping the accusation, Garrett pulled a crumpled piece of paper from his coat pocket and handed it to Ramsey. "I have a signed statement from General Mitchel. Drake will be tried in a court of law."

Ramsey glanced at the paper then gave it back to Garrett. "Does Barrymore strike you as a man who follows orders?"

Garrett shoved the paper back into his pocket. "Listen, I do not care what happens to Drake Corbin, but Alexandra does. Until Drake Corbin is brought to justice, Marlbridge is not a safe place for Alexandra."

"Is she your woman?"

Garrett stammered, "My woman? Uh…not officially, no."

"Well, Rainier, for Alexandra to not be your woman, you sure do think you know her."

"I only want her to be free to come home, where she will be safe."

"Where she'll be *safe*? You've never met Drake Corbin, have you?"

"No, and I do not wish to now. Nevertheless, circumstances require it. Drake has become a problem for an increasing number of people, including you. As we speak, Barrymore is headed this way with six hundred men. I am not telling you this for your sake but for the sake of the innocent people in Marlbridge and Cade's Mill who are going to suffer for your stubbornness."

As Ramsey reviewed everything he knew about the rich, young lawyer, one disconcerting truth loomed above the rest: Garrett Rainier was on his way to becoming the next king of Marlbridge, and as such, he could not be trusted to protect Alexandra at the expense of his kingdom. Ramsey hollered for McCabe. When the imposing Scot appeared seconds later, Ramsey ordered, "Escort this prisoner to the guardhouse."

"You are arresting me?" Garrett barked. "Why?"

"Because I know what's at stake, even more than you do."

Garrett continued to protest as McCabe led him away.

When Ramsey returned to his tent, Alexandra was still sleeping. He eased himself down onto a chair and poured a fair amount of whiskey into a tin cup. He shook his head, puzzled over what would ever possess a woman to dress like a man in the first place, but then again, he'd never tried to wear a corset and hoop skirt. He'd certainly never tried to ride a horse in that getup. He had attempted side-saddle once as a joke. The fall almost broke his hip, and his back still ached when it rained.

What was he going to do with her? The enemy was coming to take her. He couldn't let her fight, but what excuse would he give his men for why Drake Corbin wasn't with them on the battlefield? If it came to that. He still had hope that Marcus Fontaine would do the sensible thing and return to Marlbridge, but he was beginning to think there wasn't a sensible person left in the world he could count on, including himself.

The more he drank, the more he recalled all the mean things he'd said to Alexandra since he met her that night at Storm Chase, when he thought she was a boy and chastised her for shirking her duty. Ramsey shuddered when he realized he was probably the one who had given her the idea to join the army in the first place.

He set his empty cup down, groaning as he got to his feet and stretched his back. After his run-in with Red Sticks earlier, he had hoped it would be at least a day or two before he had to do battle again. It was the contemplation of bloodshed that suddenly reminded Ramsey that he had not confirmed the dried blood on her shirt wasn't hers. Finding no wounds, he took a wet cloth and gently washed away the splotches of blood that had soaked through her shirt and dried on her skin.

During his conversation with Garrett Rainier, Ramsey had not allowed himself to think about what Prichard might have done to the girl before she stabbed him. If he had thought about it, he would have dragged Rainier up to the big house and shot them both: Prichard for laying a hand on Alexandra and Rainier for not handling her well enough to keep her in Marlbridge where she belonged.

Ramsey pulled Alexandra's boots off then slid his arm under her back and sat her up. Letting her body lean against his chest, he removed her jacket and replaced the ruined shirt with one of his own. With his face close to hers as he eased her back onto the cot, he became very much aware that while his mind was having a devil of a time adjusting to Alexandra's true form, the rest of his body was having no trouble accepting her as a woman, and a desirable one evidently. Not knowing whether he wanted to shoot her or kiss her, and determined not to go anywhere near the thin cotton material that secured her breasts, he decided to forego the buttons and covered her with the blanket.

Having done everything he knew to do for the girl who was passed out on his bed, Ramsey took his jacket off and used it as a pillow as he stretched out on the ground and covered himself with a spare blanket. He hadn't closed his eyes for more than a few seconds when Alexandra started snoring as good as any man in the Confederate army. Ramsey grunted and pulled the blanket over his head.

St. Clair woke him an hour later with the news: the enemy was headed their way, and the odds were not in the Rebels' favor.

Chapter 25

Deo Vindice

April 22

Wʜᴇɴ Alexandra opened her eyes the next morning, she was tucked in a blanket, lying on a cot in a strange tent, an officer's tent judging by the size of it. Her jacket was draped across the camp chair at the table, and her head ached worse than she could remember in her life. She lifted the blanket and looked down to see that her shirt wasn't buttoned. She sprang to her feet when she realized it wasn't her shirt.

Ignoring the pounding in her head and the queasiness in her stomach, she scrambled around the tent, looking for anything that might reveal the identity of the officer with whom she had evidently spent the night. *Please don't let it be Ramsey*, she prayed as she shuffled through the papers scattered on the table. If it was any other officer, she could threaten to cut his throat if he told her secret. Alexandra clamped her hand over her mouth when she scanned the field reports. They were all signed by Captain Ramsey.

She threw the reports on the ground and was about to stomp them when a bugle sounded. Poking her head between the tent flaps, she saw Confederates throwing on their boots and jackets, collecting their weapons, and running for their horses.

Alexandra gathered the papers and put them back on the table. She pulled her boots on and grabbed her hat and jacket. There was no time to fret over whatever had happened between the time she killed Prichard and the time she awoke in Ramsey's tent. Her enemies had come for her at last, and despite the throbbing in her head, she was ready to meet them.

Once the front of the tent was clear of passersby, Alexandra slipped out and sprinted to her tent. After collecting her weapons, she slung the Henry over her shoulder and ran over to where Shadow was tethered. After she saddled him and secured the rifle in the saddle holster, she mounted and joined the rest of the men.

"Hold up, Drake." Sal rode up beside her. "Let Corporal Carter inspect ye. Make sure ye ain't forgot nothin' in all this hullabaloo. Bradford dang near went off without his left boot one time."

Carter examined her belt. "One saber, one cartridge box, one Colt Army, one pocket pistol, and a knife. Well, Drake, with all that and the Henry you're packing you ought to be set. Assuming it's all loaded," he teased.

Within fifteen minutes, they were lined up on the near side of an open field, watching the enemy amass on the other end. She turned to Carter, "Why aren't we doing anything?"

"We are doing something. We're waiting for orders."

"But the enemy is coming."

"Aw, they ain't done nothin' yet. Here, have a look-see." Sal handed her the pair of field glasses he'd won off Bouchard in a frog jumping contest.

In the distance, the enemy was divided into mounted and dismounted cavalry. Alexandra almost dropped the glasses when she saw Barrymore among the mounted contingent. He and Major Fontaine were in a heated argument. Alexandra grew excited and ordered Carter to look through the glasses. "They're in a dispute. We should attack them now." Without getting out of line, she stretched as far as she could to look for Ramsey. "I have to tell Captain Ramsey."

When Alexandra started to pull out of the line, Carter grabbed Shadow's bridle. "What do you think you're doing? You can't get out of line. They'll be sending us in any minute."

"We should attack now!"

Carter gave her the stern, fatherly look. "Drake, we will attack when Captain Ramsey gives the order and not a moment before." When Alexandra started to argue, Carter leaned into her face, "If you say another word about it, I'm gonna tan your hide when this is over."

Alexandra held her tongue.

"Looky thar, them bluebellies has got artill'ry after all," Sal observed as the Yankees were rushing around, struggling to get three pieces of field artillery in place. "Wonder how come they didn't lead with that. It's what we'd a done if we'd a had any."

"Musta just got here. Bet that's what they was arguin' 'bout. D'you see that one officer? He was mad as a hornet," Bradford chuckled.

"I cain't see worth nothing at this distance, but shoot, they best be sendin' us in mounted to stop 'em 'fore they git them guns in place, or they'll blow us clear down to Montgom'ry." Sal sat up straighter when he saw Colonel Kinkaid, a grandfather-turned-Rebel, cantering his horse in front of the Confederate line. "Yunder he comes. Git ready to ride, Drake."

"I thought you said we fight dismounted," Alexandra said.

Sal sighed. "One thang ye gotta learn 'bout officers. Half the time they don't know what they're a-doin', and the other half the time they do. I ain't decided yet which is worst."

The colonel's saber gleamed as he held it up. "Gentlemen, today, we will show the enemy the full force of our determination to live as free men in our own country. Today, we will drive him back to *his* country. *Deo vindice!*"

The Confederates responded in unison, "*Deo vindice!*"

Alexandra flinched when Ramsey appeared and wedged his horse between her and Carter. When he reached out and stroked Shadow's neck, she murmured, "You can't stop me from fighting. I've earned the right to be here."

"I never said you didn't, and I have no doubts about you charging cannon. It's the horse I'm not sure about. Can you handle him?"

Stunned that he didn't try to stop her, Alexandra said, "Yes, sir," and waited for orders.

When Kinkaid gave the order, the Confederate line lurched forward. The dismounted enemy cavalry held their fire as the Rebels advanced.

Keeping with the veteran horses, Shadow maintained his composure at the boom and muzzle flash of the cannon. The first canister shell exploded, hurling dozens of musket balls into the Confederate line. Several horses went down. A second shell tore through another section of the line. The third shell exploded on the ground sending up clouds of dirt and debris. As Shadow scrambled out of the way, he lost his footing. Just before he hit the ground, Alexandra sprang out of the saddle, desperate to avoid being trapped. She rolled to her knees, shook her head at the ringing in her ears, and stood, but the instant Shadow got to his feet, he took off without her.

Alexandra started to resume the charge on foot until she spotted a rider-less mare trotting through the lingering smoke a few yards away. She caught the horse who was evidently a veteran. The mare was twitching all over, but seemed eager enough when Alexandra leapt into the saddle and steered her toward the battle.

By that time, the rest of the Confederates were on the far end of the field about to overtake the cannon. The artillerymen got off one more round before the dismounted Union cavalry to the right of the guns fired into the Confederates. They evidently didn't kill enough of them. Seeing that his guns were about to be taken, Fontaine ordered his mounted troops into the fray.

The little mare was fast and dauntless, and within seconds Alexandra caught up to the Confederate line. She drew the Colt Army first and began firing at blue uniforms. When she had fired all her rounds, she pulled out her pocket revolver and emptied it. She couldn't tell if she had killed anyone yet, and at one point, the battle had become so confused, it was hard to distinguish one person from another as the opposing lines of cavalry crashed into each other.

Caught up in the furor, Alexandra roared as she drew her saber and swung it at the head of an approaching Yankee, but the man blocked her with such force she dropped the saber. When he raised his arm for a second blow, whether out of instinct or madness, Alexandra drew her knife and stabbed him in the shoulder. With a sharp cry, he dropped his saber.

Suddenly, a Yankee bay rammed into her mount, knocking the horse to the ground. Alexandra snatched the previous rider's carbine from the saddle as the mare struggled to her feet. When the bay's rider aimed a revolver at her face, Alexandra whacked him with the butt of the carbine, threw the weapon to her shoulder, and fired. At that distance, she was sure to hit something. She hit him in the neck.

At that moment, St. Clair and his palomino charger, Vindicator, flew past her and joined Stark's company to capture the artillery pieces. The Rebels cheered as the Yankees fell back.

Joss rode up to Alexandra and smirked as she gestured toward the male Confederates. "I don't know why they gotta yell like they done something permanent. The enemy always comes back for more."

Alexandra ignored her as she hunted for her saber. She found it a few yards away. She retrieved it and held the mud-caked tip out away from her, not wanting to get her pants dirty. When she looked down at the blood, dirt, and grass stains that covered her whole body, she went ahead and wiped the saber off on her pants before she returned it to the scabbard.

"Ain't no use in cleaning it. We're just now getting to the thick of it." Joss gazed across the field as the Yankees charged again, this time with twice as many men. "See? What'd I tell you? Men."

Colonel Kinkaid gave the order to fall back. Ramsey repeated the order. Alexandra figured she better follow orders, no matter what Joss said, but just as she was about to retreat, she spotted Barrymore in the Union battle line. She didn't have time to reload her guns. Barrymore's troops were nearly upon her. There was only one way out of this fight—she would have to kill Barrymore on the battlefield.

Grasping the empty carbine by the shoulder strap, Alexandra slung the weapon onto her shoulder, afraid to leave it on the field lest it fall into enemy hands. Apologizing profusely, she snatched a revolver off the body of a fallen comrade. Only three shots remained in the chamber.

Ramsey yelled at Alexandra to fall back, but she stayed with Joss as the Yankees descended. She fired at Barrymore twice but missed. Ramsey, Carter, St. Clair and Langley galloped back toward them. Colonel Kinkaid held back, anxiously looking toward the trees.

"Corbin!"

Ignoring Ramsey's voice, Alexandra fired the last round.

"Corbin!"

Failing to hit her target, she whipped around and saw Ramsey leaned out with his arm extended. She latched on and swung up behind him. Ramsey wheeled Solomon around to escape, but the Yankees cut him off. As Fontaine's mounted troops closed in, the small band of Rebels were moments away from being captured when Alexandra heard Sal whoop, "Hooray for Madcap Charlie! You're in for it now, Yanks!"

Colonel Whisenhunt burst out of the trees to their right, and cavalry reinforcements charged onto the field. They descended upon the outnumbered foe, and the enemy engaging the small Confederate band broke ranks, turned tail, and ran.

As the remaining Yankees fled, leaving their field artillery behind, Alexandra noticed that Joss was still firing at them, and it looked like she was enjoying it.

Ramsey turned to Alexandra. "Are you wounded?" When she shook her head, he shoved her off his horse, and she fell hard. "The next time I give you an order, obey."

With her pride throbbing as violently as her backside, Alexandra leapt to her feet and snarled low enough that only Ramsey heard her, "You wouldn't dare treat me with such disrespect if I were a man!"

Gritting his teeth, Ramsey leaned into her face and growled, "If you were a man, I would have shot you."

Angry tears threatened to well up, but Alexandra forced them down. She slipped the carbine from her shoulder and was about to throw the weapon at him when she realized he was no longer paying attention to her. She followed his gaze—Barrymore was escaping. If she had been a better marksman, and her gun had been loaded, she might have risked taking one last shot at him.

"Where's your Henry?" Ramsey asked.

"With Shadow, wherever he is."

Ramsey didn't wait for her complicity. He snatched her carbine and rode off into the woods.

"Wait!" she hollered after him.

He didn't look back.

"It's not loaded, you bullheaded oaf," she muttered.

By the time Alexandra wrenched her gaze from Ramsey, Barrymore was gone, so she turned away from it all and set out to reclaim her horse. She spotted Shadow standing on the other side of the field, near the woods, grazing away as if nothing had happened.

Alexandra hadn't gone ten yards when she was nearly run over by Colonel Whisenhunt, who, consumed with the day's glory, was dashing about the field.

"Ho, there!" he hollered and jerked his mount to a sudden halt.

Alexandra stared up at him. He could not have been more impressive if he was a bronze statue. He was tall, muscular, and wilder than anything she had ever seen in all her brother's history books, a living, breathing, unassailable war hero, and he was talking to her.

"Were you the one who failed to retreat when your commanding officer gave the order?"

Until that moment, Alexandra had been unable to look away from the man, but his question shamed her into hanging her head. "Yes, sir."

"Look me in the eyes."

Alexandra raised her head. Entranced by the colonel's other-worldly aura, she whispered, "Yes, sir."

"Were you properly reprimanded?"

"Yes, sir."

"Well, I suppose that's fittin'. If you'd disobeyed me, I'd have shot ya." Whisenhunt turned his head to gaze at a group of men chasing down a horse. "Do you know I was wounded recently?"

"Yes, sir." Alexandra didn't know that, but she figured she better say "yes" anyway.

"And do you know how I came to be wounded?"

"No, sir." Alexandra didn't care how he came to be wounded, but he seemed like he wanted to tell her a story, so she said "no" anyway.

"I was wounded because I didn't retreat when I was supposed to. But the moral of the story is I'm still here and my enemies ain't." He glanced back over the field. "Now, where the devil is Captain Ramsey?"

Still unable to complete a full sentence in Whisenhunt's presence, Alexandra pointed to the woods.

"Why did he ride off that way?" he demanded.

Finally recapturing her voice, Alexandra replied, "He saw that wicked Colonel Barrymore escaping and went after him to put an end to him."

"Barrymore? Never heard of him. Wicked, you say?"

"He's holding my town hostage."

"Well, son, if your town is overrun by the enemy, why are you here instead of there?"

Something about the man brought out the fierceness in her. Incensed that once again she had to explain why she had taken it upon herself to do a man's job, Alexandra shouted loud enough to cause his horse to flinch. "Because back there, I am only one person. Here, I am a regiment, and the enemy hides his face when I take the field." Once she got it all out, she was terrified the colonel would have her shot for yelling at him.

Instead, Whisenhunt leaned down to get a closer look at her. "If you find that thrilling, young man, you should see the enemy's face when we are a full division." He wheeled his horse around and took off across the field.

A few seconds slipped away before Alexandra recovered from her encounter with Madcap Charlie. She resumed her path only to be interrupted by Bouchard who had been filching from the dead even before the battle was over. "Corbin! Confiscate that dead soldier's boots and whatever else is of value," he ordered as he plopped a bundle of loot into the arms of Mrs. Bouchard, who was bustling along behind him.

In the heat of the battle, Alexandra had not thought of the Yankee soldiers as living beings. They were faceless bodies wielding sabers and guns, mindless creatures sent by Lincoln and Barrymore to put an end to her and her people, but the Union-clad body at her feet had belonged to a handsome young man with hazel eyes. If he had been wearing gray, Alexandra might have mistaken him for Cass. Blood was still draining from the bullet hole in his neck. It horrified her to think that she might have been the one to take his life, but then she remembered that the man she'd killed had a beard. The boy staring up at her was clean-shaven. She bent down and closed his eyes before she stepped over him and continued on her way as if she hadn't heard Bouchard's order.

Shadow perked his ears when she finally made it across the field to catch him. A smear of blood marred the white stripe that ran down the center of his head. Alexandra fussed with him to keep his head still as she examined him. He still managed to swipe a mouthful of grass. There was no wound. Alexandra rested her head against Shadow's neck. They had both come through the battle unscathed, and she was relieved to find her Henry repeater still in the saddle holster.

Alexandra raised her head when Shadow stopped eating and turned his head back toward the field. "During the battle you were over here filling your belly with grass. What on earth could've gotten your attention now?" She rubbed his ears and turned to see what he was staring at.

On foot, Sal was chasing his horse, an ornery beast named Pharaoh. Langley and Bradford, who were still mounted, double-teamed the horse until Bradford caught his reins and handed him over to his master. Sal gave Pharaoh a good cussin' as the horse danced around him. To add to the effect, Pharaoh pinned his ears back and hopped, slashing Sal with his tail. Sal finally got close enough to smack his underbelly. Pharaoh planted all four hooves in the ground and stood still. Sal snorted, "That's more like it, you dad-blamed son-of-a-mule."

Alexandra tapped Shadow on the nose. "You see what happens to horses who misbehave."

As she mounted and guided Shadow back to the Confederate side of the field, she saw Joss drag a wounded, ragtag, scarecrow of a Confederate into the woods. Alexandra followed until Joss dropped the man onto the ground and pointed her saber at his throat. He tried to scramble away but Joss stepped on his wounded leg.

"Please! Have mercy!" he yelped.

Joss glowered at him. "I been huntin' you a long time, Franklin. D'you think you could hide behind that gray coat forever?"

Franklin whimpered, "I'm sorry for ever'thang I put you through, Jocelyn, honey. Please, I don't expect you to forgive me, but if you could find it in your heart to just leave me be, I'll die out here in these woods anyway, like as not, and save you the trouble."

Joss thundered, "Who was it put meat on you when you was nothing but skin and bones? Who was it cut her fingers to the bone so she could clothe you proper? Who damned herself to hell for the lies she told when the Law came for you? Who, Franklin?" He started to cry, which only spurred Joss on. "You never was nothin' but sorry white trash—I ain't gonna fault you for that—but damn you for dragging me with you." She raised her saber to finish him off, but Alexandra raised her own saber in Franklin's defense. Franklin jumped up and skedaddled with barely a limp.

Joss and Alexandra fought until Joss gained the upper hand and drove Alexandra to the ground. She held her saber at Alexandra's neck. "I don't stand for nobody interfering with my business." Joss sheathed her saber. Her fury subsided into amusement as she helped Alexandra to her feet. "Well, now you seen the elephant. You gonna run home to your mammy, girl? Or maybe you ain't a girl no more. Maybe you're something else, now."

"You were going to murder that man," Alexandra gasped. "He was wounded and asked for mercy, and you were going to kill him."

"Some would say I'd be puttin' him outta his misery, so before you judge me, at least I didn't stab him in the gut and leave him for dead like you done," Joss sneered.

"Prichard Benefield attacked me, and I defended myself."

Joss stretched to her full height, standing so close that when she talked, spittle dusted Alexandra's face. "You shoulda finished him off. D'you think about what might happen if he survived? You think he wouldn't come after you?"

Alexandra looked back across the field at her fellow soldiers. "Let him come after me if he wants. I have friends."

Leaving Joss, Alexandra walked back towards the battlefield, leading Shadow behind her. The wounded were carried off the field on stretchers. Several women from Cade's Mill had been present during the battle, carrying buckets of water and tending the wounded on both sides. Two of the women were kneeling beside a wounded Confederate. With every step Alexandra took toward the dying soldier, her stomach got heavier. It was the elder Taylor boy, and lying dead right next to him was his brother.

Chapter 26

Threats and Parley

CRASHING through the silence of the woods, Ramsey let Solomon cut his own path through the dense hardwoods. Keeping a safe distance from the road, Ramsey rode parallel to the retreating Union column until they reached the bridge. If Barrymore escaped to the other side, Ramsey would lose his chance. But instead of crossing the bridge, the enemy troops turned aside to the adjacent field and began to set up camp.

Ramsey dismounted and lay on his stomach behind a fallen tree. Resting the carbine on top of the log, he took out his field glasses. When he spotted his target, he dropped the glasses and took aim.

A boy still in his teens was standing almost direactly in front of the colonel. Ramsey paused for almost half a minute, waiting for the boy to move. Barrymore started walking in the wrong direction. In two more seconds he would be out of range for a sure shot. If the wind shifted, he might hit the boy instead of Barrymore. "Sorry, kid."

Ramsey was about to pull the trigger when he heard a twig snap behind him. He turned just in time to catch Fontaine's apology right before the butt of his revolver smashed into Ramsey's cheekbone.

When Ramsey came to, Fontaine was crouched beside him. "You could've just told me to stop," Ramsey groaned.

Fontaine frowned. "Recall one instance in which that tactic was successful." He handed the carbine back to Ramsey. "Next time you decide to shoot someone, try using a loaded gun."

Ramsey grunted. When he took the carbine from Alexandra, his primary motivation had been to keep her from using it to go after Barrymore. He didn't stop to consider she had probably already fired it and wouldn't have had time to reload, slow as she was.

He turned to see what had become of his prey. Barrymore was nowhere in sight. After a few swear words that Fontaine took in stride as always, Ramsey stood and leaned against a tree as he dusted the wet leaves off his uniform. "Well, I hope you feel proud, Marcus. You did your duty as a good Union man. Out of all the men who should've lived today, you decide to protect the one who should've died. Now, we have to do all this again tomorrow and the next day and for however many days until Barrymore has bled both sides dry."

Fontaine sat on a log. "Barrymore wasn't the one who murdered four of my men. It was Drake Corbin and his rebel friends."

"Drake Corbin didn't murder anyone. It was the O'Dell boy that did the killing. I just sent his body back to his mama. The others are only guilty of being fools. And, it was three of your men not four. I have General Belgrave's son under house arrest at headquarters. He hasn't been harmed, and he has a featherbed, which is more than I've got."

"I'm relieved to hear of his safety. Did he tell you his real name of his own accord?"

"He did."

"When the Council finds out you're holding Belgrave's son, they are going to come after you. They might have forgiven you for unwittingly transporting the gold that was stolen from them, but Cana, if they find Edwin with one hair from his head missing, you're a dead man."

Ramsey rubbed his face. Battle rage always left him exhausted. "I've been running from the Council a long time. If they really wanted me dead, I'd be dead."

"The only reason you're still alive is because of me and St. Clair. We stuck our necks out for you, and we're fortunate the Council didn't call for our deaths, too, after what you did to Vincent Fullarton."

"I was only seventeen, and he had it coming," Ramsey muttered, snuffing out the guilt that shot across his soul like streak lightning.

Fontaine's clenched jaw relaxed. "I've never questioned your judgment on that."

Ramsey paused to study his old friend, wondering just how much he had changed over the years, if at all. He had never trusted Marcus the way he trusted St. Clair. Despite his intellectual attraction to the notions of democracy and pluralism, Marcus Fontaine was an aristocrat through and through, and when it came down to choosing between what was right by God's standards and what was expedient by the aristocracy's standards, Marcus wouldn't break ranks with his fellow elites to save his life.

Still, Ramsey wasn't sure how much Fontaine knew about the Council's operations. "Did Red tell you he was with the men who killed Barrymore's family?"

Fontaine was a master at controlling his facial expressions, but he wasn't good enough to stop his face from turning pale. "Is that what he told you?"

"Yes. He also told me Barrymore knows of his involvement. So, where do you think he's better off—here with me and my army or back in Marlbridge where there's a madman who wants him dead? I'm sorry, Marcus, but Red is the only one who can clear Drake Corbin's name, and the only person I trust to keep him alive is me."

Fontaine threw his arms up. "Why are you protecting Drake Corbin? It's because of Jonas Corbin's daughter, isn't it? You don't owe her anything. If you want to save your men from another fight tomorrow, release Edwin Belgrave into my custody, turn Drake Corbin in to Barrymore, and let justice be done. It's the only way out."

Ramsey plucked a cocklebur from the hem of his jacket and flicked it away. "If I could find a way to resolve this Drake business without harming Alexandra, I would do it, even if it meant Drake's death, but it is not possible."

Fontaine sighed and pinched the bridge of his nose, the gesture he always made when he had resigned himself to what he thought was certain doom. "Then, unless God provides a way of escape, we will fight again tomorrow."

"God offered me a chance to escape a while back, and I didn't take it. I doubt His offer still stands."

"I should have learned my lesson by now. In all those tavern brawls back in the old days, I never could talk you out of a fight."

Ramsey smiled, knowing for certain Fontaine's knuckles ached as badly as his own did when it rained. He paused to watch two squirrels fight over a nut. "Well, then, you should know that if any of y'all are still here in the morning, you and all your men are gonna die in that field over there," he said, pointing to where the Union forces were setting up camp.

When Fontaine lifted his eyes to meet Ramsey's, the wear of the past year was evident. "If there is any chance I can persuade Barrymore to withdraw, I will."

Ramsey mounted his horse. "We both know Drake Corbin won't get a fair trial until Barrymore is gone. Get rid of him, and I'll let Red go. Those are my terms."

"I'll do what I can."

"That's not enough, Marcus. I'm not going to risk Drake Corbin's life bringing him back to Marlbridge only to discover too late that you failed to hold up your end of the bargain. I already have my doubts about Red telling the truth since he lied about where Barrymore was keeping the hostages."

"How could he have known for sure where they were? There's a difference between lying and speculating."

"Not the way I see it." Ramsey rubbed the side of his face with his left hand as he extended his right hand to Fontaine. "I could have done without a cracked cheekbone, but nonetheless, it was good to see you, Marcus. I hope it's a long time before I see you again."

Fontaine shook his hand. "On that we agree."

As Ramsey steered his horse to leave, Fontaine snapped, "And tell Thaddeus to get rid of that ridiculous feather. I could've shot him three times today."

Ramsey grinned. St. Clair would die before giving up his new gigantic, bright red plume. It was too pure an expression of his gallantry.

Making his way back to the Confederate camp, Ramsey looked down to see that blood had dripped onto Solomon's white coat, forming a sizable stain. Until then, he hadn't noticed the tear in his jacket sleeve. When he removed his jacket, he saw that his shirt sleeve was soaked up to his elbow. He dismounted and rolled up his sleeve to examine the gash. It would need to be sewn up, but he didn't have the time or the utensils for that at the moment, so he tore off his sleeve and used it to bind the wound. Fortunately, it was his left arm, which wouldn't interfere with his next errand.

Whether God had sent Fontaine or Fontaine had sent himself, Ramsey counted himself lucky that someone had prevented him from killing Barrymore which would have been a major tactical error, and also an outright sin. To eliminate Barrymore in such a way would have been outside the parameters of legitimate warfare and would have tempted the enemy to reprisals. Furthermore, there was no need for Ramsey to further sully his own honor when he already had the perfect assassin in his custody.

* * *

Garrett Rainier scrambled to his feet when Ramsey jerked the smokehouse door open and stepped over the threshold, his Bowie knife glinting as he weaved between the rows of hanging meat.

"I heard there was a battle." Garrett announced in his steady, princely accent. "I presume you rebels were the victors, otherwise it would be a Federal officer sent to release me from this hellhole."

Ramsey rested the tip of his knife on Garrett's shoulder. "As you surmised, we rebels did win the battle, so the war for Southern independence rages on. However, there may be a way to alleviate some of the suffering, at least for a time."

Ignoring the blade, Garrett folded his arms across his chest. "Suffering for whom?"

"Our people, of course," Ramsey replied as he lifted the blade off Garrett's shoulder.

"You and I do not come from the same people," Garrett snipped through gritted teeth.

"I was referring to the people of Marlbridge. You have loved ones there, do you not?"

"I do. And they were safe until you rebels made a mess of things."

Tapping the blade against his palm, Ramsey ambled about the dark room. "Actually, I was not in favor of secession. Not until the president of the North sent an army down here."

"Drastic measures made necessary when you rebels fired on Fort Sumter."

Eager to oblige Garrett's hunger for a good debate, Ramsey argued, "A fort situated in the territorial waters of the sovereign state of South Carolina was occupied by a foreign power who refused to leave after numerous entreaties. The identity of the invader is of no consequence. Might as well have been the Hessians."

"How can you decry as a foreign power the federal government that was established in perpetuity by the Constitution of the United States unanimously ratified?"

"I'm sure the Rhode Islanders have a thing or two to say about how that compact was unanimously ratified. In any event, if you and I are to argue the point, I submit that when any government violates the terms of the initial agreement and spurns the one purpose for which it was created, to protect the lives and property of the people who gave their consent to its creation, that government has declared itself a foreign power and deserves whatever retribution the people and their God deem appropriate."

Garrett snorted. "Are you suggesting the people actually listen to their God? I challenge you to find historical evidence that does not suggest the opposite. I cannot know what God intends to do, but I do know the Union must be preserved at all costs. Otherwise, the American experiment in self-government is dead, and we will succumb to a tyranny far worse than the British monarchy. Surely you see that."

"Oh, I've heard all the threats," Ramsey smirked. "If any state dares to leave the Union, it is a certainty we will be overrun by the villain of the hour. Who is the current favorite? One minute it's the British; the next it's the French or the Mexicans or the Barbary pirates. Maybe, this time it will be the Indians who will band together against us."

Ramsey stuck his knife into the wall and leaned into Garrett's face. "It's all lies—Hamiltonian Federalist lies. Those sycophants in Washington may care about preserving the Union for the sake of some experiment, but it's not an experiment in self-government, and they sure as hell don't care about the Negroes. If they have so little regard for the lives and liberties of white men of property, what regard do you think they'll show the slaves once they've 'liberated' them? We both know the only reason they want to free millions of slaves is to turn them into millions of voters they can wield in whatever direction they please, trading one form of slavery for another. I'm not saying we've done right by the Negroes because we haven't. Not treating them as fellow Christians, that's our sin. Subjecting the whole country to the schemes of bankers and industrialists hell-bent on constructing the new Atlantis, that's yours."

Ramsey yanked the knife out of the wall and held it a little too close to Garrett's nose. "Now, are you going to help me make amends or not?"

Taken aback by Ramsey's speech, Garrett snapped, "What could you and I possibly do to make amends for all of that?"

Ramsey sheathed his knife. "To start with, I'm gonna see to my horse, and you're gonna put a rabid dog out of its misery."

Chapter 27

Visions of the Future

Exhaustion began to weigh heavily on Alexandra as she and the rest of the Confederate cavalry limped back to Cade's Mill. The citizens tiptoed out into the street as ambulances hauled the wounded to the church. One petite woman bustled out of her house and sailed toward the church, barely able to see over the flowing heap of linens in her arms. Several more men and women rushed out of their homes to offer assistance.

Carter had been badly wounded, so instead of riding on to camp with the rest of the troops, Alexandra stayed with Sal and Bradford, who had decided to remain in town to do whatever they could to aid their wounded comrades. As they dismounted near the parsonage, the heaviness of the day lifted a little when a starry-eyed, bashful girl named Bernice pitter-pattered up to Bradford. "Is this yer horse?"

The worry on Bradford's face disintegrated. He beamed with pride as he patted his horse, Clyde, an awkward, roman-nosed monstrosity. "He shore is. Why, Clyde, here, is a descendant of Bucephalus."

"Who?" Bernice asked.

Sal smacked Bradford's arm. "Bradford, it ain't done it. That old bag of bones ain't no more a descendant of Bucephalus than you are the progeny of Alexander the Great."

"Well, you must be the progeny of Shakespeare the way you throw them big words 'round like you know what they mean," Bradford quipped as he turned his attention back to Bernice.

"I bet Clyde's fast. Can I pet him?" Bernice tried to imitate the other girls in town who were evidently much more successful at ensnaring men than she. Her execution of the feminine arts was poor, even by Alexandra's standards, and it would not have worked on most men, but as it turned out, Bradford appeared to be supremely flattered by her efforts. He even blushed a little as he granted her permission to pet Clyde.

Bradford gulped and stammered, "Uh, if you want, I could take you for a ride later. If your folks wouldn't say it was improper."

"Oh, I'd like that very much," Bernice squeaked before she blushed and ran off.

After she had gone less than five yards, she ran back, a look of shame on her face. Keeping her head down, she blurted, "I'm sorry if I was rude for talkin' about horses and such when some of them that's wounded mighta been friends of yers. I hope you don't think me uncarin' 'cause I really ain't. I mean, I really am a carin' person. I just don't always think to show it. My mama is on me about it regular. I get all caught up in silly things and don't have enough thinkin' room for important things. That's all I wanted to say." Bernice was close to tears as she scampered away.

A moon-struck Bradford stared after her. "Well, ain't she the sweetest thang you ever saw."

Sal swatted him. "Quit ye gawkin' and tend to the business at hand. Namely, doin' what we kin fer our wounded brethren." He took hold of Bradford's sleeve and pulled him toward the church.

When Alexandra entered the makeshift hospital, she nearly vomited as the smell of blood and excrement overwhelmed her. Two healthy Confederates were toting a dead body out on a stretcher. As they moved past her, Alexandra could see the dead man's ribs sticking up out of his body. She looked away only to have her eyes fall on the pile of limbs near one of the windows where the doctor was sawing off a Union soldier's shattered arm.

"It's best ye keep ye eyes on the floor or the ceiling," Bradford warned her, too late.

Close to where the pulpit would have been, they saw St. Clair crouched beside the cot where Carter lay, struggling to breathe. Boone was lying on the floor next to the cot. As Alexandra approached, Boone raised his head just enough to rest it on her boot.

"F-f-for my g-girls," Carter stuttered and gestured to his pocket. St. Clair reached into Carter's pocket and pulled out a letter.

Without reading it, St. Clair placed the letter in his jacket pocket. "I will see ta it personally. You have my word, Lew." Carter died before St. Clair finished talking.

Alexandra thought she heard St. Clair's voice break, but the lieutenant was careful to keep his face turned away from her and the other soldiers as he stood and slapped his hat back on his head. "Help me bury him."

St. Clair insisted that the body of his friend was not to be cast into a mass grave dug by the hands of prisoners and slaves. It was well into the afternoon by the time Alexandra, Sal, Bradford, and St. Clair got Carter's body in the ground. They each said a few words and took turns comforting Boone, who refused to leave the grave.

"He had daughters?" Alexandra asked.

"Five of 'em." Sal sniffed and wiped his eyes.

Alexandra and St. Clair remained behind after the others left. They watched as Madcap Charlie and his men rode out of town.

"Where are they going?"

St. Clair scowled. "No doubt Whisenhunt thinks he has so reduced tha enemy's numbers that he can carry on with his real mission. Only reason he came here in tha fust place was for tha horses. However, it is no accident that Whisenhunt has chosen this precise moment ta move out and in tha direction that he's headed. The Yankees will be watchin' his every move, expectin' him ta attack their flank, and they know they are not strong enough ta repel him without sendin' ta Mahlbridge for reinforcements. By then, they will have decided attackin' us here is not wuth tha casualties. No, suh, they will wait for us ta move ta a more strategic location and attack us there." St. Clair smiled. "Unless we attack them fust."

"Hmm. I wouldn't have thought of that," Alexandra replied.

"That is why you are a private and Madcap Charlie will soon be a brigadier general."

"Colonel Kinkaid kept shouting 'Deo vindice.' What does it mean?"

St. Clair ran his fingers through the bright red plume attached to his hat. "It means Gawd is our vindicator."

"Do you think that's true?"

The dashing lieutenant looked down at her. "If I didn't, I would go home, for I would have no reason ta fight."

"Some would say we don't need to fight if God is going to save us in the end."

"I have no doubt He will save us, tha true sheep that is, but that particular day of salvation may yet be a long way off. Whatever Gawd does on that day, it does not change what I must do on this day."

"What are you going to do?"

"Endure, Drake, we must endure. That is what's required of everyone. In that, we are all equal. I endure tha life of a soldier as my Negro endures tha life of a slave, my sister tha life of a widow and my mother..." St. Clair cleared his throat. "Our crosses must be borne if we are ta attain what we desire tha most."

When St. Clair didn't elaborate, Alexandra asked, "Salvation?"

"Glawry." A dark shadow crossed his face. "I have contemplated tha possibility that we will lose tha great war of our time. Our glawry permanently damaged. Our descendants livin' in tha shadow of evil, held captive by gawdless men."

Suddenly, his face brightened. "Fortunately, today is not tha day of reckonin'. Today, tha seals are unbroken, tha bowls are full, and tha trumpets are silent except ta sound tha advance when our enemies turn tail and run for their lives." He rose and restored his feathered crown to its rightful place as he strode across the cemetery to reclaim his men-at-arms who were sitting in the churchyard shaking rocks out of their shoes.

Alexandra plopped down next to Boone and rubbed his ears. In the past week, she had lost three friends and her brother, none of whom had she honored with tears or her presence at their burials. She was glad she hadn't stayed home to see Cass' body lowered into the ground with folks gossiping about what really happened and what the family would do in his absence and whether or not God was bringing judgment on the Corbin house.

She looked back toward the church. Mrs. Taylor was sitting on the bottom step with her youngest boy beside her. The woman, who had been so resilient a couple days before, now looked old and weak and small. When a young woman came out of the church to fetch some water, the boy quickly wiped his eyes and jumped up to help her.

Alexandra sprang to her feet. If she sat there any longer, she would give in to the grief, and she couldn't allow that to happen, especially not if salvation and glory hinged upon her endurance. It may be that God was going to vindicate her and her loved ones, but she wasn't going to sit around and wait on Him when there was fighting still to be done. If she wanted to keep fighting as Drake, it seemed to her that it was Cana Ramsey she would have to convince, not God. As of late, God was the only one who hadn't told her what to do or commented on her apparel or pointed out how terribly she had failed at being a woman. He had only spoken to her once in her whole life that she knew of—the night they brought Jonas Corbin's body home and she had fled to her room to bury herself under a pile of quilts. In the midst of her tear-soaked, patchwork tabernacle, she thought she heard God say, "Don't cry, little girl. You still have a father who loves you, and he will never leave you." Alexandra must have believed Him because she had never cried since.

* * *

Alexandra found Ramsey in the barn that sat next to the "big house," the small one-and-a- half story dogtrot in the middle of camp that served as battalion headquarters. He was dipping a brush into a bucket of water and scrubbing dried blood off his horse as he sang the chorus to "We Are a Band of Brothers" in a fairly decent baritone.

Hurrah, hurrah, for Southern rights, hurrah.
Hurrah for the bonnie blue flag that bears a single star.

He dropped the brush in the bucket and wiped his hands on the towel thrown over his shoulder. The blood had stained a large swath of Solomon's coat, turning it pink. Ramsey patted him on the shoulder. "Of course, I had to pick a white war horse."

"Is Barrymore dead?" Alexandra asked.

Ramsey pulled out a flask, took a drink, and cut his eyes toward the door where she was standing. "Turns out you know a little something about war after all. How many of the enemy did you kill today, two, three?"

"Just one that I know of. I stabbed another one in the shoulder, but I don't think he died."

"Not altogether bad for a girl, especially a girl who can't shoot worth anything. You're pretty quick with that knife, though." He flipped one of the buckets over and motioned for her to come and sit next to him.

Assuming he was about to tell her how he did away with Barrymore, Alexandra complied. She waited. He remained silent. She stared. He caught her. When she looked down to avoid his gaze, she saw his forearm. "You're wounded."

She reached over to examine the wound, but he pulled his arm back and looked away. "It's all right."

"Shouldn't you clean it? Maybe if you poured whiskey on it—"

"I'll tend to it later." He took another drink.

"But I really think you should—"

He glared at her from the corner of his eye, repeating his words slowly. "I said I'll tend to it later."

Alexandra raised her hands in surrender.

"Where d'you get the name 'Drake'?"

Alexandra's throat tightened. "Cass gave it to me when I was at Miss Daschle's School for Girls. I used to dress up like a boy and sneak into the boys' school to see him. He was going to call me Alexander, but that was too close to my real name; so, he named me after one of our ancestors who was something of a troublemaker back in England."

"Troublemaker? Why, that doesn't suit you at all." Rolling his eyes, he took an extra-long swig and wiped his mouth on his good sleeve.

Unable to help herself, Alexandra smiled. Then she hated herself for it. A self-respecting woman should be offended at such teasing.

Ramsey reached out and wiped a streak of dirt off her face. "You know, you do sorta look like a woman—in the right light."

He held the flask out to her. Her fingers brushed his as she accepted it. When he didn't take his eyes off her, she thought for a moment that maybe he wasn't upset after all to find out she was a woman. Her relief was fleeting. While Ramsey did not embody the full gamut of attributes one should expect of a Southern gentleman, Alexandra would not allow herself to hope that he was rebel enough to let a woman fight in his army. So, she took a tiny sip and carried on with what she'd come to say. "I'm not—"

"I heard about Carter," he interrupted.

Unprepared for the abrupt change of subject, Alexandra paused for a long moment before she added, "The Taylor boys are dead, too, and it happened just like their mama said it would. Well, it would have if you hadn't spared the youngest boy."

Ramsey shook his head. "Ol' Carter. He was a good man. Had a good voice, too. Whenever he was reciting something, anything, he always put a lot of feeling into it. Damn near had me crying over the *Federalist Papers* once."

If she thought his language would improve with the realization that she was a woman, she was mistaken, but not surprised. As she took another sip, she caught him looking down at the blood on the shirt she was wearing. She had forgotten it was his. "I'm sorry. I'll wash it before I give it back."

Ramsey looked down at the shirt he was wearing. It was in worse shape than hers. "Might as well keep it."

After a few moments of exchanging the flask back and forth in silence, Ramsey drained the last of the whiskey. Then, he looked straight into her eyes and said quietly, "You should've told me, Alexandra."

Her heart quickened when he spoke her name. "Told you what?"

"Everything. If you had told me everything, you wouldn't have had to leave Marlbridge, and you wouldn't have had to stab ol' Prichard."

That traitor Joss must have told Ramsey about Prichard to get back at her. Alexandra frowned. "He had it coming."

"Why didn't you finish him off then?"

"He's still alive?"

"Fortunate for you, yes."

"How is that fortunate for me?"

"Hard to believe, but he's worth more alive than dead."

"Not to me." She could feel her cheeks flush. Ramsey wouldn't run the Yankees out of her town, but he saw fit to preserve the rogue who had attacked her. Cass would have killed Prichard for what he did.

Ramsey read her expression. "I want Prichard alive," he warned.

"What are you going to do with him?"

"None of your business."

"Did you kill Barrymore?"

Ramsey studied her for a moment before he answered. "Is that what you were hoping?"

"I can't deny that I want my people to be free and I can't keep sitting here playing soldier while Barrymore holds them captive." She stood and folded her arms across her chest as she began to pace.

Ramsey didn't bother to stand. "You complain about playing soldier, but it was you playing sheriff that got your friends killed."

Before she could catch herself, she slapped him. She had never slapped anyone. Not even the dozen or so males who had frustrated her beyond deliverance at various points in her life. Punch them in the face, yes. Punching them made her feel equal with them. She was ashamed that she had slapped Ramsey. Not because it was disrespectful, but because it seemed as if she was acknowledging that he was a man and she was a woman and that the distinction gave him some kind of authority over her.

Alexandra balled her fists, ready for his counterattack, but none came. Instead, Ramsey gave her a crooked smile. "Well, I'm glad to know all this fighting like a man hasn't ruined your ability to fight like a woman. Heck, if all the women start fighting like men and forget how to fight like women, then we'll really be in a fix. Or, maybe we should all just lay down our weapons and stop fighting over the Land of the Feathered Serpent. It's all gone to the Devil anyway."

"What are you talking about?"

"Amaruca. It's what the people in South America called this part of the world long before the white man came. It means Land of the Feathered Serpent."

"That's not true. America was named for Amerigo Vespucci."

"You know, if you'd quit worrying so much over what Barrymore and the Yankees are doing to *your* town and *your* people and *your* land, you might come to realize that there's a whole lot going on all around you that you don't know about."

"Maybe I don't know about any feathered serpent, but I'm fully aware that it is impossible to have a conversation with you where I'm not accused of being cowardly, selfish, or stupid."

Alexandra turned and marched out of the barn. What to do about Ramsey's ongoing dismissal of her mission to save Marlbridge, she didn't know, but there was a thing or two she could do about Prichard Benefield.

* * *

As Alexandra stepped onto the back porch of the little big house, she paused when she heard the clank of silverware on porcelain and bursts of laughter coming from the direction of where she imagined the dining room must be. She peered through one of the windows to see St. Clair, Captain Stark, and several other officers sitting around the dining table eating and drinking and merrymaking. It wasn't until she got over her initial disdain for their revelry in the aftermath of battle that Alexandra spotted the source of the entertainment.

Seated at the head of the table, with his back to Alexandra, an enemy soldier was telling jokes between gulps of wine. Alexandra stood back from the window and leaned against the wall. Everywhere she went people she had trusted were fraternizing with the enemy, carrying on as if there were no war at all.

Alexandra pressed her hat down on her head, drew her knife, and slipped into the house through the back door. She found Prichard dead asleep, sprawled out on a bed in one of the rooms at the back of the house. At first, Alexandra had been surprised to find there was no guard, but there was no need. Even if the wound in his stomach failed to confine him to his bed, he wouldn't make it very far.

Blood had soaked through his bandage and onto the sheets. His feet stuck out from under a pink-and-blue quilt and hung off the end of the bed. His right arm dangled from the leather strap that tied his wrist to a bedpost. In that state, snoring softly with his eyes closed and his lips opened up in a distorted "O," he was stripped of his menacing power, so much so, that Alexandra almost regretted that she had come to finish him off. Nevertheless, it had to be done.

When he coughed suddenly, the whole bed shook and squeaked. Alexandra jumped back into the shadows and knocked over the baby carriage that had been shoved into the corner. A host of dolls spilled out and landed near the fireplace. Alexandra ducked into the shadows until she was certain that Prichard was still asleep. She picked up one of the dolls that had fallen into a mound of ash. Soot soiled the doll's white-and-pink dress. Alexandra brushed it off as best she could, not that it mattered. Bradford had told her the tragic tale of the home's previous inhabitants. Little Mary Clarisse would not be coming back to reclaim her dolls.

Alexandra tossed the doll back into the carriage. Earlier that day, she had killed two men who hadn't really done her wrong except wear a different uniform from hers. They were far less deserving of death than was Prichard, and if it hadn't been for Alexandra's failure to finish the job the night he attacked her, he'd already be dead. Yet, Alexandra hesitated as she held her knife near his throat.

Feeling as if there ought to be the pretense of ceremony before she put her enemy to death, she said, "As the Lord delivered Sisera into the hands of Jael, so you have been given into my hands, Prichard Benefield."

Her hesitation was a mistake. Prichard's eyes popped open. With his free hand, he caught her wrist and twisted the knife away from her. Alexandra yelped. When she tried to pull away, Prichard sprang out of the bed, but he fell back as the leather strap pulled taut. Alexandra escaped his grasp and scrambled to the door. Prichard broke loose from the bedpost and charged as Alexandra ducked toward the hallway. The knife slashed her thigh. She fell, and he fell on top of her. He sneered as he wrapped his beefy fingers around her throat and set the knife down on the floor at her head. When she reached for her gun, Prichard straddled her, pinning both her arms to her side. She struggled to get away as he buried her mouth under his fat lips and sweaty beard that tasted like rank pecans.

She bit his lip, and as the foul blood filled her mouth, her enemy roared and backhanded her cheek. As he reared back for a second blow, Alexandra saw his eyes widen as a man's boot smashed into his jawbone. When he fell back, Alexandra snatched up her knife and scrambled out of the room. Prichard charged, but the man who rescued her hit Prichard in the face with the plate of food he was carrying, yanked the door shut, and held onto the doorknob with all his strength. Prichard was pounding on the inside of the door, failing to realize the door opened to the inside.

Alexandra staggered to her feet, ignoring the pain shooting through her leg and dreading to face Ramsey almost as much as she dreaded to see Prichard break through the door, but she was shocked to discover that the man who was standing between her and Prichard was wearing a blue uniform.

When the man saw her face, his jaw dropped. "You."

Alexandra yanked her revolver from its holster and waved her Yankee rescuer away from the door. The second Prichard opened the door and poked his head out she cracked him on the back of the head. He collapsed into the hallway.

Alexandra leveled the gun at the Yankee's chest and pulled the hammer back.

The voices coming from the dining room ceased until Alexandra heard one of them holler, "Hey Yank, what's happening back there?"

The Yankee stared at Alexandra in disbelief. "Nothing. All clear," he announced as he shoved Prichard's unconscious mass back into the room and closed the door.

Alexandra jerked her gun toward the door. "You're coming with me, Red."

Chapter 28

That Girl's Gonna Be the Death of You

Ramsey paused at the mud puddle in front of Johnny Knowles' tavern, thinking back to that night when he was sixteen, the last time he'd gone to the Broken Eagle outside Marlbridge to drag his father away from the poker table. He'd had to step over a muddy trench that night, too. Back then, Ramsey had avoided the puddle because he didn't want to get his new boots dirty. The boots he wore now had tread through far worse things than mud puddles.

When Langley had come to him earlier and told him who was waiting for him at Johnny Knowles', Ramsey had at first intended not to show, but then Langley had given him the bloodstained boll of cotton. "The man said you would know what it meant."

As Ramsey stood at the edge of the puddle, he turned the yellowed boll over in his hand. After fingering the brittle, but still sharp casing, he rammed the stalk through the buttonhole on his lapel and splashed through the mud.

The man at the poker table greeted Ramsey with clouds of cigar smoke and kingly disdain. The amber glow from the lantern made his expensive suit shine like plate armor. He donned his savior garb with such perfection that he could have very well been mistaken for a hero in the right lighting.

"Good evening, Captain," he drawled as Ramsey took a seat at his table.

The way he slung "Captain" out of his mouth amused Ramsey. "You're too late, Elias. All those horses are no longer in my possession. Madcap Charlie has absconded with the whole lot."

"I didn't come here for the horses." Elias rolled his cigar in his mouth. "I came for the girl."

"I don't keep girls in this outfit."

"Don't tell me after all this time you haven't noticed Drake Corbin isn't like all the other boys."

"Come to think of it, he is a lot meaner than the rest."

"I imagine so." Elias chuckled, the brief, genuine smile altering the man's whole persona for a moment. He poured a shot of whiskey from the full bottle that was sitting on the table and settled back into his chair. When he brought the glass to his lips, he wrinkled his nose at the smell but drank it anyway.

"I've come to make you an offer." Elias pulled a document out of his coat pocket and handed it to Ramsey. "Hand the girl over to me and Storm Chase is yours again."

Ramsey held the jaundiced paper as if it would disintegrate and blow away in his hands. It was his past and his future written out by lawyers like Garrett Rainier. For a brief moment, he considered taking the deal. It was a chance to set everything right, to rebuild the past as if it had never been destroyed, as if it had existed in the first place. "Is it the girl you want or her land?"

Elias exhaled a ring of smoke. "If the acquisition of property was all I cared about, the deed to Storm Chase would not be on the table. Even in its current condition it's worth three times what the Corbin plantation is worth."

"If Storm Chase is so valuable why did you let it sit up there on that hill and rot? If you weren't going to maintain the house, you should have torn it down and built a palace on top of the ruins."

"I would sooner build on top of a graveyard," Elias mused. "A memorial to the dead— that's its only suitable purpose now. The blood we spilled to protect our loved ones will never go away." He poured another shot of whiskey, but instead of drinking it, he slid it across the table to Ramsey. "Give Alexandra to me, or it will be your blood on my hands this time."

With his fingertips on the rim, Ramsey rotated the glass for several turns. "What are you going to do with her? Carry her off to Chattanooga? Charleston? Singapore?"

Elias ground the end of his cigar into the tabletop. "What I do with her is my concern, not yours."

Ramsey rested his elbows on the table. "How do you imagine all this is going to play out, Elias? You think you can take Alexandra away from her family, away from the past, away from me, and when she finds out the truth, she'll forgive you?"

"I don't believe she will forgive either one of us which is why I'm willing to bet my life that you aren't going to tell her the truth. Why, I imagine by now you've got more to lose than I do."

"I don't have a kingdom to lose."

"Marlbridge is not my kingdom."

"My apologies. I suppose it is more of a fiefdom. How much of your soul did you have to part with to stay in the good graces of your feudal lords? Or does the Council not know about your arrangement with Prichard Benefield?"

"I didn't hire Prichard to steal the gold from the Council. I hired him to steal it back. I do things like that on occasion to keep myself in the good graces of the powers-that-be. Just like I occasionally try to do right by my fellow man, but you and the girl keep getting in the way."

Ramsey leaned forward. "Who was standing in the way when you let Cass die?"

Elias almost blinked. "I offered the boy a way out, and he didn't take it. So, the way I see it, his death is on his own head. Just like yours is going to be. Now, for the last time, give me the girl."

"No."

"You're going to get her killed, or worse," he snarled. "One female in the midst of all those…homesick men. An unattached woman might get mistaken for a camp follower. Maybe they'd start to think they had a right to her."

The danger had entered Ramsey's mind, but he knew his men, and more than that, his men knew him. "They don't know she's a woman, and if they did, they still wouldn't touch her."

"You understand why I'm not inclined to have the same faith in your men as you do. Can you guarantee they won't touch her?"

"I stand a better chance of protecting her from her own comrades than you and Garrett Rainier have of protecting her from Barrymore."

Anger boiled beneath Elias' placid façade before he finally subdued it with a smirk. "I don't know what I was expecting. You never did know when to get out of the way." His chair screeched as he pushed it back from the table and rose to leave.

Ramsey stood and blocked Elias' path to the door. "We're not finished here," he announced as he reached into his pocket and retrieved the land deal documents Alexandra had given him. He slapped them on the table. "You haven't heard my counteroffer."

Elias sat back down.

Ramsey remained standing as he flipped through the documents. "This is bold even for you, Elias. Why, I'm surprised you put your name on it."

Elias clenched his jaw.

"Truth is," Ramsey continued, "I don't care what happens to Marlbridge. Barrymore can torch it as far as I'm concerned, but I do care what happens to Alexandra, whose life is in danger because you let a snake in your garden. So, here's my proposal: either you kill the snake so Alexandra can go back home where she belongs or I'm going to send these documents to the Council. I can only imagine their reaction when they find out what you've been doing behind their backs."

A smile played at Elias' mouth. "Do it. I'm sure nothing would please the Council more than for Cranston Ramsey's heir to stroll up to their front door and save them the bounty on your head."

"There's no need for me to go in person when I can send Prichard. I doubt he'll have any qualms about squealing on you when he sees his name marked out on page three." Ramsey held up the corresponding page.

Elias' poker face never cracked. "A good bluff only works if you don't show all your cards."

Ramsey slammed his fist on the table. "Elias, I don't know what game you're playing, and I don't know whose side you're playing for; but, this isn't stud poker, and I'm not bluffing. If Alexandra gets hurt because of you—"

Elias sprang to his feet and leaned across the table. "You're the one who's going to get her killed!"

"What's that to you?"

It wasn't until Elias punched him that he saw the truth. At first he could not accept it, but it was there, staring him in the face. Curiously, in spite of the eternal enmity between their families, Ramsey felt a passing twinge of pity for the man. "You love her."

Elias looked away as he rubbed his knuckles. "Jonas wasn't a perfect man, but we were friends once, and I owe it to him to look after the girl. So, here's my proposal: You let her go, or that girl's gonna be the death of you." He plucked the cotton boll from Ramsey's lapel and twisted the stalk between his fingers as he strode out the door.

Chapter 29

Female Warrior Bold

Alexandra and Red rode for several miles before Red broke the silence, "This is the gratitude I receive for saving your life? I was quite comfortable among my captors. At least they didn't hold me at gunpoint and force me to ride around in the dark with a rainstorm brewing."

"Quiet, Red."

Red twisted in the saddle to look back at her. Ignoring the rifle Alexandra pointed in his direction, he inquired, "What were you planning to do with that beastly Prichard, anyway?"

"None of your concern."

"Perhaps it is more of my concern than you realize, but what is of greater concern to me is our destination."

Alexandra considered withholding her plan from Red, but his hands were tied, and they were already several miles from camp. She also figured if he knew he was heading toward freedom and not away from it, he might cooperate. After all the trouble she had gone to, she hated to shoot the man. "I'm taking you back to Marlbridge."

Red stared at her for a moment, presumably to ascertain whether or not she was serious. "I don't think that's a good idea."

"What you think doesn't matter. Colonel Barrymore's holding my people hostage, and he won't free them unless I bring you back."

"You think I'm worth it?"

She didn't know how to respond to that. It seemed unlikely that one man's life could purchase freedom for the whole town, but it was the only path she could see, so she had to go through with it.

"What if I escape?" Red asked. "What are you going to do then? Return to Marlbridge empty-handed? Barrymore will kill you for certain."

"I'm trying to set you free, Red. Don't talk me out of it."

"I know who you are and what you're trying to do, but Captain Ramsey has a plan, and it is better than yours."

Alexandra jerked Shadow to a stop and lowered her rifle. "What do you mean Captain Ramsey has a plan? He hasn't said anything to me about a plan. A plan for what?"

"Nothing. I meant nothing."

She had assumed Red had escaped Storm Chase, gone back to his unit, only to be captured in battle, but nothing about Red suggested that he had been in a battle that day. His uniform was as clean as the day she and the Home Guard had captured him. "How long have you been a prisoner?"

"Since you kidnapped me."

"How did you escape?"

"I didn't. Captain Ramsey found me and brought me here. You know, you never asked me my name. Everything would be simpler if people would only ask who I am."

Alexandra rested the barrel of the rifle over her shoulder. "I don't care who you are, Red. I just want to save my town and get this war over with so I can go home and finish reading *Jane Eyre*."

Red raised his eyebrows. "You read?"

The level of incredulity with which he asked insulted her. "Of course, I read. I come from a very respectable family, and I was a protégé of Miss Josephine Daschle." It was the first time she had ever thought to brag about that.

"If she could only see you now," Red mused.

"I never would've had to wear pants in the first place if it hadn't been for Miss Daschle, so I hope she's got a good view from down there." Alexandra pointed to the ground.

"Well, I've heard of students wanting to send their schoolmasters to the Devil, but I've never heard of one actually achieving it."

"I didn't send her to the Devil. She went of her own free will."

"I don't believe it. Why would she do that?"

"Some man she was in love with ran off with another woman. What does it matter to you?"

Red chuckled. "It's not a regular occurrence for a woman so refined to do such as that. I like stories in which the protagonist has unusual motivations. Do you really think Barrymore will abandon Marlbridge for good if you turn us both in? You're putting a lot of faith in Barrymore's estimation of my worth, which is even more remarkable considering you don't know who I am or what I've done."

"Barrymore said he would punish the town until you were returned and Drake Corbin was brought to justice."

"What's to stop him from continuing the punishment once you give in to his demands?"

Alexandra had no answer to that.

"Furthermore, why are we going to Marlbridge when Barrymore is here?" Red continued the barrage.

"Because I don't know where the enemy is camped. If they haven't taken heed of the weather and gone back to Marlbridge already, they will go back eventually. I didn't see Heppinstahl with them, so the logical conclusion is he stayed in Marlbridge. If I can't find Barrymore, I'll turn you in to Heppinstahl."

"What if they haven't gone back and they attack Cade's Mill? Will you abandon your post?"

"My post was back in Marlbridge. I wanted Captain Ramsey to help me get it back, but he doesn't care about me or what I'm supposed to do. Apparently, I only exist to serve him, not the other way around."

"The Scriptures do say that woman was made for man, not man for woman."

Alexandra scowled. "That doesn't really help me much, Red, seein' as how lately I've had to be both. Now, is there anything else you want to gab about, or can we ride in peace?"

Red was about to answer when he suddenly stopped at the bend in the road and held up his hands. "This was not my idea."

"Who are you talking to?" Alexandra urged Shadow forward until she saw St. Clair and Ramsey blocking the road.

St. Clair dismounted and yanked Alexandra off her horse. "Well, I never took you for a spy, Drake."

Alexandra rolled over onto her back and opened her eyes. Out of all the harrowing events she had endured lately, never had she felt as close to death as that moment when she looked up the barrel of the gun St. Clair was pointing in her face. Everything about him from his green-gold eyes to his clenched jaw to the way he squared his shoulders told her that he was about to pull the trigger.

"St. Clair, let her go." Ramsey ordered the instant St. Clair pulled the hammer back, ready to shoot Alexandra in the face.

"Cana, this boy is a——" he argued.

Ramsey interrupted, "I know what she is."

"He's a spy——" St. Clair stopped abruptly and looked at Ramsey. "Did you say 'she'?"

"That's what I said." Ramsey stepped closer to Alexandra, who was still sitting on the ground trying not to show how terrified she was.

The rain started to fall.

St. Clair stared at Alexandra for several moments, cocking his head as if to find a better vantage point from which he might ascertain Alexandra's true form. Finally, he holstered his gun and sank to his knee to meet her at eye level. He brushed away the strands of hair that had fallen across her face. "I've heard stories of tha mythical Female Warrior Bold. How could I have mistaken you for mortal man? Forgive me, m'lady."

Ramsey groaned and kicked at St. Clair's boot. "Get up. Don't encourage her." He grasped the back of Alexandra's collar and jerked her to her feet. He didn't notice the gash in her thigh until she winced and tried to hop away from him.

"What happened?" he demanded, his hand still gripping her collar.

"I saved this woman from Prichard Benefield," Red chirped as he looked down at her from atop his horse. "Or maybe, I saved him from her. Either way, she repaid my gallantry by kidnapping me. Again."

Alexandra glared at Red, who seemed to be enjoying himself. "Traitor," she hissed.

"I told you to stay away from Prichard," Ramsey growled.

Alexandra narrowed her eyes, ready to defend her actions, but when she tried to stand up straighter, she swooned.

Ramsey let go of her collar and caught around the waist to keep her from falling. With his arms still around her, he looked down at her wound. "That's gonna have to be sewn up." He turned her head to face him. "Can you ride?"

Alexandra glanced at Red who had curiously made no attempt to escape. She was tempted to make one last effort to break free from Ramsey and take Red back to Marlbridge, but her heart was still racing from her encounter with St. Clair. With every pulse, she felt weaker. "I can make it."

Before she could protest, Ramsey picked her up and placed her on Shadow's back.

As he mounted Solomon, Ramsey charged St. Clair with escorting Red back to camp and making sure he didn't catch his death in the rainstorm. St. Clair complied, but expressed for the record that it was against his better judgment to leave Ramsey and the lady to find their way back to Cade's Mill alone.

To reassure him, Ramsey added, "This storm's gonna be a bad one. I need you to secure the camp in my absence." Without another word, St. Clair rode off toward camp with Red leading the way.

By the time Ramsey and Alexandra reached the edge of town, the rain was so heavy they could scarcely see five feet in front of them. Shadow had spooked twice, once at a thunderclap, and once again when a tree limb fell across the road. Fortunately, Ramsey had been riding close enough to help Alexandra stay in the saddle.

He made no mention of Prichard or Red or her insubordination. They weren't very far from the parsonage when Alexandra got up the nerve to say what had been swirling in her head for the past twenty minutes. "You had Red the whole time. We could have saved Marlbridge days ago. Now, they're probably dead."

Ramsey stopped the horses in front of the parsonage and pulled Alexandra out of the saddle. Bud came out to greet them, and without a word, he took the horses to the barn.

Alexandra tried to limp along by herself, but when she stumbled, Ramsey picked her up and carried her the rest of the way. For the first time, as she let her head fall against his shoulder, she was grateful for that stubbornness in him that she had fought so hard against since their run-in at Storm Chase.

When Ramsey banged on the door with his boot, Henrietta called out from inside, "Who is it?"

"Cana. I got a wounded soldier."

Henrietta flung the door open and leaned her musket against the wall. "Well, why didn't you say so 'stead a bangin' on de do' like you some riffraff? Git on in dis house."

Evelyn entered the room with a revolver. Relief flooded her face when she saw Ramsey. She set the gun down as Henrietta muttered to herself, "Comin' 'round in de middle a de night. Bangin' on de do'. Scarin' folks half to deaf. Drippin' water on de flo'. Mmph. I tell you what all dat is—dat's how folks git shot."

Evelyn must have seen the battle stains on Ramsey's rain-soaked jacket. Alexandra was too weak to turn her head enough to get a good look at Evelyn's face, but she heard her gasp, "Please tell me all that blood is not yours or his."

"Yankee. Mostly."

Evelyn touched Alexandra's head. "Get him upstairs."

Alexandra felt Ramsey's heart pounding more forcefully from the strain of carrying her. Not wanting to drain his strength further, Alexandra insisted she could make it up the stairs herself, but Ramsey went ahead and carried her to an upstairs bedroom and laid her on the bed, muddy boots and all.

Evelyn ordered, "Take his clothes off."

Ramsey hesitated. "I can't."

"Cana Ramsey, you do what I say. Quick now."

"I can't. See for yourself."

Alexandra interjected weakly, "I can take care of myself."

Evelyn ignored her and started to unbutton Alexandra's shirt. Alexandra tried to push her hand away, but it was too late. The binding on her chest was already exposed.

After standing agape for a moment, Evelyn whirled around and tore into Ramsey. "You knew? And you let her fight? She could've been killed!"

"She didn't give me much choice."

Alexandra grimaced as she tried to move her leg. "He's right. I chose for myself."

Evelyn continued to direct her attack at Ramsey, "Do you have any idea what would happen to her and her family if word got out that she's been dressing like a man, living in an army encampment? She might as well be a prostitute!"

Evelyn's words struck Alexandra. She had assumed that when she turned herself in, she would explain her actions, and even if Barrymore executed her, at least she would be absolved in the eyes of her people. It had never occurred to her that she might not get a chance to explain. For her own image, she took little regard, but to tarnish her father's name was unconscionable. She had to try harder to get back to Marlbridge. Whether she saved the town or not, she could at least justify her actions and redeem her father's name. She struggled to sit up.

Ramsey pushed her back down onto the bed, keeping a firm hand on her shoulder. He spoke to Evelyn with that tone he frequently used with Alexandra. It surprised her that he would dare use it with Evelyn. "I don't have to justify my actions, not to her family and not to you. I let her fight because she needed to."

Evelyn didn't back down. "The newspapers will brand her an adventuress who has no husband, no family that would claim her, no prospects, no money. Even if they don't go so far as sending her to an asylum, a woman has no future without a good name. How could you have been so stupid?" She shook her head furiously and held her hand up. "I can't talk to you right now. Go downstairs and get out of those wet clothes. Go on."

Alexandra couldn't tell if Ramsey was incensed or ashamed. Whatever his feelings were, he did as he was told.

Evelyn turned back to Alexandra and shifted her pant leg to get a better look at the knife wound. "I'll have to sew that up."

Alexandra nodded and fumbled with her garments until she was finally free of them. Evelyn took a wet cloth from the water basin on the bedside table and began cleaning the wound.

The older woman seemed close to tears, and Alexandra felt it was her duty at the moment to apologize for Ramsey, knowing he would never do it on his own accord. "I don't think he really means to be a bear. He just acts that way sometimes. I always take it personal, but maybe I shouldn't."

"I shouldn't chastise him. He's a good man, and he carries his wounds better than most."

After she made a couple of stitches and Alexandra hadn't cried, Evelyn looked up at her. "What's your real name?"

"Alexandra," she panted, trying not to yelp.

"You must be a decent enough soldier to fool all those men into thinking you're one of them."

Alexandra shrugged. "Oh, you don't have to have any special skills to pull that off."

Evelyn made one last stitch and bound up the wound. "Well, it's not my best needlework, but Doc Yancey has too many patients already, so it'll have to do. Rest if you can, and I'll see if I've got anything that will help with the pain." Evelyn tossed the bloody rags in the water basin.

"Thank you," Alexandra whispered. Even with the pain, she wasn't close to tears, but her throat was so tight, it was all she could do to breathe. When Evelyn left the room, Alexandra laid her head back on the pillow intending to spend the rest of the night formulating a new plan. She blinked three times and fell asleep.

Chapter 30

What Have You Done?

WHEN Evelyn appeared in the doorway, Ramsey was sitting at the table, staring into his cup of coffee, still in his wet clothes. He took a sip. Evelyn poured herself a cup and sat down.

She gave him an apologetic look. "I know you did what you thought was best under the circumstances."

He begrudgingly accepted her apology with a cut of his eyes.

"Does anyone else know?"

"Just St. Clair." Then Ramsey remembered Red. "And Red, the soldier she kidnapped, and Prichard Benefield, the man she stabbed and left for dead." He ended the list with a bitter chuckle. "And, of course, Elias." He rested his head on the table.

"Elias? The man who took your family's land?"

"He didn't take it. My father gambled it away."

"Do you think he would harm the girl?"

He didn't answer.

Evelyn continued, "You know, she's actually quite handsome. She followed you into battle, suffered a wound, and she still followed you here."

Ramsey raised his head. He could tolerate Evelyn's interference up to a certain point, but not about this. "She suffered that wound trying to finish off Prichard Benefield after I ordered her to stay away from him."

"Prichard Benefield is a bad man, and as far as I can tell, no one is doing anything about it. Are you surprised that a woman like Alexandra would take matters into her own hands?"

"I'm gonna make sure Prichard gets what's coming to him, and in doing so, I might even save Marlbridge, if Alexandra would get out of my way."

"Cana, I know you have a plan and I know your plan will work, whatever it is, but she doesn't know that. You've kept her in the dark. No wonder the girl is acting on her own—your silence has convinced her she is alone."

"She should trust me," he mumbled.

"Yes, she should, but maybe you haven't given her a reason to."

Ramsey stared into his coffee cup.

"What are you gonna do with her?"

Ramsey opened his flask and poured whiskey into his coffee. "I don't know."

"Do you love her?"

He nearly choked on his coffee.

Evelyn smiled and touched his wounded forearm. When he winced, she pushed up his jacket sleeve. "Did you really think you could hide that from me?" she scowled.

Giving her a wary look, he turned in his chair to put more distance between Evelyn and his wounded arm. "I'll tend to it later."

"When?"

"Soon as I leave here."

"You're not leaving this house until that arm's taken care of."

"And just how do you plan on making me stay?"

Evelyn's eyes narrowed as she got up from the table and walked over to the doorway. "Henrietta!"

* * *

Exhausted, aching, and irritable, Ramsey didn't spare his horse as he rode back to camp. Despite the weather and Evelyn's admonitions, he had flatly refused Evelyn's invitation to remain at the parsonage for three reasons, not counting his ill-humor.

One, while Ramsey loved Evelyn as he had loved his own mother, she was not his mother, and it just wouldn't look right for a bachelor, whose reputation was already less than desirable, to take up residence even for one night with a married woman whose husband was off serving his country as a chaplain.

Two, while Ramsey was not above parting with his honor to do what needed doing, he could not bring himself to sleep in a warm, dry bed while his fellow soldiers slept out in the rain.

However, it was his third reason that was perhaps the most compelling—there was a woman in a warm, dry bed, and Ramsey meant to keep his distance. If he was depending on Alexandra's ratty uniform and her muddy boots and her short mane to prevent any kind of attraction on his part, he knew his faith was misplaced when he carried her in his arms and she laid her head on his shoulder.

As Ramsey rode into camp, the rain had so impaired his vision that he almost ran over Sal and Bradford who were scurrying like squirrels to relocate their suspiciously large hoard of foodstuffs to the barn. Across the way, St. Clair was helping Langley and McCabe secure a tent that had been dismantled by the wind. When St. Clair saw Ramsey, he abandoned the tent and came over to stand next to his captain.

Extending his good arm, Ramsey reached down and yanked the rain-soaked plume out of St. Clair's hat. "You better get this turkey feather to shelter. Another storm's brewing over in Paul Jordan's field."

St. Clair snatched his feather. "Paul Jordan's field? Is that where tha enemy has settled himself? Why, that's a terrible place ta camp, especially in this weather. We oughtta attack now lest a whirlwind beat us to it. If I'm gonna have ta bury dead Yankees in the mornin' anyhow, I'd ruther not have ta pick 'em outta tha trees fust."

As Ramsey dismounted, he spotted Bradford returning from the barn and ordered him to see to his horse. Pitiful as a drowned rat, Bradford took Solomon's reins and led him away without a peep.

"I fear tha loss of Lew Carter has significantly reduced morale," St. Clair observed.

The captain nodded as his own weariness began to sink into his bones. "Marcus will do the best he can to prevent an engagement, but Barrymore will not listen, I'm sure of it. So, it falls to us to prevent a bloodlettin' that will benefit no one."

"How do you propose we do that?" St. Clair followed Ramsey to his tent and lit the lantern on the table.

"Are you sure you want me to answer that? I know how you abhor dishonorable tactics." Ramsey took off his hat and jacket and hung them on a hook he'd fastened to one of the tent posts.

"What have you done?" St. Clair asked as he took a seat at the table.

Ramsey sat on his cot and kicked his boots off. "I turned Garrett Rainier loose with the information that we have reinforcements coming. He is to use that information to convince Barrymore to withdraw. If Barrymore doesn't withdraw, Rainier will kill him."

"An assassination? Have you abandoned your senses? Garrett Rainier is tha wust possible choice for such a mission. Why, you'd do better ta send Bradford 'n' Sal, and let them talk tha man ta death.

"Well, I can't do it without inviting reprisals from his men. If, however, it looks like an accident, then I'll have the satisfaction of saving Marlbridge at no cost to us. As for Rainier, when it comes to breaking the law with impunity, I challenge you to find anyone more suited in knowledge and disposition than a lawyer."

"I understand your reasonin', but what will be tha cost ta your honor?"

"Honor is a luxury reserved for those of your kind, my friend."

"Why are you so eager ta avoid an engagement? It's not like you. We've been in wust scrapes than this. Other men might go soft after Shiloh, but not you, so tell me tha truth. What has happened ta you?"

"Before, it was just you and me. Now, I have a hundred men to keep alive, and there's Cade's Mill, Evelyn, Marlbridge. I don't know how to move forward without bringing unnecessary harm to all of them."

"Whisenhunt will not allow Barrymore ta succeed. If there ever was a time ta play tha hand you've been dealt, it's now. Everything is in our favor."

Ramsey took a deep breath, mostly to buy himself some time away from St. Clair's insights into their situation. "Would you have shot her?"

"What? Who? Drake?"

"Alexandra. Would you have shot her?"

"Yes, but I didn't know she was a woman," he replied, sounding a little flustered.

"Neither do they."

"Cana, if this is about tha girl, maybe sendin' her away is tha best thing for everyone. Keepin' her here doesn't make sense. You should let her go."

"I made a promise that I would look out for her, and for twelve years I neglected my duty. I'm not going to abandon her now."

"Then let her abandon you. Who knows? Maybe she'll want ta go back ta Mahlbridge and marry Garrett Rainier or some other gentleman. Either way, your duty is fulfilled, and we can get on with fightin' this war."

St. Clair paused for observation. "Or perhaps, tha problem is you don't want her ta marry some other man. If that's tha case, you should marry her yourself. At least then she'd have ta do what you say."

Ramsey laughed at the absurdity of the suggestion. "She doesn't do what I say now, and I'm her commanding officer. It wouldn't make any difference if I was her husband. She's gonna do whatever she has a mind to do, and I can't stop her."

"Then change her mind. She's evidently changed yours: tip-toein' around tha enemy, plannin' assassinations, and avoidin' conflict altogether when you have every reason ta fight. I declare, I don't know you anymore."

"Alexandra is an ever-present reminder of who I was."

St. Clair scoffed, "You've only known her for a day."

Ramsey pulled Alexandra's letter out of his pocket and handed it to his friend.

St. Clair read the letter then gave it back to him. "So, a little girl wanted you ta stay and protect her town, and you didn't do it. I don't see that anything's changed—she still wants you ta save her town, and you're still not doin' it."

"She isn't trying to save Marlbridge because it's her town. She's trying to save it because it's Jonas Corbin's town. If Marlbridge falls, it will be because Jonas Corbin wasn't there to stop it. It's not her fault that he's gone, but it doesn't make it any less her responsibility to do whatever she can in his stead."

"But, it isn't her responsibility, and it isn't yours either, so why do you insist on makin' it so?"

"Because, all his contradictions aside, Jonas Corbin was a good sheriff. He would've managed enemy occupation better than Elias, and

I'm the reason he's not here to fulfill his duty. I can't save his town, but I can save Alexandra."

"Cana, what your father did, that wasn't your fault."

Ramsey let some time pass before he answered. "It doesn't matter who pulled the trigger. The truth is, if I hadn't been there, Jonas wouldn't have died, not that night anyway."

St. Clair got up from the table. "Well, tha reality is we still got ourselves a Yankee problem, and all this reminiscin' ain't solvin' it."

Ramsey leaned back on his cot with his hands behind his head. "Worst comes to worst, we can always rely on the cannon."

"We only have three, and I don't know what good they'll do unless you plan on hurlin' twelve-pound fieldstones at tha enemy."

Ramsey grinned. "Madcap Charlie and I came to an agreement. He needed horses. We needed artillery shells, and judging by the amount of black paint and sawdust on Sal's uniform, we should have at least a dozen cannon by now."

Chapter 31

Dealing With Devils

ABOUT the time Elias shut his eyes, a thunderclap brought him back to the realm of the living, though there was little about an army encampment that didn't remind Elias of death. For the hundredth time, he asked himself why he had agreed to accompany Heppinstahl's men while the colonel himself was back in Marlbridge, no doubt wallowing in his overstuffed featherbed at this very moment.

It had only been a few hours since Elias had left Ramsey and returned to his quarters. He had hoped to be well on his way to Chattanooga by now, but he had underestimated Ramsey's feelings for the girl. It was a costly miscalculation. Not until Garrett Rainier appeared later that night, recounting the details of his incarceration at the hands of the renegade, did Elias realize how much he had underestimated Ramsey.

If Garrett's report was accurate, out of all the players at the table, Ramsey had the best hand. In addition to the leverage he currently had against Elias, Ramsey had allies and spies in Cade's Mill and Marlbridge. He had the ear of Madcap Charlie, who was eager for any opportunity to reduce the numbers of the enemy. He had Prichard Benefield, wanted by Barrymore. He most likely had General Belgrave's son, wanted by Heppinstahl, and he had Alexandra, who was wanted by everyone though undoubtedly such knowledge was lost on the girl herself.

Why Ramsey hesitated to use his advantage, Elias could not figure out, and it made him nervous. Perhaps, Ramsey really did believe the girl would be safer surrounded by an army rather than sitting in her aunt's library in Chattanooga with nothing to do but read more history books. Jonas, God love him, should have never allowed the girl to read in the first place, filling her mind with war heroes and battles and knights and castles. No wonder the girl fought so bravely for the South. She probably thought the mythical country she'd read about in her books was a real place and Marlbridge its miniature.

"Did you hear me? He wants me to kill Barrymore." Garrett spoke more loudly than he should have.

Elias had only been half-listening to Garrett's account of all that had transpired during his harrowing imprisonment, but the mention of Barrymore's demise caught his attention. "Who wants you to kill Barrymore?"

"Ramsey," Garrett replied, exasperated.

"Why would he pick you? What else did he tell you?"

"He would not give me Drake."

"I expected as much."

"Then why did you send me on a fool's errand?"

"Because all the other fools were busy doing other things, and you were the only one I could spare at the moment." If Elias hadn't been in such a terrible mood, he would have laughed at Garrett's reaction. "Do you contest that you are a fool?"

Garrett drew his shoulders back and stuck his chin out as far as it would go. "I do contest it. Furthermore, I submit that if I am a fool, you are the bigger fool. Why are you here risking your life to capture Drake Corbin for the benefit of Colonel Barrymore, whom you detest as we all do, when you could be at home nestled in your library devising sundry ways in which you might profit from these ungodly times that have befallen our nation?"

"I might ask you why Alexandra risked her life to leave Marlbridge when she could have stayed behind with you." Elias had been somewhat surprised when Alexandra ran off to the army, but he had been more surprised when she let go of the boy she was sweet on.

"Alexandra fled to Chattanooga to escape the dishonor Drake Corbin has brought upon her and her family."

Under other circumstances, Elias would have enjoyed toying with the young man a little longer, but his patience with less intelligent beings had expired. "Alexandra *is* Drake, you idiot."

"That is absurd. Ramsey would never allow a woman in his ranks."

"And I would never allow a woman to ride in the county horserace."

It took a few moments for the blood to fully retreat from Garrett's face. He sat in the chair next to the field desk and covered his face with his hands.

Elias got up from his cot and handed Garrett a cigar. "Consider this your initiation gift."

Garrett pushed the cigar away. "I already feel sick."

Elias lit the cigar for himself.

"What are we going to do?"

"About what?"

"About Alexandra being..." Garrett stumbled over the words, "in the army! She could have been killed!" He shook his head violently. "No, surely Ramsey did not let her fight in the battle today."

"Oh, I'm sure he tied her to a tent post first, thinking that would work."

"Dear God, what are we going to do?"

"Why are you asking God for help? Most likely, He's the one who arranged all this calamity to bring about our ruin."

The affront propelled Garrett to his feet. "Our ruin? What have I done to offend the Almighty?"

Elias exhaled a cloud of smoke. "You're a Rainier, and God doesn't like Rainiers and Kelsons any more than he likes Hittites and Amalekites. You and I were born on the wrong side of the river. Whatever heaven we get, we better get it for ourselves while we can because if there is a heaven, you can be sure God isn't going to share it with us, not after what we've done."

Garrett waved the smoke away from his face. "What are you talking about? Alexandra is in trouble and you are going on about Amalekites! There are no more Amalekites!"

"That is my point. All that is left of them is their name. The funny thing is it won't be the Kelsons and the Rainiers that the people of Marlbridge will remember. It will be the Corbins and the Ramseys. For while we were amassing our fortunes, they were tragic figures doomed to become legends, and the people will feast on their stories 'til doomsday."

By this time, Garrett looked about ready to shoot himself if he didn't shoot Elias first. "My father is right. You are completely mad."

Elias grinned, his cigar clenched between his teeth. "Then who better to navigate this sea of madness we're all drowning in?"

Garrett yanked the cigar out of Elias' mouth and threw it on the muddy floor. "You will do whatever it takes to get Alexandra out of this predicament."

Elias folded his arms as he eyed Garrett, trying to decide if he should box the pup's ears for his insolence. "And if I don't?"

The pup showed his teeth. "I will tell the Council it was you who killed Jonas Corbin."

Elias smirked, even though Rainier the Younger's words amounted to a death threat. "And here I thought you weren't like Hanson at all."

As Elias anticipated, Garrett recoiled. "I am nothing like my father."

"No, come to think of it, Hanson doesn't typically make death threats. In that regard, you are more like your mother."

Garrett stared at Elias, his eyes blazing with contempt. "Take back your disparaging remark regarding my mother."

"No."

"Take it back, sir, or I will strike you!"

"I might respect you more if you did."

"I have no need of your respect, nor do I desire it," Garrett snarled.

Elias stepped closer until he was almost nose-to-nose with Garrett. "But you do desire Alexandra's respect. Question is: how far are you willing to go to get it?"

"I resent your implication that she does not respect me already."

"How else would you interpret her actions? She ran off and joined the army, for heaven's sake." Elias put his hand on Garrett's shoulder and forced him to sit back down on the cot. "Don't worry, Rainier. I have a plan to get her back. Shall I deal you in or not?"

Garrett took a deep breath. "Does your plan require me to kill anyone?"

"No."

"Then your plan suits me better than Ramsey's."

"Well then, Rainier, it's time to make a deal with the devil."

"Which one?" Garrett scowled.

"The one who's least likely to drag us to hell with him when he goes."

After sending Garrett away, Elias slipped into his great coat and slogged his way to the heart of the Union camp. If Ramsey hadn't been so stubborn, if he had just given up the girl, the deal that Elias was about to make wouldn't be necessary. Yet, there he was, risking his life in the middle of a lightning storm, muddying his favorite pair of boots. Fortunately, Ramsey was not there or another death would be counted against Elias' soul.

As Elias ducked inside Joab Barrymore's tent and sat down at his table, it was some consolation that the colonel was just as loath to make a deal as was Elias, being that he and Elias had no mutual interests except in the removal of two seemingly insurmountable obstacles: Cana Ramsey and Drake Corbin. So, when Barrymore heard Elias' plan to kill two birds with one stone, he was eager to oblige, just as Elias had predicted.

Chapter 32

Quaker Guns

EARLY the next morning, as Ramsey waited for Langley to return from his scouting mission, he inspected his battery of Quaker guns. "Good work, Sal."

Sal grinned and patted one of the logs that he had cut and painted to look like a real field gun. "Reckon she'll do." He squinted over Ramsey's shoulder. "Yunder comes Langley and in a hurry, too."

Ramsey tensed as Langley rode up and dismounted. "What news, Langley?"

"Good news, sir! The enemy has fled."

"See! I told ye, Langley, these here guns would do the trick, and ye didn't believe me, did ye?" Sal hooted.

Langley snorted. "There is no evidence it was your stick artillery that caused the enemy to retreat."

"They ain't no sticks. Look at the size of them barrels."

"They're the wrong color. Napoleons are bronze."

"Well, I ain't got no bronze paint, and besides, who said they's s'posed to be Napoleons? Since these here are Confederate-manufactured howitzers, I say they oughtta be painted black like iron. Don't you think so, Cap'n?"

Reining-in the banter that could conceivably last until noon, Ramsey ordered Sal to get back to work while Langley gave a full report. The enemy had retreated back across the river sometime before daybreak. Where they were headed, Langley didn't know. The rest of the report covered relevant storm damage.

"Find Lieutenant St. Clair. Give him the news, and tell him I'll meet with him directly."

"Yes, sir." Langley saluted, but before he dashed off, he handed Ramsey a sealed letter. "From Miss Evelyn. She said it was important."

A knot twisted in Ramsey's gut. He dismissed Langley then paused to reassure himself before he tore into the letter. Surely, Alexandra hadn't died. It was just a flesh wound, and Evelyn was as good as any doctor. After he opened the letter and scanned it, he leaned against the closest Quaker gun and finally released the breath he'd been holding.

Sal came over and stood in front of him. "Cap'n, you all right?"

"Doesn't matter. I'm needed in town. Tell St. Clair I'll be back as soon as I can."

"Yes, sir." Sal put down his paint brush. "Uh, sir, I wasn't gonna say nothin' 'cause I don't want to start no trouble, but we ain't seen Drake since yesterday afternoon, and he don't strike me as a deserter. Reckon me and the boys oughtta go look fer him?"

Ramsey carefully folded Evelyn's letter and slipped it into the pocket where he kept Alexandra's letter. "That won't be necessary, Sal."

* * *

The parsonage was dark and silent. Ramsey sat with his head in his hands. He jumped to his feet when St. Clair entered the bedroom.

Glancing at Ramsey, St. Clair walked over to the bed and touched Alexandra's forehead.

"The fever comes and goes." Ramsey came over to stand next to St. Clair. He reached down and brushed clumps of matted hair away from Alexandra's face.

"How long has she been like this?" St. Clair asked, his concerned gaze alternating between Alexandra and Ramsey.

"Evelyn sent word this morning."

"You should've told me, Cana. I would've come sooner." St. Clair put his hand on Ramsey's shoulder. "It's near midnight. Go get some rest. I'll sit with her."

Ramsey shook his head. "I can't sleep anyway." He slouched back down in the chair. "It was just a flesh wound."

"On top of everything else." St. Clair stiffened and set his shoulders the way he did when he was exasperated. "Have you not considered what all she's been through? She lost her brother, got attacked by a ruffian, and then we threw her onto tha battlefield and expected her ta fight like a man—and she did. No one could take all tha tribulation that's come upon this poor girl in a matter of days, and you have no right ta expect it of her."

Ramsey glowered at his friend. "Expect what? Expect her to live? I do expect it because the alternative is out of the question."

"Come over here then, and start barkin' orders at her. I'm sure she'll respond ta that," St. Clair snapped.

Ramsey's eyes widened in shock. "You blame me for this."

"I do. You're too hard on her."

"Me? You were the one who nearly drilled her to death."

"I didn't know she was woman."

"Neither did I."

"When did you find out?"

"The night we found Prichard in the woods. I took her back to my tent and saw she wasn't hurt."

"You looked upon her nakedness?" St. Clair gasped, scandalized.

"Her—" Ramsey cupped his hands and held them close to his chest, but couldn't bring himself to say the word. He lifted his chin, daring St. Clair to contradict him. "They were covered. Besides, who appointed you the protector of her honor? You would have shot her if I hadn't been there to stop you."

St. Clair's face flushed. "Well, these are unusual circumstances in which we have found ourselves. I trust you will forgive my sharp tongue. All I really meant ta say was that whether you consider her a lady or not, we oughtta treat her as such because we are gentlemen."

"Thaddeus, I know you think I should've sent her home with Garrett Rainier, but…" Ramsey closed his eyes and pinched the bridge of his nose. He didn't have an explanation that would satisfy St. Clair's chivalry. As he watched Alexandra shiver beneath the blankets, he began to doubt his decision. Maybe he should have sent her to Chattanooga after all.

"I know, you don't trust anyone ta care for her but you." St. Clair took a deep breath as he turned to leave. Pausing at the door, he looked back at Ramsey. "Cana, we have a war ta fight. You can't keep this woman as a soldier. So, unless you intend ta keep her as a wife, it's best you let her go."

When St. Clair stepped out of the room and closed the door, Ramsey got out of his chair and moved to the edge of the bed. He lifted Alexandra's head and gave her a drink of water from the glass he'd taken from the nightstand. Her eyelashes fluttered, but she immediately fell back asleep. Ramsey set the glass down on the nightstand then leaned over and rested his forehead against hers. "What am I going to do with you?"

Chapter 33

Dreams

April 26

ALEXANDRA *was sleeping in the tall grass, a candy stick dangling from her mouth. Shadow tried to steal the candy stick, leaving a streak of grassy horse slobber on her nose. She scrunched her face and playfully pushed Shadow's nose away, giving him the stick. Without opening her eyes, she wiped the slobber off her nose. She heard a faint jangle. Then a shadow crossed her and something tickled her nose.*

She reached to push Shadow away, but instead of a soft muzzle, she felt a hand. She opened her eyes to see her brother standing over her.

Cass grinned and popped her on the nose with his enlistment papers. "What do you think?" he asked as he showed off his new Confederate cavalry uniform.

Alexandra squinted up at him. "I think Mama is gonna fuss about gray. You know it stains so easy."

Cass chuckled at Alexandra's impersonation of Laura Catherine and plopped down next to her. "I think Mama is gonna be too busy fussing at your outfit to even notice mine." He gestured toward her shirt and pants.

"It's not as if I wear them in public where anybody could see me, and I only wear them when I'm riding. Have you ever tried riding in a hoop skirt?"

Cass looked down at his legs. "Hmm…"

"Of course, it doesn't really matter what I'm wearing," she sniffed, giving him her haughtiest expression.

"No, no. I will always be the better rider."

Alexandra tossed her long mane. "Who won the Jackson County horserace?"

"If I remember correctly it was my long-lost 'cousin' Drake who rode in that race, and he came in second if I recall."

"Only because I pulled back at the last moment to spare your pride," Alexandra declared.

Cass laughed. "Alexandra, I know you. You would not have pulled back for any reason. Admit it, sis. I beat you in a fair race, simple as that."

"If it makes you feel better to think of it that way, go ahead." Alexandra twisted her hair on top of her head and shoved her hat down over it. She stood up, nearly as tall as Cass. She paused just long enough to catch her brother unawares then jerked his hat down over his face and leapt onto Shadow's back.

They raced across the pasture and over the fence. They splashed through the creek and wove through the forest. The trees grew thicker, and they had to slow their pace. They had just entered the darkest part of the forest when they ran into a bear.

Alexandra gasped for air and sat up in bed, her body drenched with sweat. A bird was chirping right outside her window indicating that it was still morning, though the heavy drapes were keeping out most of the light. Forgetting her wound, she swung her legs to the edge of the bed. The stiffness and the pain forced her to wait a little while before she eased onto her feet again. There was also a weakness in her chest that she hadn't noticed before. Alexandra hobbled to the washstand and poured fresh water into the basin. Her reflection was paler than it had been since she was ten and had that bad fever.

Evelyn had left a clean shirt and trousers on the chair. After Alexandra washed, she slipped into the clothes and crept downstairs. By the time she reached the dining room, she was tired all over again.

"Mornin'."

Alexandra jumped when Ramsey spoke. He was sitting at the table, surrounded by a newspaper and several empty plates. Despite the odd bit of contentment in his voice, he looked as if he hadn't slept well. When Alexandra took her place at the table, he got up and fixed her a plate of eggs and two biscuits.

He plopped the food in front of her along with a cup of coffee.

She took a bite of her biscuit and closed her eyes, repenting of all the times she had wasted biscuits in the past by hoarding them for days until they were hard as rocks. Whenever her mother forbade her to play in the yard with the boys, Alexandra participated in their mock battles by hurling the biscuits from her bedroom window. Due to her strategic location, she was often one of the first to be picked when the boys divided up into Patriots and Redcoats, but the Redcoat leader eventually stopped picking her because she always jumped sides to fight for the Patriots.

Ramsey poured himself another cup of coffee. "Did you get attacked by a bear at some point in your life? You kept going on about a bear."

Alexandra ducked her head. "Did I hit you?"

"Ha. You tried." He sat back in his chair and blew on his coffee before he took a sip. "So, what about the bear?"

Alexandra picked at her food. "Whenever I have the bear dream, it means something bad is going to happen."

Ramsey peered at her over the top of his coffee cup. "Like what?"

"Usually, someone dies."

"In the dream or in real life?"

"In real life. No one ever dies in the dream. The bear jumps out at me, and I wake up." She shrugged, embarrassed that Ramsey knew yet another one of her secrets. "Garrett says it doesn't mean anything, that it's just a coincidence."

Ramsey swirled his coffee. "Does the bear ever attack you?"

Until that moment, Alexandra had always tried to push the bear dream as far away from her mind as possible. She had never actually analyzed the dream. She set her fork down and closed her eyes, allowing the images to enter her mind. When she opened her eyes, Ramsey was staring at her in anticipation, as if he genuinely cared to know. "No, he doesn't attack me. He just stands there and huffs and tosses his head at me."

Ramsey sipped his coffee, his brow furrowed.

"What do you think it means?" she asked hesitantly.

"Well, I don't know anything about bear dreams; I dream about whirlwinds. If bear dreams are like whirlwind dreams and someone's gonna die, in my experience, the best you can do is pray it won't be you doing the killin'." He finished the rest of his coffee and set his cup down on the table. "I'll be back later to make sure you're ready for tonight."

"Ready for what?" The thought of another battle depressed her.

He gave her the look he usually gave her when he didn't think he owed her an explanation and strolled out the door, leaving her with the dishes.

The moment Alexandra finished eating, Henrietta appeared and took her plate. "Sorry dey ain't no milk. Ol' Milly up an' died on us lass week. Ms. Evelyn's bruthuh, he's da sheriff in dese parts, he 'sposed to bring another milk cow this evenin' when he come fo' da shindig."

"What shindig?"

"You don't know 'bout da shindig? Folks come from all over dese parts to hear da music. We been doin' it fo' near on twenty year now. We thought we was gwine have to cancel on account a da battle, but da Yankees up an' lef' when dey seen all dem Quaker guns Cap'n Ramsey set out fo' 'em."

Henrietta lowered her voice and tried not to laugh. "Dem cannons was nuthin' but logs. I ain't neber seen dat befo'." She shook her head. "Mm-hmm. Dat Cap'n Ramsey, he somethin'. I don't know what, but he somethin'."

"I have to agree with you there," Alexandra muttered.

"Now, if you wants milk, I hear dey gots some down at da tabern, but I don't go to dem places whar I know da Debil been recruitin' souls fo' da pit. Course, I don't reckon he come out dis time a day, so's if you gwone now, you might gitchee some milk wiffout da riffraff."

Alexandra thanked Henrietta for the information and headed for Johnny Knowles'. She hadn't had a glass of milk since she left home, and it sure sounded good—until she remembered that the tavern was more than a mile away, too far for her injured leg. She was about half-way across the yard when she saw Evelyn hanging sheets on the line.

"Need a hand?" Alexandra asked.

Evelyn smiled and handed her one end of a sheet and some clothespins.

"Henrietta said there was a shindig tonight? Am I expected to attend?"

"If you feel up to it." Evelyn glanced over at her. "Have you seen Cana?"

"At breakfast," Alexandra replied as she hung her end of the sheet on the line.

"Good. I tried to tell him you were going to make it, but evidently, he didn't believe me. Boy nearly worried himself to death."

Alexandra stared at her in amazement. "Did I really come close to dying? It was just a little gash. How long have I been here?"

"Three days."

Alexandra let a clothespin slip from her hand.

"You came down with a fever. You must know how Cana—" Evelyn hesitated as if she was about to divulge a secret and decided to say no more than she already had. "Well, he was worried, that's all."

"Why was he worried about me? It wouldn't be a great loss to the war effort if I died. I may not be the worst soldier of the bunch, but I'm a far cry from being as good a soldier as Lieutenant St. Clair."

Evelyn watched Alexandra lean on her good leg to retrieve the clothes pin. "For you to be so good at imitating men, you sure don't know much about them."

More confused than ever, Alexandra snatched a shirt from the laundry basket and placed it on the line.

"What are you doing here?" Evelyn asked.

It hadn't occurred to Alexandra that Evelyn may have been annoyed and greatly inconvenienced by her extended healing time. "I'm sorry if I've been a burden. I'm sure Captain Ramsey meant for me to be here only one night. As soon as I get to the bottom of this laundry basket, I'll be on my way."

Evelyn gently clasped Alexandra's shoulders. "I meant, what are you doing in the army?"

Alexandra sighed and sat down on an overturned washtub. "I started out trying to convince Captain Ramsey to come back to Marlbridge and liberate the captives there, but he won't, and every time I think I've found another way, it turns out wrong."

"Is that what you were doing out in that storm?"

"I know my tactics and timing need improving, as Captain Ramsey never fails to point out, but I saw an opportunity to save my people and I took it."

"You keep saying it's your town and your people, but it seems to me if any of those folks really were your people, wouldn't they come looking for you?"

"They think I'm in Chattanooga with my aunt. At least, that's what my mother would have told them when she saw that I was gone."

"Does any of your family know where you are?"

"Only Wilson, my stepfather," she answered. "It's strange, while everyone else would judge me for being —what was it you called it?—an adventuress?—Wilson Metcalf, the last man in the world to pick up a gun and fight, is the only one who really understood what I had to do." Alexandra set her jaw. "I hoped Garrett would understand, but, of course, he didn't."

"Is Garrett your beau?"

"No."

Evelyn unfurled the last sheet in the basket. "So, how do you figure on helping Marlbridge if you're here in Cade's Mill?"

"I didn't want to come here, but I can't save Marlbridge by myself."

"And you thought if you proved yourself to be a good soldier then Cana Ramsey might do what you want him to do?"

Alexandra shrugged.

"Mm-hmm. What rank are you?" Evelyn asked as she reached into Alexandra's laundry basket and pulled out a pair of trousers.

"Private."

"That's the lowest, isn't it?"

"Yes." Alexandra scrunched her brow, uncertain about where this conversation was going.

"Well, suppose you keep on proving yourself and you get to be, what's the next rank, sergeant?"

"Corporal, then sergeant."

"Oh, well, let's suppose in the next battle you really impress the lot of them and become a captain, Ramsey's equal. You think he would listen to you then?"

Alexandra's shoulders drooped. "No."

"Do you think there is any man in this world who could convince Cana Ramsey to do anything he didn't want to do?"

Alexandra tossed a leftover clothespin into the basket. "No."

"Well, then, it seems to me that if God intended for Cana Ramsey to save the people of Marlbridge, he wouldn't send a man to convince him." Evelyn shook out one of Ramsey's shirts and hung it on the line.

"Now, as a matter of conscience, I can't approve of what you're doing, but I understand that for you, it may also be a matter of conscience, and that is between you and God. So, whatever I may do to help you sort it out, you may rely on me to do it."

Evelyn picked up a pair of white gloves and a double-breasted Confederate frock coat that was hanging on the back of a chair. She handed them to Alexandra. "Henrietta did the best she could with your uniform, but it just wasn't presentable, so Cana sent you these to wear tonight. How he managed to wrench them from Bouchard's clutches, I shudder to think. I daresay Bouchard was not happy to part with them."

"Are they mine to keep?"

"For as long as you want them."

Alexandra held them for a moment, admiring the craftsmanship. The coat and gloves were a little too fine for a lowly private, and Alexandra was sure to endure a little ribbing from Sal and Bradford, but they were hers.

She had never been so happy to receive an article of clothing since the day her father had bought her that white dress with the lavender flowers on it, the day Meredith Kilroy had made fun of her for... Alexandra couldn't remember what, but it probably had something to do with her unruly hair or her muddy hem or her manure-caked shoes. Her father had come home with the very same dress she had been admiring in Pop Brady's window for weeks. She hadn't said a word to anyone about how much she wanted that dress, and she hadn't done anything to earn it. Her father had gotten it for her for no other reason than to make her happy. She had worn that dress every chance she could. It was all Lellen could do to convince her to wear something else. Even when she played with the boys, she had worn it like it was her uniform.

Chapter 34

The Dance

THOUGH it was a small community, Cade's Mill boasted the prime venue for strumming, picking, fiddling, and dancing in the surrounding counties. The back wall of the large pole barn, which served as a livestock auction barn throughout the rest of the year, had been dug out of the hillside to create a curved backdrop to the stage so that anyone within town limits could hear the music, whether they wanted to or not. Years ago, the town had collected a special tax to add walls and doors for use during the winter, and several of the ladies had used the leftover money to add flower boxes to dress it up during the spring and summer.

This year, as Alexandra had been informed by several townspeople, all the best musicians in the area were lined up to perform: the Densons, the Waldrop Brothers, the Sand Mountain Fiddlers, and a host of other groups, a few of whom had traveled three days to get there. The best of them all was Cade's Mill's own Buck Kennedy who could pick a banjo better than anybody on either side of the Mississippi, and Buck's eighty-five-year-old grandfather was still the best harmonica player who had ever lived.

Standing at the punch table, Alexandra had a full view of the barn. Bernice was sitting on a bale of hay, giggling as Bradford spun her a yarn that would surely never work on any of the other girls. Langley and St. Clair were taking turns impressing the ladies with stories of gallant deeds.

Mr. Finch, an elderly man whose cane was bigger around than he was, fussed about celebrating when there were so many wounded.

"The dead wasn't even cold in their graves," he remarked as he devoured a handful of cookies.

As Alexandra looked around at all the musicians and dancers, she found herself enjoying the event—a surprise to her as she had never cared much for social events back home, except for the races and the baking contests. Maybe it was because, for the first time in her life, the gossips huddled in the corner were not talking about her. Just to be sure, she tucked a few loose strands of hair behind her ear.

Even with its short length, Alexandra's hair was barely manageable. Evelyn had tied it in a ponytail. The style was outdated for the mid-nineteenth century, but for a girl who missed her defining feature that she had sacrificed to enter a man's world, the ponytail, short as it was, made her feel like her long tresses were still there.

As she flipped the nub of her ponytail around her gloved finger, Alexandra caught Ramsey staring at her from across the dance floor. It was impossible not to stare back. He had traded his shell jacket for a double-breasted frock coat, cinched at the waist with a crimson sash, the gold braid on the sleeves signifying his rank. His unruly black hair was clean and tame, and no trace remained of the dark stubble that usually adorned his chin and jaw line. He was every bit as striking as the night he had held her at gunpoint at Storm Chase and no less threatening. She could feel the heat creeping up her neck and cheeks, but as much as she wanted to hide her blushing face, she couldn't bring herself to look away.

He didn't look away either, until a moment later when something else drew his attention. He smiled as a woman—with whom he was evidently already acquainted—walked up to him and extended her hand. She was the most beautiful woman Alexandra had ever seen. If Drake had actually been a man, he would have been smitten with her, but as it was, Alexandra despised her immediately for no other reason than the effect she apparently had on Ramsey. He kissed the girl's hand and instructed the band to play a waltz.

Every male in the place looked on Ramsey with jealousy as he danced with the other woman. When the music changed, Ramsey led his dance partner toward the table.

Alexandra turned around to avoid him while Evelyn handed him a cup of punch and greeted the girl, "Good evening, Miss Patience. You are as beautiful as ever."

"Isn't she though," Ramsey agreed. He took the cup with a slight bow. "Why, thank you, Miss Evelyn." After one sip, he stifled a cough and raised his eyebrows at Evelyn who gave him an innocent look. Ramsey turned to Alexandra. "Private Corbin, I was starting to think you weren't gonna show up."

Alexandra refused to look at him. "And disappoint the ladies? I wouldn't dream of it. *Sir*." She cringed when Patience approached her.

"Why, who is this dashing young man? I've never seen you before. Are you one of Captain Ramsey's gallant cavalrymen?" the girl asked with her little voice.

Alexandra tried not to look her in the eye, but it was impossible. The girl would not be ignored. "Yes," Alexandra answered begrudgingly.

Patience stared at her for a moment before she demanded, "Well, aren't you going to ask me to dance?"

Alexandra could think of nothing else to say beyond, "I don't like to dance."

"Oh, you are only being shy. Now, ask me to dance, or I'll have Captain Ramsey order you. You would do that for me, wouldn't you, Captain?" She turned her big brown eyes on Ramsey who seemed to be enjoying Alexandra's discomfort.

For a moment, Alexandra thought Ramsey would give in, but to her relief, he said, "You'll have to forgive Corbin, Miss Patience. It's not that he doesn't like to dance. He doesn't want to admit that he was wounded and dancing is just too painful. So, you must relent and find yourself another partner."

"Wounded? Why, you poor dear," Patience cooed as she took Alexandra's hand. "I shall always remember your sacrifice for your country." Her solemn look vanished the instant she directed her attention back to Ramsey. "You know, I wouldn't dream of causing this gallant young man any more pain, but I'm afraid that still leaves me without a dance partner, so it seems I must content myself with you, Captain," she flirted as she offered him another cup of punch.

Ramsey grinned. "If I keep on drinking Ms. Evelyn's punch, I'll be too drunk to do anything but lean against this post and admire you from a safe distance."

Patience gasped, pretending to be scandalized as she looked at Evelyn.

Fortunately, they were spared any more of the girl's chatter when Langley appeared and requested the next dance. Alexandra ignored Evelyn who was smiling at her with intrigue.

"How are you getting on?" Ramsey asked. Alexandra snubbed him as she sipped her own cup of punch with a little more offended daintiness than she should have for someone pretending to be a boy. He held out his empty cup for Evelyn to pour him another.

Evelyn commented on the turnout: who all was there and what they were wearing and who all was missing because of the war. Ramsey was on his third cup of punch when Bradford scooted up to him.

"Hey Cap'n, mind if I ask your advice?" Bradford squeaked.

Ramsey set his empty cup down. "What do you need, Bradford?"

"Well, sir, and Drake, you kin weigh in on it if you want, but well, I's dancin' with Bernice. I reckon you all's noticed I'm kindly sweet on her, but we was dancin' and all of the sudden she starts to goin' on about some feller named Mr. Darcy and she talked about him like I's supposed to know who he was, like he was a famous politician or some such. Now, I believe a man oughtta know his rivals, but I never heard of the man. Do you know him?"

Alexandra bit her lips to hold in her laughter as Ramsey put his hand on the poor fellow's shoulder. "Bradford," he said with a solemn expression, "you might as well retreat as fast as you can 'cause there ain't a man alive who can beat Mr. Darcy. Except maybe St. Clair," he added as the dashing lieutenant himself approached.

"What's that you say? Me up against Dahcy? I'd put money on it." St. Clair clasped his hands behind his back and graced them all with a regal smile.

As Bradford walked away, his shoulders drooping, Alexandra felt a little sorry for him. If Bernice meant to arouse Bradford's jealousy, she could have done it without threatening him with Mr. Darcy.

The moment Bradford was out of earshot, Ramsey chortled, "Can you see Bradford's head sticking up out of a cravat?"

"And him ridin' around in a phaeton and ponies," St. Clair guffawed.

The ridiculous imagery made Alexandra smile, and she nearly forgot her anger until Ramsey said, "I never did like Darcy. Now Rochester, that's a man I can relate to. Poor soul can't escape his past, he loves no one but his horse, and he's forced to live with a crazy woman he can't get rid of."

Recovering from her shock that Ramsey and St. Clair had even a smattering of knowledge of literature, Alexandra blurted out, "Jane is not crazy!"

"I wasn't talking about Jane." Ramsey paused. "I was talking about Rochester's wife."

Alexandra's heart sank. Surely Mr. Rochester wouldn't marry that horrid Miss Ingram. Suddenly realizing that *Jane Eyre* was not the sort of book with which Drake should be familiar, Alexandra lowered her voice to a fierce whisper. "Rochester's not married. He can't be. He's supposed to marry Jane in the end."

Ramsey was standing close enough to kiss her. "You haven't read the book," he teased.

Alexandra stiffened as her anger and grief came flooding back. "I was reading it to Cass the morning he died, so forgive me if I didn't take time to finish it before I left my home and everyone I care about and came all the way out here to do what was supposed to be *your* job!"

Fortunately, the music was loud enough that no one except St. Clair and Evelyn overheard her outburst. Otherwise, Ramsey would have to punish her for her insolent disregard for the protocols that governed the relationship between a captain and an enlisted person, though he appeared to be more stunned than angry as he stared back at her.

Without waiting for a reprimand, Alexandra slammed her empty cup down on the table and, assuming her best Cass Corbin impersonation, she limped across the room to the homely brunette who had been standing by herself all night. The girl smiled and followed Alexandra onto the dance floor.

For the rest of the evening, Alexandra danced with every wallflower in the room, and all of them were impressed that Drake managed to dance in spite of his wound. Even when he wasn't dancing, all the ladies, including the pretty ones, crowded around Drake as he entranced them with tales of battle. Alexandra fit right in with the men, too, until it came time to smoke a cigar. It took everything she had not to choke to death.

On the rare occasion that she looked for Ramsey, he was nowhere to be found. Neither could Miss Patience find him. Alexandra pitied the girl for spending every dance looking around the room for the vexing captain when there were so many better partners to be had.

As the evening wore on, Alexandra's wound began to ache so badly that she finally bowed out and returned to the parsonage. She hopped up to the porch and sat on the top step, grimacing at the pain shooting through her leg.

She didn't notice Ramsey sitting in a chair in the dark corner of the porch with a bottle of whiskey until he spoke, "That's what happens when you don't know when to quit." He looked at her for a moment, got out of the chair, and walked over to her.

When Alexandra scrambled to her feet, Ramsey caught her around the waist and pulled her closer to him. "You aren't fixin' to run, are you?"

Assuming he meant desertion, she released an exasperated sigh. "No, I'm not fixin' to run! What else do I have to do to prove myself? Have I not earned my place already?"

When she tried to get away, he pulled her into the house and kicked the door closed as he held her tight against his chest. "Promise me you won't run."

She glared at him for several moments before she mumbled, "I promise I won't run."

He released her slowly, but held onto her hands long enough to remove her gloves. When he laid her gloves on the chair and proceeded to unbutton her coat, she tensed. "Let me go before someone sees us."

"Everybody's at the dance."

"I think I should go back to the dance."

"You're not going back."

"You're going to stop me?"

"Mhmm." He slid his hands under her collar and slipped her coat off her shoulders.

"What are you doing?" she breathed.

He tossed her coat onto the chair and tossed her over his shoulder.

"Put me down!" She pounded his back with her fists, but he ignored her protests and carried her upstairs.

Chapter 35

No Going Back

UNAFFECTED by Alexandra's rage, Ramsey eased her onto the bed. "Take your pants off." She stared at him in disbelief. He repeated the order, this time speaking more slowly, "Take your pants off."

She slapped him. He set the bottle of whiskey on the bedside table and started to unbuckle her belt. She fought him. "You are a devil after all! Turn me loose!"

"Stop fighting me. You're gonna make it worse." He held her wounded limb steady as he waited. Blood was starting to seep through her pant leg. She took her belt off and began unbuttoning her pants. He helped her slide them off. He knelt down and removed the blood-soaked bandage. Several stitches had come loose. He poured some water into the washbasin and handed her the bottle of whiskey. She held it in her lap until he ordered her to drink it. She took a swig and started to hand it to him.

He pushed it back into her hand. "More."

She grimaced but obeyed.

After he washed his hands in the basin, he kneeled and began sewing up the wound with a needle and thread from his pocket field kit.

To take her mind off the pain and the sensation brought on by the touch of his hand on her thigh, Alexandra decided she might as well get some answers to what had been nagging her all night. "Now that you've already ruined the story, just go ahead and tell me if Jane marries Rochester in the end."

She winced as he pulled the first stitch tight. "If I tell you they don't, are you gonna finish the book?"

"Probably not."

"It's a good story, and you shouldn't disregard it just because there's a chance it might not end the way you want it to."

No longer in the mood to discuss literature with a ruffian, Alexandra took a few more swigs. "Most men wouldn't have let a woman on the battlefield."

"You didn't exactly give me a say in it."

"You could've locked me up."

"I thought you would sleep through it, and if you didn't, I figured after all you'd been through, maybe you wouldn't have any fight left in you. I was wrong about that."

Alexandra smiled. The whiskey was beginning to take effect. She stared at Ramsey's hands—wide palms with long, slender fingers, more befitting a musician than a soldier.

Ramsey started to laugh. "I remember that time I saw you at Pop Brady's, running all over the place. I'd never met a girl with a black eye before."

"Ha. Well, you should've seen Braxton Benefield. He's Prichard's brother, you know. He had two black eyes." A sudden and unexpected melancholy came over her. "I wonder whatever happened to Braxton. His family left town right after that. You think he turned out as bad as Prichard?"

"No, last time I saw Braxton, he'd turned aside from his brother's ways. I reckon the whippin' you gave him did him some good."

Ramsey leaned down to break the thread with his teeth. Alexandra closed her eyes as his lips brushed her skin. He took his time as he wrapped a fresh bandage around her leg.

When he finished, Alexandra stood up and caught his wrist. "Take your shirt off."

"What for?"

"Take your shirt off." She reached for his collar.

Looking up at her, Ramsey let her unfasten the top two buttons before he slapped her hand away and pulled his shirt over his head without her help. When Alexandra handed him the bottle of whiskey, he turned on his knee and sat on the floor beside the bed. Alexandra dropped to her knees and laid his wounded arm in her lap. She could feel his eyes on her as she removed the bandage on his forearm. The stitches were still intact, and it didn't look like infection had set in, not that Alexandra knew what to look for.

"It's all right," he reassured her. As she replaced the bandage with a clean one, he smiled. "You know, you could've just asked me to roll up my sleeve."

Alexandra blushed and handed him his shirt.

He looked at her for a long time. She averted her eyes, but only for a second. He set the bottle down and tossed his shirt aside. He leaned toward her and touched the back of her neck with a tenderness that compelled her to place her hand on his chest, not as a defense but as an acknowledgment that the safe distance between them had been breached. If he was about to kiss her, she was going to let him, but the moment she closed her eyes the comforting sensation that had filled her vanished as images of Prichard flooded in. Before she could get control of her senses, she shoved Ramsey away.

She braced herself for his swift exit, but if her actions upset him, he made no move to pull back any further than arm's length. Instead, he got up from the floor and sat on the side of the bed. He took her hands and drew her to him as he lay back on the bed with her on top of him. Still unsure of herself, Alexandra started to move away, but Ramsey held her fists against his chest. "If you aren't gonna let me kiss you, then you kiss me."

"No," she breathed.

"Kiss me."

"You can't order me to kiss you."

He thought about that for a moment.

"You can't," she insisted.

"You're afraid."

"I'm not afraid."

"Yes, you are, and not because of Prichard Benefield, not all of it. What happened to that strange girl who left the dead behind to chase down a man who was clearly unworthy of the task she laid at his feet? Where is that girl?"

"You made a soldier out of her."

"That's not what I intended."

"You can't go back and undo it."

"I don't want to go back."

The longer he gazed at her, the more flustered she became. "I don't understand you. What do you want from me?"

"I want you to do what I say, not because I made you do it, but because you want to."

"So, you only want me to kiss you if I want to."

"No, what you want doesn't change what I want. It just changes how I go about getting what I want."

"Well, even if I had wanted to kiss you at some point this evening, the desire got lost somewhere in this long, tiresome conversation."

Ramsey grinned. "You must have a little desire left unless there's some other reason you're still laying on top of me with your pants off."

Alexandra jerked away from him and scrambled to retrieve her pants. She clutched them to her waist, allowing the pant legs to dangle in front of her bare limbs. "You may leave now. I'm quite exhausted, and I wish to retire for the evening."

" 'Retire for the evening?' With that kind of talk you must have gotten good marks in finishing school." Ramsey sat up and reached for the whiskey bottle.

Alexandra snatched the bottle and backed away from him.

"Give that back," he protested.

"I think you've had enough."

After a long pause, Ramsey got up and walked over to her. She froze when he reached out and took hold of her chin. He gently pressed his lips to hers and pulled away. When she didn't fight back, he kissed her again, this time with greater force.

Alexandra was surprised that she had no desire to punch him. She had always thought that if a man tried to kiss her against her wishes that she would punch him, even if it was Garrett. It horrified her to entertain the possibility that Ramsey might know more about her wishes than she did.

He didn't release her until he had her pinned against the wardrobe. He studied her face for a moment before he drawled, "You know you don't look anything like Jonas Corbin. Are you sure you're his?"

Out of all the things Ramsey could have said at that moment, he chose the most destructive. No one knew better than Alexandra how far she had fallen from her father's image. She had grown accustomed to falling short of the lauded image of Southern womanhood. Disappointing her mother was so commonplace that Alexandra had made a game of inventing new ways to engender disapproval, but disappointing her father, the sheriff, the war hero, the man who would have led the Confederacy to victory in the west—whatever tender feelings she had for Ramsey plummeted. Hearing the judgment come from his lips took the fight out of her.

"Get out," she said in a small voice.

"I had no call to say that. I'm sorry."

"I said get out."

"I didn't mean what I said."

"Well, I mean what I'm saying. Get out. I don't want to see you."

When he still didn't move, she gave him the whiskey bottle. She grabbed his discarded shirt and threw it at him. Then, she drove him out into the hall and slammed the door. She waited at the door, ready to reject him again when he begged her to let him back in, but after several moments, she heard his retreating footsteps. Her hand trembled on the doorknob. Ramsey had wounded her more deeply than anyone else could have. He was the last person in the world she wanted to see at that moment, but it was the pain of that moment that made her want Ramsey to come back—and stay.

Angry at herself for being a female and having female feelings for a man who clearly did not know anything about females or their feelings, she hobbled over to the bed, pulled her nightgown out from behind the pillow, and plopped onto the mattress. As she stared down at the patchwork quilt, she caught herself fussing to God about her man problems.

Just as she was really laying it on good, shame hit her like a howitzer blast. For her whole life, it seemed that not a day had gone by that someone wasn't fussing at her about something—her hair, her shoes, her disregard for the rules of polite society. After all she was trying to do for her people, did they appreciate it? No, instead they complained, and if they weren't complaining to her, they ignored her. She was quite put out with them for it. When she realized that maybe God felt the same way about her, she snatched the quilt and pulled it over her head as she used to do when she was a kid, thinking neither God nor her mother could find her under there.

After a brief, but heartfelt confession, Alexandra sprang out of the bed. Tossing the nightgown on the floor, she slipped into her pants and was about to make things right with Ramsey when there was a knock on the door. Alexandra smiled. Ramsey must have known what was in her heart and returned to claim it.

Alexandra opened the door and immediately caught her breath. The man at the other end of that Smith & Wesson was not Ramsey.

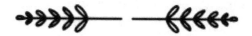

Chapter 36

―――

Bloodlettin'

RAMSEY stepped off the front porch and almost fell when he tripped over the last step. He was angry with Alexandra, but he knew he had gotten what he deserved. If he hadn't been drunk, he still would've kissed her, but he wouldn't have said that about Jonas. Fortunately, he was just sober enough to know better than to stay and fight it out with her, but that meant he would have to prove.... Whatever he was trying to prove, he would have to prove it to her some other way.

The music from the shindig at the other end of town could still be heard from the parsonage which meant anyone brave enough to try to stop Ramsey from doing what he was about to do was too preoccupied to notice he was gone—except Boone. Struggling to keep his balance, Ramsey reached down to pat the dog's head when he came trotting up and licked his hand.

"You'd give your life to bring Carter back, wouldn't you?" Boone leaned against Ramsey's leg as dogs do when they want you to forget about whatever it was you were heading out the door to do and focus all your attention on petting them.

Ramsey was making his way to Evelyn's barn with Boone close on his heels when St. Clair blocked his path.

"Well, did you change tha girl's mind about all this soldierin'?" the lieutenant drawled.

Ramsey grumbled, "I'd have had greater success convincing Red Sticks to pull a pony cart."

St. Clair shook his head. "Then what's ta be done? She can't stay in tha army, and you can't send her home." He hesitated before he continued, "There is one solution, but I'm not sure you're gonna like it."

"I don't want to talk about it." When St. Clair started to follow him to the barn, Ramsey added, "It's not your fight anyway."

"Cana—"

"You're dismissed."

Ramsey didn't look back to see if St. Clair had obeyed, mostly because he knew being dismissed so gruffly and without satisfactory explanation hurt his feelings, not that the lieutenant would let on. St. Clair was a sensitive soul, but he wouldn't dare let his sensitivity interfere with his honor, or pride, whichever was at stake.

The guilt over abusing his most trustworthy companion hastened Ramsey in finishing off the rest of the bottle by the time he reached Evelyn's stable. He pushed open the door, sauntered over to Solomon's stall. Solomon snorted his disapproval when Ramsey picked up the bridle.

* * *

Prichard sat up in the bed when Ramsey burst into the room. "What the devil—"

Ramsey cut his exclamation short when he dragged him out of bed at gunpoint.

"Cain't a man git some sleep 'round here? What's that gun for? You ain't gonna shoot me." Prichard snarled.

Ramsey didn't reply as he forced Prichard out of the house and into the back yard.

Wearing nothing but his long johns, Prichard shivered in the night air as Ramsey marched him across the yard. He didn't say much else until he saw that Ramsey was taking him into the woods. "Wait a minute. What are you plannin' to do, Ramsey?"

Ramsey still didn't say a word.

Prichard began to panic. "Wait. Now, let's talk about this. You ain't thinkin' straight, Ramsey. Think about what you're doin'. What will it profit you to kill me? Ain't no profit in it."

Ramsey shoved Prichard onto his knees and aimed his Colt at the back of his head. "I don't kill people for profit. I kill people to stop them from killing other people."

"What are you talkin' about? Ramsey, you done lost your mind. I ain't got no plans to kill nobody. Now, I admit I ain't no stranger to sin, but when it comes to bloodlettin' all I ever done is defend myself. I ain't kilt nobody in cold blood. You the one that's done that. Not me."

"You attacked Alexandra."

"The Corbin girl?" Prichard wailed. "You mean to tell me that's what this is about? Good night, I don't know what she told you, but I didn't hurt the girl! Not a-purpose."

"She almost died."

"Why, it was just a little 'ol flesh wound. Besides, she was the one attacked me. I's just defendin' myself."

Ramsey pulled the hammer back.

Prichard's eyes went wide. "You gotta believe me! I didn't set out to hurt the girl, even after she tried to kill me, twice. I's just defendin' myself, like I said. Ramsey, you gotta git your mind right. You gotta think about this. Now, why would I hurt the girl a-purpose when I don't get paid 'less I bring her back alive? D'you think about that?"

That caught Ramsey's interest. He knew Prichard worked for Elias, but that didn't mean he only worked for Elias. "Paid by who?"

"Don't act like you don't know who I work for," Prichard sneered. "You know it was Elias Kelson hired me to fetch the girl and bring her back along with the documents she stole from him. Reason I grabbed her at Johnny Knowles' was so she wouldn't get away. You actin' like I'm the danger 'round here. You oughtta take that knife away from her 'fore she sticks it in somebody ain't as forgivin' as me. You know for a fact anybody else in my profession woulda kilt that girl by now."

Ramsey released the hammer. So, that was what Elias meant when he said Alexandra was going to be the death of him. If Ramsey didn't give her up willingly, Elias was going to take her by force. "Well, then Elias must mean for you to kill me. 'Cause the only way you're gonna walk out of here with Alexandra is if I'm dead."

"Gosh-a-mighty! Don't anybody 'round here have a lick of sense?" Prichard got to his feet and spun around to look Ramsey in the eye. "Elias don't want you dead. You're the only thing standin' between him and…" Prichard's voice trailed off when he looked over Ramsey's shoulder.

Ramsey turned to see Red coming up behind him with his arms raised.

Nels, the hefty Confederate charged with keeping a watch on him, was chugging along behind him.

"Halt!" Nels hollered at Red. His face fell when he saw Ramsey. "S-sorry, Cap'n," he stuttered. "Ol' Red here's a mite quicker'n I thought, but I'm on to him now. He won't be gettin' away from me agin."

"Leave Red to me. I'll deal with you later, Nels."

"Yes, sir," Nels muttered as he shrank away in shame.

"Hey, Yank, you better watch yourself," Prichard called out to Red. "The Cap'n here's done gone a little cockeyed. Might be you and me oughtta go on back to the house, and let him sleep it off. What do you say, Yank?"

Red eyed Ramsey carefully. "I'd say Captain Ramsey looks sober enough to realize the hornet's nest he stumbled into when he boarded that train bound for Chattanooga. You have a habit of doing that, Captain, stumbling into hornet's nests, I mean. This time, I don't think you're going to get out of it, not without a little help."

Ramsey lowered his weapon, but he didn't holster it. "Help from who? Your father and the rest of the Council? I might as well sell my soul to the Devil."

Instead of answering Ramsey directly, Red turned to Prichard. "What do you think, Mr. Benefield? Do you think Captain Ramsey could take us both in a fair fight?"

Prichard grinned. "Naw, I reckon not. What you got in mind, Yank?"

"Nothing, if Ramsey cooperates. Do you intend to cooperate, Ramsey?"

"As far as my conscience will allow," Ramsey growled.

Red chuckled. "From the stories I've heard, your conscience will allow quite a lot, Cana Ramsey."

Ramsey stepped closer to Red. "Get on with it then."

"My request is as before. Release me so that I may go to my father. You have my word that you and Alexandra will be absolved, and Barrymore...will be dealt with. I'll even put in a good word for Mr. Benefield here."

"Release you. That's it? That's all you want?" Ramsey studied him with a wary look.

Red hesitated, watching his words. "That's all I want. I have no hidden agenda. Moreover, I would prefer that you don't mistake me for my father, for I am no more like Edwin Belgrave III than you are like Cranston Ramsey."

Surprised that Red would openly express any deviation from the path of his forebears, it always pleased Ramsey to hear he and his grandfather were nothing alike. Not that he would admit it to Red. "How do I know your word will be good enough?"

Red shrugged. "Because it has to be. It's all you've got. Oh, you've got men and horses and guns and a stubborn streak as wide as the Amazon, but we both know it is on my word alone as to whether Alexandra lives or dies—whether *you* live or die. So, what will it be, Ramsey?"

* * *

Having made his decision, Ramsey left the big house and returned to the parsonage with Prichard riding in front of him on a mule.

"If you mean to haul me all over the creation, you could've got me a better mount than this flop-eared jackass," Prichard fussed as he strained against the rope binding his hands behind his back.

"I'm not wasting a good horse on your sorry hide, Prichard."

"Where are you takin' me anyway?"

"You heard the deal I made with Red. He requires proof that I'll live up to my end of the bargain. He wants to know I'm committed."

"Committed to what?" Prichard turned in the saddle to face Ramsey, a look of terror in his eyes.

Ramsey dismounted in front of Evelyn's barn and yanked Prichard down from the mule's back.

"Committed to what?" Prichard yelped as Ramsey dragged him into the barn. "You mean to hand me over to the Council? You're makin' a mistake. Ramsey, don't you make a deal with them devils. I didn't let on when he come up, but I recognized the Belgrave boy. Sure enough I did. I know who his father is and what him and the Council are plannin'. Do you even know? Have you thought about it? Have you thought about what they're gonna do to you and me and Elias and ever'body? And what about the girl? Have you thought about what they're gonna do to her when they find out who she is?"

Ramsey slung Prichard on the ground. "Shut up."

Prichard continued to squirm as Ramsey bound his feet and tied him to a post. He begged and pleaded, but Ramsey would have none of it. He grabbed the cloth sitting next to the leather soap and stuffed it in Prichard's mouth.

Leaving Prichard in the barn, he made his way across the yard to the house. It was time he told Alexandra the truth. About Red, about the Council, about what Elias was really after, and worst of all, the truth about what he'd done the night Jonas died. He would sooner cut his arm off, but he had no other option.

The moment he set foot on the back porch, a cold dread came over him. The back door was open and a desperate whining and scratching sound was coming from the closet door under the stairs. Ramsey drew his gun and opened the door.

Boone jumped out. He sniffed the air for any whiff of malevolence that would lead him to the intruder. Having caught the scent of something or someone, he charged up the stairs.

Ramsey followed Boone to Alexandra's room. The bedroom door was already open. Ramsey cocked his revolver and eased into the room. The bed was empty and her nightgown was crumpled on the floor. At first, he thought he might have gotten the wrong idea. Instead of someone taking her, maybe she had run away and locked Boone in the closet to keep the dog from following her. It wasn't until he stepped closer to the bedside table that he saw the broken vase on the floor. When he reached down to examine the pieces, he froze, fear settling in his gut like lead. The red splotch on the white ceramic wasn't paint. He ran through the house, checking every room. She was gone.

His mind drowning in a storm of rage and terror, Ramsey stopped at the bottom of the stairs and leaned against the rail. He had been in this state of mind once before. If he went down that road again, his soul would not survive. Before he could stop himself, he prayed, and he didn't stop at "Lord, help" either. He hadn't dared approach the Almighty to ask for anything since he was seventeen. Then, in the middle of eleven-years-worth of pent up regrets, including his recent attempt to murder Prichard, it was as if God had whispered the name. *Elias.*

The peace Ramsey had experienced with the knowledge of who had taken Alexandra quickly subsided into anger. He walked over to the cabinet where Evelyn hid her extra ammunition and grabbed a handful of cartridges. Elias Kelson had taken from the Ramseys for the last time.

Calling to Boone, Ramsey stormed out of the house. Just as he was about to step out onto the back porch, he felt the cold barrel of a revolver at his temple.

Out of the corner of his eye, he saw Luke Kelson standing alone on the porch. Boone growled, but when Luke hollered and stomped in his direction, he darted back. He kept barking until Luke threatened to shoot him unless Ramsey shut him up. When Ramsey commanded Boone to hush and lay down, the dog obeyed after a final, defiant woof.

"You shouldn't have crossed my father, Ramsey." Luke grinned as he pressed the barrel harder into Ramsey's head.

Grateful for the confirmation that it was Elias who had taken Alexandra, Ramsey snatched the gun away and seized Luke by the throat. Luke yelped and gurgled as Ramsey held him against the wall. "Where is she?"

Luke was half-crying, half-laughing. "Not where she belongs. They all want her to be safe in Chattanooga, but you and I know that's not the best place for her, so I came here to make you an offer." When Ramsey loosened his grip slightly, Luke continued, "I know you don't want a girl in your army, and I know you hate my father, so help me take Alexandra away from him. I'll take her off your hands, and you can go back to whatever it is you renegades do."

Ramsey jerked Luke away from the wall and threw him off the porch. "Where is she?" He stood over Luke and lowered the gun to his forehead.

"*They* are keeping her on the train."

" 'They' who?"

Luke tapped his finger against his lips. "You know who 'they' is. It's *them* plus what's left of the Benefield gang."

"Elias ought to know better than to make deals with devils he can't control."

Luke shrugged. "He wants Alexandra. They want Prichard."

"He doesn't have Prichard, and he has no way of getting him. What is he planning to do about that?"

"Oh, he never said he had him. He just told 'em you were keeping Prichard at a warehouse on the other side of the river. By the time they find out it was all a trick, Elias will be halfway to Chattanooga, and they'll be walking right into Barrymore's trap. Oh, I forgot to mention the part about Barrymore being in on it. I bet you thought it was your Quaker guns that convinced Barrymore not to attack, but it was all my father's doings. Of course, Barrymore doesn't know about Alexandra. He still thinks Drake Corbin is hiding out in Cade's Mill somewhere. I wonder what he'll do to this town. I've been here less than five minutes, and I can tell it's overrun with 'rabid secessionists.' "

Ramsey studied Luke. "You said if I helped you take Alexandra away from Elias, you would do me a favor and take her off my hands. Assuming that's what I want, looks to me like Elias has beat you to it, so why would I put myself in harm's way to get her back just to turn around and give her to you?"

Luke looked at him as if the answer was obvious. "Because, finally, it would be you doing the giving instead of Elias doing the taking."

Ramsey considered for a moment how pleasurable it would be to smash the butt of his Dragoon into the whelp's teeth. Instead, he hauled Luke to his feet and drove him toward the barn.

"So, do we have a deal?" Luke's eyes lit up with eagerness as Ramsey opened the barn door and shoved Luke through the entrance.

Luke's eyes went wide when he saw Prichard. "What's he doing here?" he gulped.

Ramsey grabbed a rope and pulled it taut to test its strength. "Boys who rob trains have to pay the piper."

Luke began to panic as Ramsey walked toward him with the rope. "Wait. Stop. What are you doing?"

"There's bloodlettin' needs to be done." Ramsey shrugged with chilling indifference. "I can't have you getting in the way."

Chapter 37

Who Is Alexandra?

DESPITE the curtain sash covering her eyes, Alexandra recognized her surroundings by the whiffs of burning coal and the steady clickety-clack of the iron horse. A pair of rough hands pulled her to her feet.

"Get up!" he yelled. The stench of his breath told Alexandra he was the same scoundrel who had kidnapped her. She flailed her arms, hoping to strike the man's ear that she had wounded when she threw Evelyn's vase at him.

"Stop!" a woman's voice commanded.

Alexandra struggled out of the man's grasp and ripped the blindfold off. She threw it at her mother.

Laura Catherine looked as if she was about to cry. "They didn't tell me you cut your hair. It was always so beautiful. How could you have done such a thing?"

Without arguing, Alexandra pushed past her mother and flung the car door open. She stepped out onto the platform and was about to jump from the train when Garrett grabbed her.

"Alexandra! What are you doing?"

The shock of Garrett's voice almost caused her to fall. "Garrett? You took part in this? To kidnap me?"

"We did it for your own good."

She shoved him. "Stop this train and take me back at once!"

"I can't. Elias—"

"You're in collusion with Elias?"

Avoiding the fight, Garrett opened the door to the adjacent passenger car and stood back, waiting for her to enter ahead of him. Alexandra stormed down the aisle and met Elias head on as he reclined near the front of the car. She ripped the newspaper away from his face. "Take me back."

"You don't belong back there." Elias jerked the newspaper away from her, folded it, and laid it aside. "Your mother wants you to accompany her to Chattanooga."

"How much did she pay you?"

"Pay me?" he scoffed. "Laura Catherine Corbin is the most tight-fisted woman I've ever met, unless she's in the market for a new dress."

Alexandra stared at him for a moment, baffled as to why Elias would take such an interest in her to the point he would leave Marlbridge at such a perilous time to escort her and her mother to Chattanooga, a task that Wilson could have fulfilled. Her heart sank when it occurred to her that in her absence something might have happened to Wilson. Maybe Barrymore had found out he had given Alexandra the rifle. "Where's Wilson?"

Laura Catherine ducked her head. Only when Alexandra pressed her did she admit the truth. "I told him what we were doing. He said he wanted no part of it, so I left him behind. He's got his books. I'm sure he'll be quite happy."

Alexandra plopped onto the nearest seat, shocked that the matriarch of propriety had involved herself in such a scandal.

"I don't know why you're surprised. That willful constitution of yours didn't come from Jonas," Elias muttered. Alexandra was ready to show Elias exactly how willful she could be when the train began to slow down and finally screeched to a halt.

Alarmed by the unplanned stop, Elias drew his revolver, a .44-caliber Remington, not the pocket pistol he normally carried. He shoved Alexandra down into the seat as Laura Catherine hid behind Garrett.

The door burst open, and a crowd of miscreants flooded in from the back of the car.

Elias raised his weapon. "This isn't what we agreed to. I already told you where you could find Prichard," he growled.

"Yeah, I sent a man up ahead to see if you was telling the truth about that, and you know what he found? A nest of bluebellies! Now, you give us Prichard or we're gonna take the girl." His mouth twisted into a hideous smile, "We're *all* gonna take the girl."

Elias cocked the revolver.

"Wait. There is no need for bloodshed," Garrett intervened.

"Stay out of this, Rainier."

Garrett ignored Elias' warning. "I am Garrett Rainier. My father is Hanson Rainier of Marlbridge which means I am worth more to you than anybody else on this train."

The big man leered at him. "I know who you are. All you Rainiers are alike. If somethin' don't go yer way, you think you kin buy yer way out of it."

A smaller, but uglier man near the back hollered, "Now wait a minute, Walters. He shore is a dandy. Why, we might rather have him than the girl anyways."

The gang's rumbling laughter was cut short when the door at the front of the car swung open, and Prichard himself appeared, dressed in his long johns.

"Whar d'you come from?" Walters stammered as he gawked at Prichard. "We was beginnin' to thank you was dead."

Prichard glared at Alexandra, "I ain't dead."

"Yet," the man standing behind Prichard finished, as he shoved him into the aisle.

Forgetting the danger of the situation, Alexandra smiled when she saw that the man with a Colt Dragoon aimed at Prichard's head was Ramsey.

Somehow the ugly snarl on Walters face actually improved his appearance. "So, you come to make a trade, Ramsey?"

Ramsey kept his eyes on Walters. "I haven't decided yet. Depends on how much Prichard's worth to you."

"Well, now let's look at this sitiation we got here. It's gonna be mighty hard fer you to do all the bargainin' when thar's twenty a us and only one a you."

"And only one of me!" Prichard bellowed. "Do as he says, Walters!"

Walters huffed and hem hawed for another minute or two, but finally he and the rest of the gang filed out of the car and stood waiting for Ramsey to send Prichard out to the field where the train had stopped. Ramsey ordered them all to get their heads down, pushed Prichard off the train, and bolted the door.

"What are you doing?" Elias exclaimed. "They'll attack us the moment Prichard is safe!"

Just before Ramsey lunged across the aisle to cover her head, Alexandra saw a row of flashes in the middle of the field. The distinct, cracking sound of gunfire immediately followed. A few stray shots shattered the car windows, and the rumble of a hundred horses shook the car. Laura Catherine screamed.

Within seconds, Confederates were swarming the train, picking off the renegades, who had no chance of escape. The fight lasted no more than a minute. When Ramsey let her up, Alexandra ran to one of the windows. Several members of the Benefield gang lay dead. The rest were moaning and grasping at their wounds, except Prichard who was swearing something fierce as the Confederates surrounded him.

When St. Clair saw that Ramsey and Alexandra had emerged from the car and Prichard was yet unscathed, he stalked over to the rogue and threw his hat on the ground. The lieutenant did not hold back on his wrath. "Do you hear tha blasphemies spewin' from this scourge of tha earth? How, in tha name of decency, is he not dead? I cannot abide this loathsome cockalorum. Pray, let me run him through."

Before Ramsey could answer, Garrett stepped between St. Clair and the miscreant. "I cannot allow you to murder this man in cold blood."

St. Clair stormed, "And I cannot allow an interloper. Now, stand aside that I may put this lawless mongrel ta death."

Garrett turned to Ramsey. "Is this your justice? Murder?"

"He attacked Alexandra," Ramsey replied as he retrieved St. Clair's hat and returned it to the fuming lieutenant.

Laura Catherine gasped and looked as if she was about to faint.

"Who's Alexandra?" Bradford asked.

The color began to drain from Garrett's face. "Was she...harmed?"

Prichard huffed, "For the last time, I didn't hurt the girl!"

Annoyed that they were talking about her as if she wasn't present, Alexandra was about to speak up for herself when Ramsey started laughing. He kicked Prichard's boot. "Go on, Prichard. Tell us who did all the hurtin' in that fight."

Alexandra ducked her head at Garrett's shocked expression.

Bradford turned to Sal. "What're they talkin' 'bout? Who is Alexandra?"

"Must be Cap'n's girl," Sal muttered loud enough for everyone to hear.

"That is none of your concern," Garrett snapped before he resumed his argument with Ramsey, though he continued with less enthusiasm. "The depravity of the man does not abate his right to be tried in a court of law."

Ramsey waved his arm over the bloody mess of bodies at his feet. "Who's law?"

"God's law!"

"When has mankind ever bowed the knee to God's law except someone had to cut their legs off first?" Ramsey drew his saber.

Prichard yelped, "Now wait! We done talked about this, Ramsey. It don't profit you none to kill me. You remember that."

"If I really meant to kill you, Prichard, I'd have done it by now. Good thing I didn't, though. I'm sure the bounty on you and the rest of these plug-uglies could feed a cavalry company for at least a week, but I don't recall reading anything about y'all having to be in one piece."

Prichard turned red with rage as he glowered at Alexandra. "This is all your fault, you hussy. I ain't gonna meet my end because of you. I just ain't havin' it. I deserve better. On second thought, Ramsey, why don't you just go ahead and hand me over to the Council. Let me tell 'em all about Jonas Corbin's daughter."

"Oh, this is absurd!" Laura Catherine drew a pepperbox from her purse and shot Prichard in the face.

Everyone stared at Laura Catherine in shock until a man suddenly appeared and shone a light in their faces. They were relieved to see that the man was only the train conductor. "Y'all done killin'? I got a schedule to keep."

"Well, go on then. For heaven's sake, don't let all this bloodshed keep you from your schedule," Laura Catherine commanded him. "Go on and leave me and my daughter to fend for ourselves. That seems to be the way of things these days."

"Mr. Kelson, can I go now?" the conductor asked.

Elias seemed to accept the pronouncement burning in Laura Catherine's eyes that he was as much of a failure as the rest of them. "Rainier, escort Mrs. Metcalf to Chattanooga."

"I've changed my mind. I will return to Marlbridge at once," Laura Catherine declared with disdain as she made eye contact with every man present. "My late husband, Jonas Corbin, was the sheriff of Jackson County, and he would have never allowed such things to carry on right under his nose. My son is dead. My daughter has joined the army. And I have nothing decent to wear because of that damned blockade! So, the lot of you will set things right, or so help me, I will shame you in front of the gates of hell!"

As if nothing else needed to be said, Laura Catherine marched over to the conductor, her pistol still in her hand. "Take me to the next stop where you will hire me a carriage and a driver who has more sense than these tomfools."

The conductor hurried to obey.

"I will escort you, Mrs. Metcalf," Garrett volunteered.

"Do as you will. Isn't that the real law by which men govern themselves?" she snapped with disgust as she marched back toward the train. "Come along, Alexandra."

Sal and Bradford gasped when Drake dared to answer the woman. "I'm staying."

Laura Catherine whirled around, but paused just long enough to allow Garrett to speak first. "Alexandra, you have to stop this."

Alexandra glanced at Ramsey to see if he would agree with Garrett. He didn't argue.

Bradford looked down at Alexandra. "Drake?"

"My real name is Alexandra."

All the Confederates who had accompanied Ramsey stared at Alexandra in disbelief. Sal scratched his head. "Ye mean ye been a girl all this time? Well, I never woulda thought it. How come ye to know how to ride and shoot? Well, ride. Ye still cain't shoot worth nothin' even for a girl. Cap'n, d'ye know Drake was a girl?"

"Yes, Sal. I knew."

"Well, that sure 'nough is a relief. I's startin' to wonder."

Garrett implored her again. "Alexandra, this is no place for you."

Alexandra looked to Ramsey. "Is that true?"

When Ramsey hesitated, Bradford spoke up, "Maybe it ain't my place to say, and I cain't speak for ever'body, but we sorta gotten used to Drake. Let her stay, Cap'n. I don't reckon we kin let her fight in no battles, but maybe we could find somethin' for her to do. Why, Miss Evelyn would take her in, I'm shore of it."

Sal chimed in. "I agree, Cap'n. Ain't no cause to send her away. Less'n she wants to go."

Laura Catherine pushed Garrett out of her way as she addressed Ramsey directly. "My daughter has two choices. She may go with her mother to Chattanooga, or she may choose a husband and stay with him."

She turned to Alexandra. "Which will it be? I have tolerated your rebellious ways, but regarding this I will not be dissuaded. If you stay, you may not do so as a free woman. So, you will marry one of these men here and subject yourself to his dominion, or you will go to your relatives in Chattanooga. Choose."

Thinking that she could outwit her mother, Alexandra smirked, "I don't see a preacher around here, so who's going to officiate?"

"Isn't a train conductor the same as a ship captain?" her mother replied.

"Laura Catherine—" Elias objected.

Laura Catherine cut him off. "I will choose what's right for my daughter." Turning back to Alexandra she added, "Go on. Choose. If you want to stay, choose."

"No," Alexandra declared through clenched teeth.

"Very well, I will choose for you."

"That won't be necessary. I will marry her," Garrett announced.

Laura Catherine rejected him. "You had your chance, and if you had taken it, none of this would have happened. I practically bribed you, and still you dragged your feet. On what grounds do I trust you to keep her in her place when you couldn't keep her in Marlbridge? Instead of picnics and buggy rides with you, she chose *this*!" She waved her arm at the band of cavalrymen who hadn't even dared to murmur amongst themselves as Laura Catherine took command of the field.

"No, the choice is clear. Though it doesn't please me, I take minimal solace in the hope that it would have pleased Jonas. Cana Ramsey, you will be Alexandra's husband."

Alexandra was mortified as Laura Catherine took her by the arm and set her in front of Ramsey. When she dared to peek at her comrades' faces, she was shocked to find that St. Clair appeared unmoved by the announcement. Instead, he seemed to find the idea amusing. As did the others, except for Garrett and Elias. Alexandra couldn't bring herself to look at Ramsey.

Elias pulled Laura Catherine close. "I might expect this rashness from her, but I thought you had better sense. You cannot force her to do this."

"I am her mother. She will do as I tell her."

Ramsey finally spoke. "On what grounds do you object, Elias? Her mother consents to the match. As for her father, I can only wonder what he would have to say about it."

Elias glared at Ramsey. "We would all be eager to know what Jonas would think. He would be here now, if you hadn't killed him."

Ramsey's face turned white at the accusation, but Alexandra didn't know if it was from fear or rage. Either way, she did not allow herself the opportunity to validate Elias' words. "Liar! Everyone knows it was Miles who did it. Cana respected my father. He wouldn't have killed him." She turned to Ramsey. "Tell him the truth. Tell him you didn't kill my father."

Finally, Ramsey brought himself to look her in the eye. "It wouldn't do any good to tell him. He already knows I didn't kill your father. He also knows that what happened that night had nothing to do with the feud or land or horses. It was all about you, Alexandra."

"What about me?"

"Go on, Elias," Ramsey said. "Tell her what you and Jonas Corbin fought about. Tell her why you don't want her to marry a Ramsey."

Before Elias could answer, a lone, mounted Confederate came galloping across the field, yelling for help. As he drew closer, Alexandra saw that it was Lieutenant Shelley, Colonel Kinkaid's aide.

"Captain Ramsey! The enemy has attacked Cade's Mill!" Shelley panted. "We fought them, but we were overcome. All of our number who didn't escape are carried off. And Colonel Kinkaid—" Close to tears, the officer paused to collect himself. "The colonel is dead, sir. His last order was to bring you back, so that you might deal with the enemy face to face and redeem the captives. Those were his words."

When Ramsey didn't respond right away, the young man asked, "What are your orders, sir?"

Ramsey stared across the field as if Shelley had put two rounds in his chest.

"Captain, shall we fust bury tha dead?" St. Clair prompted.

Ramsey turned his head in St. Clair's direction but didn't look at him. "Not these dead," he answered, referring to Prichard and the rest of his ilk who were strewn out in every direction. "Collect their weapons and leave their carcasses for the birds. Take the live ones to Sheriff Matthews and get what bounty you can for 'em."

St. Clair pointed his thumb to Garrett, Laura Catherine, and Elias. "Shall I detain these civilians, or shall I send them back ta Mahlbridge?"

"I don't care what happens to them," Ramsey replied as he mounted his horse.

"What about Drake, er, Alexandra?" Bradford asked.

Ramsey looked down at Alexandra. When he offered her his hand, she accepted it and climbed up behind him. Solomon snorted at the extra weight, but made no more fuss as the Confederates rode off toward Cade's Mill.

Chapter 38

Let the Dead Bury Their Dead

THE sun had just begun to appear when all the Confederates who were left came together at Cade's Mill to see what ought to be done. Of the three hundred men who comprised Kinkaid's battalion, nearly a quarter had been captured or killed, including most of the officers. Captain Peterson had been killed during the attack, and Captain Stark had been captured, leaving Ramsey as the highest ranking officer.

Some parts of the town had been burned, but Alexandra was relieved to see that the church and the parsonage were unscathed. When she saw Joss struggling to drag a wounded soldier into the church, she trotted over to help her. To Alexandra's surprise, Joss accepted her help.

"I thought you left the army to go after your husband," Alexandra said.

Joss snorted, "I ain't no deserter. Besides, someone had to take charge of the wounded. Most of the officers are either dead or captured." She glanced over Alexandra's shoulder. "Where's Ramsey going?"

Alexandra looked toward the end of town where Ramsey and St. Clair had summoned the rest of the Confederates along with a dozen or so civilian men from Cade's Mill. "They have to stop Barrymore before he escapes to Marlbridge."

"You aren't going with them?"

"Captain Ramsey told me to stay here and help with whatever needs to be done."

Joss eyed her warily, "And you obeyed?"

"My secret's out now, so I had to do what he said."

Her eyes widened. "They all know?"

"Only the men in Ramsey's company."

"How did they take the news?"

"Well, I'm here, aren't I?"

Joss frowned as they laid the wounded man on the floor. "I wish I wasn't."

Alexandra spent the rest of the morning doing whatever she could to help the people of Cade's Mill recover from the attack. Bradford had volunteered to stay behind and help wrangle the horses and other livestock that were running loose all over town, but he spent most of the morning helping Bernice find her cat that had gone missing during the attack.

Fortunately, no civilians had been killed, though a few had been wounded. Three buildings had burned completely, and two more had sustained reparable damage. Alexandra later found out that one of the townsmen had accidently ignited the fire when they rallied to fight off the invaders.

It was almost noon when Ramsey and the rest of the exhausted Confederates returned. The captives were not with them. Sal rode over to Alexandra and told her the story of how the enemy escaped, but he omitted his usual embellishment.

By the time Sal finished the tale, Ramsey had dismounted and was walking toward them with St. Clair following close behind him. After dismissing Sal, Ramsey grasped Alexandra's hand and led her to the parsonage at a brisk pace.

Evelyn greeted Ramsey, Alexandra, and St. Clair at the door and hurried them into the parlor where her brother-in-law, Sheriff Matthews, was pacing about, pausing only to check his timepiece. He gawked at Alexandra's shirt and pants in astonishment. "Is this the *girl* you told me about?"

Evelyn replied, "Yes, Robert, but that is a very long story that we don't have time for. Perhaps we should just get on with it."

Alexandra jerked her head around to look at Ramsey who was keeping his eyes on the rug. Evelyn pushed Alexandra closer to him.

Sheriff Matthews cleared his throat and pulled a small Bible out of his coat pocket. "Let's get on with it then. We'll perform the ceremony first, after which the two of you will sign this Bible as a record. Then... well, y'all know what comes after that."

"Wait," Alexandra squeaked. When Ramsey looked at her, she said, "You don't have to do this. I know what my mother said, but I don't listen to her anyway."

"I'm not here because someone said I had to be. I'm here because it's the right thing to do. You don't agree?"

"I hadn't thought about it."

"Because you thought you were gonna marry Garrett Rainier."

Alexandra blushed. "I meant I hadn't thought about what folks would say if I got caught. I didn't think about it being a disgrace to my father and my brother. I was only thinking about..." She started to say Marlbridge, but she might as well own up to the truth that her saving Marlbridge was more about her saving Marlbridge than it was about Marlbridge getting saved. "I was thinking about myself."

Sheriff Matthews offered, "Seems like y'all got some things to discuss before y'all tie the knot. I'm gonna get a cup of coffee, and when I come back, y'all can decide if y'all gonna do this or not."

Evelyn and St. Clair followed the sheriff out of the room. Alexandra waited for Ramsey to speak first. "I've done some hard things. Some of them I regret, and some I don't. I'm not asking you to say any vows that can't be taken back. It's about the same as enlistment papers: a temporary covenant made for a time until things are set right again."

Alexandra nodded that she understood. "So, it's not a real marriage then."

"It's real in the sense that it gives me the right to look out for you."

"Do I have to do what you say?"

He scowled. "If you don't do what I say as a soldier when I have the authority to shoot you, I don't anticipate you'll do what I say under less threatening circumstances."

"Well then, I will consent to this arrangement if you will answer one question." She paused when he gave her an anxious look. "Seein' that we might get ourselves killed before this war is over and I might not get a chance to find it out for myself, then I need to know: does Jane marry Rochester?"

Ramsey relaxed. "What would be the purpose of the story if she didn't?"

"You didn't answer the question."

"You already know the answer. You just won't believe it."

"Answer the question anyway."

"Is this how it's gonna be? A constant battle to determine who's more stubborn? Because if it is," he took hold of her shirt collar and pulled her close to his face, "you're gonna lose."

Alexandra was ready to prove him wrong, but she hesitated when he took her hand. The cold, unflinching blue eyes to which she had grown accustomed faltered, revealing a soul-weariness she hadn't noticed before. Unable to break away from his gaze, she barely acknowledged Sheriff Matthews' return and spent most of the ceremony in a daze. She said all the words she was supposed to say, even the part about "love, honor, and obey," and she vaguely remembered Ramsey saying all the words he was supposed to say, but beyond that, she heard very little until Matthews announced, "You may kiss the bride."

"Wait," she objected.

Ramsey waited, but kept a tight grip on her hand. He knew Alexandra Corbin would never run from a fight, but he wasn't so sure about the girl who was now standing in front of him, panic welling up in her eyes. He had never seen this girl before, and he wasn't quite sure how to deal with her. Without breaking eye contact with Alexandra, he spoke to Sheriff Matthews. "Would you give us a minute?"

Ignoring the sheriff's exasperated sigh, Ramsey pulled Alexandra out of the parlor and into the adjacent dining room. He placed his hands on her upper arms. "Look at me."

She shook her head.

"Alexandra, we're going to stay in this dining room until you look at me."

She put on her brave face and raised her eyes to meet his.

"There's nothing to be afraid of. It's only temporary."

She lifted her chin. "I'm not afraid. It's just, well, if it's only temporary, I don't think you should kiss me."

Taking a deep breath, he let go of her arms. "We may think of it as temporary, but to everyone else it has to *look* real."

"Then tell me what a real marriage looks like."

The coldness in her eyes confused him. He had assumed she wouldn't want an arrangement that couldn't be undone. Maybe he'd been wrong about that. "Do you want it to be real?"

She closed her eyes and balled her fists. "I want to go home, and I don't want to see any Yankees when I get there." Relaxing her fists, she gave Ramsey a look of understanding. "But, I know now what it would cost, and I had no right to ask it of you. It's not your place. It never was."

Ramsey drew a piece of paper from his pocket and pressed it into her hand. "Turns out it is my place."

Her eyes widened as she read the orders from Madcap Charlie. "No," she gasped. "Does he not know how strong the enemy is in Marlbridge? How can he expect you to drive out a thousand Yankees with a force of three hundred?"

"Less than three hundred, and we don't have to drive them out, just delay them in sending reinforcements to Bridgeport."

"We?" Her eyes sparked with hope.

"You didn't think I would leave you behind, did you?"

She threw her arms around him and hugged him so tightly he thought she might crush his ribcage, but it was her brilliant smile that got him as she looked up at him, her fighting spirit instantly revived. "Real marriage or not, 'til death do us part' anyway," she declared, right before she gave him a peck on the lips and dragged him back into the parlor.

After the ceremony was completed and Henrietta had served the small party a good meal, Evelyn sent the newlyweds off to the woodland cottage that had recently been vacated by the circuit preacher who ministered to Cade's Mill once a month in the absence of Evelyn's husband. While Ramsey's men knew Alexandra's true identity, the rest of the battalion did not, so to keep up appearances, Alexandra and Ramsey rode out to the secluded cottage on horseback as if it was just another mission.

Alexandra was about to dismount, but Ramsey ordered her to stay put. He opened the cottage door and searched the place. When he returned, he took hold of Alexandra's waist and started to lift her out of the saddle, but she leaned away from him. "You don't have to help me. I can dismount by myself. Besides, no one's looking, so we don't have to pretend to be married." He rested his arm on her thigh. "Why do you have to fight me on everything?"

"I wasn't fighting you! I was just saying—"

Ramsey snatched her out of the saddle and carried her into the house. She didn't protest this time, but when he set her down, she started to back away. He caught her by the collar. "Alexandra, be still. Please."

She complied, but not without comment. "When I fight you, most of the time it's not on purpose. It's just that I don't know what you expect of me until you start barking orders at me. Maybe if you told me ahead of time what you wanted…"

"As you are so quick to do." He immediately wished he hadn't said it when he saw the flicker of hurt in her eyes.

"Well, I've learned my lesson about that." She clamped her mouth shut as she removed her gray coat and draped it over the chair. Without another word, she picked up the wash bucket and went outside.

Ramsey remained standing in the middle of the room until she returned with a bucketful of water. He watched her pour the water into the wash basin, and he didn't look away when she took off her shirt and pants.

While the binding still covered her breasts and her knee-length drawers covered her hips, Alexandra felt a twinge of guilt for not feeling ashamed to undress in front of Cana Ramsey, until she reminded herself that he was her husband, in the eyes of the law at least. He had already seen most of her anyway.

She could feel his gaze as she soaked the washcloth in the water and proceeded to wash. He waited until she finished then slowly approached her. When she didn't move away, he took the cloth out of her hand and set it on the wash table. After seating Alexandra on the bed, he picked up her discarded garments, folded them, and placed them on the chair with her coat.

Returning to the bed, he pulled the quilt back and gestured for Alexandra to get in. When she obeyed, he tucked the covers around her. He locked eyes with her for several moments then took a deep, decisive breath. "There's something I have to do. Stay here and get some sleep." Alexandra opened her mouth to argue, but Ramsey gently pressed his fingertips to her lips. "I'll send for you."

She clutched his hand. "What about the bear dream? I told you someone always dies."

"Someone has."

Alexandra's chest tightened. "Who?"

He pulled a small Bible out of his pocket, the one they had signed as a record. He placed it in her hands. "When Elias took you, I knew it would be impossible to get you back without the rest of the company finding out the truth. I had to choose between you and Drake. I chose you."

She stared at her real name next to Ramsey's on the record of marriage. He was right. Her true identity had been made known. Even if she put her uniform on again, her fellow soldiers would only see Alexandra from now on. Drake no longer existed. Cass had told her the day would come when she would have to choose between Drake and Garrett. She had sacrificed them both to stay with Ramsey and hadn't given a thought to either of them.

She remained silent as Ramsey left her bedside. He paused in the doorway and turned back to her. "I'm sorry. It should have been your choice." And then he was gone.

Alexandra pressed the Bible to her chest and drew the quilt over her head. No tears, she had promised herself the night she had stood in front of the mirror and sacrificed her hair to the image of Drake Corbin—a false image. Alexandra had believed Drake would save her people from the enemy, but it wasn't Drake's actions that had compelled Ramsey to return to Marlbridge. All it had taken was a piece of paper—orders from Madcap Charlie—orders made necessary because of General Mitchel's attacks on Bridgeport, a turn of events that had nothing to do with Alexandra's crusade to save her town. Alexandra could have stayed in Marlbridge, kept her hair, and—. She covered her mouth to stifle her wail. *If I had given up Drake sooner, Cass would still be alive.*

Several tears fell before she realized she was crying. Twelve-years worth of tears fell before she stopped to listen in case there was anything else God had against her. Of all the sermons and lectures she had heard over the years, the one that came to mind was the one about a woman's hair being her glory—Laura Catherine's favorite Bible verse.

As if the death of her dear brother wasn't bad enough already, Alexandra had traded her glory for nothing in return. God must be greatly disappointed in her. He was the One Who had given her all that beautiful hair. How could she ever make it up to Him? Suddenly, two thoughts popped into her head: *One, your hair will grow back, and two, let the dead bury their dead.*

Alexandra dried her eyes and came out from under the quilt. She walked over to the writing desk and finding a broken pencil in the drawer, opened the Bible to the record of deaths. She wrote them in order, starting with Jonas Corbin. As she wrote their names, she cried over each one: Cass, Chance, Bryce, Quinn, the Taylor boys (she didn't know their first names), Carter. She paused when she thought of Prichard Benefield. Though she had no tears for the scamp, she was a tiny bit sad that her mother had murdered him, even though she had planned in her heart to do the same. She went ahead and wrote his name, partly out of guilt and partly because it was unlikely that his death would be recorded in anyone else's Bible as his mother was no longer living.

Just as she began to think her task completed, she remembered the Yankee she had killed in battle plus the three Yankees that Quinn had gunned down. And, the Yankees killed during the failed jailbreak—she might as well add their names to the list. Running out of room on the page and not knowing any of their names, she simply wrote, "Unknown Yankees."

Finally, at the bottom of the page, she recorded the most recent death: "Drake Corbin, April 27, 1862."

Chapter 39

Reckoning

NIGHT had fallen, and Marlbridge was buzzing as Yankee soldiers scurried about. Elias was nearly run over by horse-drawn artillery as he rode down the street to Union headquarters. He dismounted and barely got out of the way as Fontaine barreled out of the house and marched toward the street.

As Elias stepped into the foyer, he overheard Heppinstahl's explosive rant, "This is all your doing! I had everything under control, and you, you lunatic!—"

Elias crossed the threshold into the office where Heppinstahl was stuffing his maps into bulging leather bags.

Barrymore cut Heppinstahl off. "Our highest priority must be to eradicate those bent on destroying the Union. There is no other cause to which we must devote our time and efforts."

Heppinstahl shifted his weight, and the floorboards creaked as he babbled on, "Colonel, if you had not attacked Cade's Mill, the Rebel Army would not now be on their way here."

Barrymore coolly replied, "They are not an army. It is only Cana Ramsey with a few hundred men."

"A few hundred men with cannon that you left in the field!" Heppinstahl yanked his maps out of his satchel and flung them across over the room. Calming himself, he ordered one of his underlings to pick up his maps.

"Ramsey wouldn't fire on his own people," Barrymore reassured his irate colleague. "Even if he did, I daresay General Mitchel would be delighted to hear of this wretched town's destruction, and he not having to lift a finger. He might even give you a commendation."

Elias cleared his throat and waited for Heppinstahl and Barrymore to acknowledge him. "I wouldn't be so quick to assume anything about Ramsey."

Barrymore cut his pale gray eyes at Elias. "I assume nothing. We all know with certainty that wherever Cana Ramsey is, there will Drake Corbin be also."

"Drake Corbin! Curse that name! May I never hear it again!" Heppinstahl plopped down into his chair. "Confound the Rebels for causing this trouble. I've not had a wink of sleep and I've completely lost my appetite. I find pleasure in nothing since that Drake Corbin and Captain Ramsey started this mess. Woe to them indeed if I ever get my hands on them. They will be sorry they vexed me. Now, get out, both of you. Leave me to my contemplations." He pulled out his field manual and began reviewing the standard battlefield tactics.

As Elias and Barrymore left headquarters, Barrymore halted on the porch and pressed his riding crop against Elias' shoulder. "I was perplexed that Cass Corbin sacrificed himself so quickly to save a wayward cousin that strangely no one has ever seen. I was further perplexed when you, whose only pursuit is self-interest, didn't bring Drake Corbin to me, when it was clearly within your interests to do so, but instead you tried to help him escape to Chattanooga, the very city to which the Corbin girl was supposed to have retreated to mourn her brother. Yet on the night her brother died, she didn't strike me as one who would choose mourning over vengeance." Barrymore stepped closer to peer down his long nose at Elias. "I am going to attack Ramsey at the first opportunity and if the girl is with him, I won't make allowances. Thus, my recommendation is that you bring the girl to me. After I have destroyed Ramsey, I will give her an opportunity to give an account of herself. Perhaps, she will be found innocent after all."

Elias shrugged. "The girl is of no consequence to me, but I'll see what I can do." The moment Barrymore mounted his horse and rode out of town with his men, Elias fled to his plantation.

* * *

Luke stood in the doorway of the library as Elias shoveled stacks of papers into the fireplace. He stuffed another mound of papers into a satchel, failing to notice Luke's presence until Luke announced, "I'm going to tell them the truth about what happened to my mother."

"What?" Elias was more startled by Luke's presence than by what he said.

"I'm going to tell them you killed her," Luke smiled as he crossed the room and set his own satchel down on the desk.

Elias resumed his packing. "I warned you the last time we had that discussion to never mention that woman to me again. Now, leave me. I've got more pressing matters to attend."

"Like taking Alexandra for your wife so you can have a legitimate heir?"

Elias took a deep sigh. How many more times would he have to explain? "Your mother reaped the natural consequences of her actions: giving birth to you. So, if anyone beyond herself is the cause of her demise, it's you."

Luke turned away from the desk to face Elias with a boldness no sane person would have risked at that moment. "When did you find out I was your nephew? Before or after Uncle Andrew died?"

With more annoyance than outrage Elias flipped the satchel shut and growled, "Andrew Kelson died in a fight he shouldn't have been in."

"I won't let you have Alexandra."

"What's gotten into you? You've turned into an ungrateful waif overnight. Now you straighten up."

"You take what you want. Why can't I?"

Elias seized Luke by the back of his neck and shoved his face against the window. "If it seems like I'm cruel, it's because the world is cruel, and I want you to be ready for it because when I die, this land and all the people on it will be your responsibility. As of late, instead of proving yourself worthy of such an inheritance, you've done nothing but pout and pine after a girl you can never have." Elias released him. "Now, is there anything else that needs to be said?"

Luke glared at him. "You've said enough."

Elias snatched up his satchel and gave one final order before he left. "Make sure those letters burn completely. Melissa thinks I don't know about Whit teaching her how to read, and I don't want her getting a-hold of anything she shouldn't." He was just about to leave when he got that sick feeling in his gut, the one he got whenever he knew he'd been outplayed. He returned to the library.

Luke was perched in his chair with one hand on the desk and one hand behind his back. His open satchel lay discarded on the floor.

"I wondered how Barrymore knew about Alexandra and my plans to take her to Chattanooga. *You* told him." Elias accused him.

Luke gave him an innocent expression. "I tried to help her. I went to Ramsey and tried to convince him to let me take her away from all this, but he is such a mean, cold-hearted devil. I don't know how he's lived so long. Still, my unauthorized excursion to Cade's Mill wasn't completely unsuccessful. While you were busy running off with Alexandra and all the Rebels were busy fightin' Yankees, I snuck over to the Rebel camp, and what do you think I found in Ramsey's tent?" From behind his back, he brought out the land deal documents and a small sack. When he dumped the sack over, gold pieces scattered across the desk. "You see, instead of abusing me, you should be thanking me because if all this evidence of your schemes had made it into the wrong hands, I wouldn't be sitting in your chair right now. I would be sitting in *my* chair."

Elias acknowledged the dilettante's achievement with a decorous nod before he laughed. "Do you even know which hands are the wrong ones? To whom were you going to present this 'evidence'? Barrymore? You were right there with Prichard Benefield when he robbed that train, and you've seen for yourself what Barrymore does to his enemy's associates. Heppinstahl already knows about the land deal because he is the party of the second part." Elias opened the set of documents to the last page and tapped Heppinstahl's signature. "To inform a malefactor that you are privy to a misdeed he's involved in would only tempt him to eliminate you as he would any threat. So, you see, instead of abusing me, you should be thanking me because if this evidence had made it into the wrong hands, well, they don't even have chairs where you'd be going."

The smug look on Kelson the Younger's face grew as he lifted his other hand away from the desk to reveal the blood-stained boll. "Miles Ramsey didn't kill Jonas Corbin, did he? I'm bettin' he didn't kill himself either. Was he even in the room?"

Elias took a letter opener and pinned Luke's sleeve to the desk. "What's done is done. If I could take it all back I would. I would give my life to bring Jonas back because he was my friend. I betrayed him, and I got him killed. If there was anything I could do to atone for it, I would, but there's not. So, I'll live with what I've done, and whatever I do tomorrow, I'll live with that, too. You remember that the next time you kick up your heels at me."

Elias grabbed the documents, gold, and cotton boll and shoved them in his satchel. Leaving Luke in the library, he stormed out of the house. He hadn't taken two steps onto the porch when he suddenly drew his Remington and spun to his left. Sitting in one of the rocking chairs was Cana Ramsey—with a Colt Dragoon.

Chapter 40

I Am Alexandra

April 28

At dawn the Confederates crossed into Jackson County and passed through the rusted gate to Storm Chase. The earth there was dark, uncultivated, and hard as rock. Cannon rolled over it easily except where ten years of rainstorms had washed out the narrow, serpentine drive. As far as last stands went, Storm Chase was more than suitable, if preserving the house wasn't a priority. The crest of the hill was bare and flat with the house at the center. Fallow fields stretched across the bottomland, about two hundred yards behind the house on the backside of the hill. Pastureland stretched out on either side of the house.

Once they finally made it to the top of the hill, St. Clair gave the men no time to rest, but immediately set them to digging earthworks all along the crest of the hill. Several men from Peterson's company eyed Alexandra with suspicion. Word had gotten around that Drake Corbin was actually a woman named Alexandra pretending to be a man. However, it wasn't about her true identity that they gossiped. Of greater concern to them was how she had managed to rope Captain Ramsey into marrying her. Only Ramsey's men seemed to accept her marriage to their captain as "fittin' and proper" and had no problem with her wearing pants, declaring that it would take them some time before they could imagine Drake wearing a dress.

Alexandra bombarded St. Clair the moment she caught him out of earshot of the other men. "Where's Cana? You said he would meet us here."

St. Clair clenched his jaw and repositioned his hat. "As I have already told you, ma'am, our captain wasn't any more forthcomin' with me than he was with you regardin' his whereabouts. He said he would meet us here, at some point. He did not say when. He did not say what he was doin' nor why. So, the best you and I can do in tha meantime is ta follow orders." He handed her a shovel.

About mid-morning, while the Confederates were making their final preparations, Alexandra spotted St. Clair in earnest conversation with McCabe. Not willing to spend one more minute waiting on them to tell her their battle plans, she marched up to them.

As she approached, McCabe turned around and almost plowed into her. "Aye! Lass, what are ye doin' here? I thought the cap'n wasna going to let ye fight?"

"He isn't," St. Clair replied. "McCabe, escort Mrs. Ramsey ta tha house where her husband is waiting for her."

McCabe's eyes bulged. "So, the rumor's true, then." He scrunched his thick, red eyebrows. "When have ye had time for a weddin'? And when did ye—" He stopped short when Alexandra blushed. "Never mind. There'll be time for that later, let's hope, if we dinna die today defending this God-forsaken hill," he rambled on as he escorted Alexandra to the house.

When they reached the porch, McCabe removed his hat. "It's been a pleasure serving with ye, lass, and I ask your forgiveness for any crude words I may have spoken in your presence back before I kent who ye were." He kissed her hand and marched off to holler at Sal and Bradford who had been doing more jawing than digging.

Alexandra found Ramsey in the library. He was standing at the window watching as men and horses traipsed through the patch of weeds that had once been a beautiful garden. Instead of facing Alexandra, he turned back to the desk and poured wine into two tin cups. "I couldn't find any glasses that weren't broken," he explained as he handed her one of the cups.

Alexandra accepted the cup and took a sip. Expecting the dry, unpleasant taste she had come to associate with wine, Alexandra was shocked at the sweetness.

Ramsey gazed at her as she took two more sips. "Do you like it?"

Alexandra nodded, her eyes never leaving his face. "I've never tasted anything like it."

"That's because there's not another one like it in the world."

Alexandra was by no means knowledgeable of such things, but if what Ramsey had given her was the only one of its kind then it must have cost a fortune. "Where did it come from?"

Turning back to the window, Ramsey pointed at a tangled mess of greenery that many people mistook for ordinary bushes until they got close enough to see the dark purple berries. "You've never tasted muscadine wine?"

She shook her head. "You made this?"

"My father made it. He hated the stuff, but Mama loved it, and he could never bring himself to refuse her anything until the day she died. After the burial, he came back to the house, lined all the bottles up on the fence, and used them for target practice. He missed this one." It wasn't until he ran his thumb along the neck of the bottle that Alexandra noticed the chip at the top.

Taking a moment to get up the courage, Alexandra touched Ramsey's hand. "I'm glad." When she held out her cup, he filled it. Neither of them spoke as they sat on the desk and drank the rest of the wine.

They had just finished the bottle when Langley strode into the library and saluted. "It's half past the hour, sir. Shall I bring him in?"

Ramsey nodded and drained his cup. He waited until Langley left the room before he took Alexandra's cup and set it on the desk. Too lightheaded to resist, Alexandra waited patiently for him to make the next move.

He fingered the chip in the bottle. "I know you've heard all the stories, but none of them are true. Jonas Corbin didn't sacrifice himself to end the war between the Kelsons and the Ramseys."

He left the desk, walked over to the fireplace, and rested his hand on the mantel, his back to Alexandra as he spoke into the charred stone hearth. "The fight wasn't between Elias and Miles. It was between Elias and Jonas. You already know that, but I never thought it was my place to tell you what they fought about. You and your brother were part of it, but the real fight was about who was the better man."

"My father, clearly!" she exclaimed as she hopped off the desk and moved to the other side of it, setting her foot near where Jonas Corbin had fallen.

"I imagine Jonas had always been the better man, but he wasn't that night. That's why I had to stop him. I couldn't let him become what he had spent his life fighting against. He was a man of the law, and he hated those who thought they were above it. But, even righteous anger can blind a man."

Alexandra leaned against the desk to steady herself. "You stopped him from doing what?"

"Elias was unarmed, but Jonas was blind with rage. I don't know how I knew that Jonas was about to the pull the trigger, except that it was as if in spite of what his flesh was about to do, his spirit spoke to me, and I…" He closed his eyes for just a moment before he looked at Alexandra squarely. "I had to stop him."

Even as she rejected what he was saying, the moment she looked in his eyes, she knew in her heart he was telling her the truth. She started to cry. Her father had left her, her brother had lied to her, Garrett had abandoned her. She couldn't bear to lose Ramsey. Why had he told her the truth here at the last? Why didn't he take the truth to his grave? They would probably both die in battle anyway.

"You should have let him kill Elias," she declared. "Elias is no good. Everyone would have been better off without him. Everything is his fault. You should have let him die. He doesn't deserve to live, but my father was a good man. How could you take him away from me to save a man like Elias?"

Alexandra jumped when Elias himself appeared in the doorway. "Because Cana did what Jonas trained him to do: defend the law, no matter who's trying to break it or hide behind it. In a way, Cana was the only one who did right by Jonas that night." He directed his attention to Ramsey. "As far as I'm concerned, the war between the Kelsons and the Ramseys is over."

"It's finished then." Without looking at Alexandra, Ramsey tossed the empty bottle into the cold hearth and made his way to the door.

He turned and looked back, at Elias first, then Alexandra. "Alexandra, when I said I didn't kill your father, I wasn't lying to you."

Without further explanation, he left.

A moment later, the house shook when cannon fire erupted. At the jolt, Alexandra forced herself to stop crying. She wiped her eyes on the sleeve of her uniform and marched to the window. Unable to get a clear view of the battle, she ran upstairs to the bedroom at the front of the house. From there she saw the enemy coming, and she made a choice. Her heart could not bear to lose one more man at Storm Chase. She had to stop the battle even if it meant her death.

"Alexandra."

She whirled around to face Elias who had followed her into the room.

"Leave me alone," she warned.

He took a hesitant step toward her. "This isn't your fight. It's Ramsey's fight, and it's a long time coming. He should have burned this house to the ground while Jonas' blood was still wet, and when he didn't, I should have. Cranston Ramsey and Montague Kelson brought a curse on this land neither you nor I nor Ramsey can undo."

"Whether this land is cursed or not, that has nothing to do with me. But those men, those war heroes, they are going to die out there because of me, because of what I did. I kidnapped Red, and I could have turned myself in. I was the one who gave Barrymore a reason to attack Cade's Mill. Ramsey was right. It was me trying to do what wasn't mine to do. Protecting Marlbridge wasn't my place. It was my father's place, and I know the only reason it even entered his mind to put an end to you was because you were a threat to Marlbridge."

Elias shook his head in wonder. "You stupid girl. You think everything is about you except for the one thing that really was about you."

Alexandra drew her saber. "I hate you, and I hate Cana Ramsey for sacrificing my father so that you could live."

Whether or not she had really intended to bring the saber down on Elias' head, Elias caught her wrist with surprising strength and speed, as if he had expected such a move. The tension in his face relaxed as he pulled her to his chest with a gentleness and a sadness that Alexandra had never before witnessed in the man.

"Jonas Corbin wasn't your father." He carefully took the saber out of her hand and tossed it away. "That's what the fight was about."

At first, Alexandra didn't believe him, and yet, the longer she looked at him, the more she could see for herself. Elias had Cass' face, and he was giving her the same look Cass had given her the night he died for her. But mostly, it was his eyes. The resemblance was irrefutable. The Corbin twins weren't identical—Alexandra favored Laura Catherine—but everybody swore they could tell they were brother and sister by their deep-set, hazel eyes. Evidently, no one had noticed they were Kelson eyes.

Unable to accept that Jonas Corbin, the war hero, was not her real father, Alexandra jerked away from Elias and ran for the door.

Elias grasped her arm. When she fought him, he wrestled her to the ground. "Alexandra, listen to me."

She kicked him in the face.

Fleeing the room, she made it down the stairs and into the foyer without stumbling, but before she reached the front door, an artillery barrage shook the house to its foundation. The blast ripped through the front corner of the main floor, scattering bricks and mortar across the parlor.

Alexandra fell and cut her forehead on one of the bricks. Another blast and another, but no rounds hit the house again. She lay on the floor until smoke from the battlefield began pouring into the house from the hole in the parlor wall. She dragged herself to her feet and staggered to the front door. It took all her strength to open it.

Between the smoke and the blood that was dripping into her eyes, Alexandra could hardly see anything except two distinct lines of men firing at each other. Bullets zipped past her ears. Smoke rings wobbled above her head. A stray horse almost trampled her as it ran from the battle.

As Alexandra stumbled across the field to where the enemy lines were preparing for an infantry assault, one of the Yankees yelled at her. "Hey, get out of there, you stupid Rebel! Your side is over yonder!"

When she didn't stop, one of them took a shot at her. She froze and called out the only name she knew. "Major Fontaine! Major Fontaine! It's me! Alexandra Corbin! I surrender! Please stop the battle! I surrender!"

Someone yelled for a cease fire, and the battle stalled when the bugle sounded the command. During the lull, she heard Sal holler at the Yankees, "What's goin' on over thar? D'yall come to fight or didn't ye?"

Every enemy soldier in that section of the line looked at Alexandra, then looked at each other, then looked at their officers, then looked back at her until Fontaine appeared. He rode out to her in the middle of the field and heaved her onto his horse. Once he got her to safety, he dismounted. "What were you doing out there?" he demanded as he gave her his handkerchief.

Wiping the blood off her face, Alexandra confessed, "Major Fontaine, there is no Drake Corbin. It was just me. I was there when those Yankees were killed. I didn't do the killing, but I did have a hand in kidnapping Red."

Fontaine pulled her away from the Union soldiers who were still gawking at her. "Belgrave? Where is he?"

"Stop the battle, and I'll tell you everything." Alexandra gripped Fontaine's arm. "If you don't stop the battle, I can't promise that Red will remain alive. Let the Confederates go, and Red will be returned to you. Ask anyone in Marlbridge, and they will tell you this place is not worth even one man's life. Certainly not the hundreds you will lose trying to convince Ramsey to surrender. You know the man, so you tell me if forcing him to see things your way is worth the cost." Alexandra prayed that God would make Fontaine believe her. She had not seen Red since the dance at Cade's Mill, and he had not accompanied them to Storm Chase. For all she knew, he was already dead. Wherever he was, maybe God had saved him, and if God had saved him, maybe God could bring him back to Marlbridge so that everything could be set right in spite of Alexandra's contribution to the trouble that had come upon her town and her people.

Before Fontaine agreed to her terms, Barrymore rode up. "Major, this girl is Drake Corbin. Arrest her then destroy the Rebels across the way who are polluting this land. You will not cease until every drop of their blood has been spilled."

Alexandra opened her mouth to inform Barrymore that Red was safe, but Fontaine held up his hand for silence as he stood between her and Barrymore. "I know who she is, Colonel, but I don't answer to you. I answer to Colonel Heppinstahl."

"Heppinstahl is not here," Barrymore growled.

"Whether my commanding officer is present in the flesh or not, he gave me the authority to carry out his orders and equipped me with the resources to do it. If you insist on driving Ramsey off that hill, go ahead, but I will not aid you." Fontaine gave orders for his men to fall back.

As his men started to leave the field, Barrymore fired at the ground in front of them. "You may do as you please, Major. These men are under my command now, and I order them to stay and fight like men."

One of the soldiers stood up to Barrymore. "Shoot me if you want, but I'm not taking orders from you. I enlisted to serve under Marcus Fontaine."

When several others voiced their agreement, Barrymore shot the man. "Anyone else?"

By that time, Barrymore's men had fallen in behind him and formed a line that might as well have been a firing squad. Fontaine ordered his own men to stand down. "Very well, Colonel, I have stated my objections for the record. Whatever consequences befall you are on your own head."

Fontaine took Alexandra by the arm and dragged her away from the battle line.

"No!" Alexandra screamed as she pummeled Fontaine with her fists. "You have to stop the battle!"

Fontaine caught her hands. "Stop!"

She didn't keep fighting when he released her, but her eyes were still blazing. "How can you let him bully you like that in front of your men? He's going to get them killed."

"It's out of my hands."

"Why are you afraid of him?"

"The men under my command are shopkeepers and farmers with muskets. It doesn't matter that they outnumber Barrymore's men. His men are killers. If he turned them loose on Marlbridge, they'd burn it to the ground before we could stop them. Is that what you want?"

Horrified, Alexandra kept silent. She had assumed that if she turned herself in and returned Red unharmed that Barrymore would leave Marlbridge. Yet, he hadn't even asked about Red. It hadn't occurred to her that maybe the reason he had come after her in the first place wasn't because of anything she did but because he enjoyed hunting people down and bringing them to justice whether they had it coming or not.

Fontaine rubbed the back of his neck as he looked up at the dark clouds gathering overhead. "Let Barrymore wear himself out trying to take that hill from Cana Ramsey. He won't succeed."

"But it won't be his men wasted in the process; they'll be yours."

Fontaine replied with cold pragmatism, "That's why I left one third of them behind to guard Marlbridge and sent another third to aid Mitchel's advance on Bridgeport. Whatever I lose at Storm Chase is acceptable."

Alexandra stared at him in disbelief. "Don't you care that their lives are going to be wasted?"

"Dying in a pointless battle is still better than dying of dysentery." Without another word, he escorted her back to Marlbridge.

Chapter 41

Let It Fall

As Elias paced in front of the Rainier mansion, he rubbed his hands, trying to stop them from shaking. Only an hour had passed since he had watched his only daughter run out onto the battlefield at Storm Chase, and he had been powerless to stop her.

For the past two decades, he had not allowed himself to care for anyone very deeply, except Jonas, but despite his efforts to harden his heart, he loved the girl. Being separated from her and her brother for all those years had made it easier for him to numb the pain at watching his children give their love to another man, a man who was far more worthy of their love than Elias had ever been.

In his desperation to save Alexandra, he hadn't allowed himself to grieve over Cass. It was a consolation that the boy knew what he was getting into and had faced the consequences of his actions with honor and courage. In spite of his justifications, a lump began to form in his throat, and his vision grew blurry. He shook his head and raked his sleeve across his eyes. Fortunately, the Rainiers' butler was slow coming to the door, giving Elias time to quell any counterproductive emotions.

The butler finally opened the door, and Elias stepped into the foyer just as Garrett was coming down the stairs. He balked when he saw the blood on Elias' face and shirt. "If you've come to see my father, he's…indisposed."

"I didn't come to see Hanson. I came to see you," Elias replied, his usually patronizing tone buried under guilt and weariness.

"If you have come to entangle me in any more of your schemes, the answer is 'no,' " Garrett answered coldly as he gave Elias his handkerchief.

"Do you truly love Alexandra, or are you only playing?"

Taken aback, Garrett stared at Elias for a moment before he lifted his chin, daring Elias to doubt him. "Yes, I truly love her, but what concern is it of yours?"

"She's been captured."

Garrett's face went pale.

"And you, Rainier, are going to set her free."

"How?"

Clutching the bloody handkerchief, Elias pointed in Garrett's face. "By doing exactly what I tell you to do."

* * *

The people of Marlbridge stood aghast as Major Fontaine led the Rebel-clad Alexandra down the middle of the street to Union headquarters. Alexandra smiled when she stood on the porch of the Commodore Mansion.

"I used to think this place was haunted. I never met the Commodore, but when I was a child, Mort Grimshaw, who's the closest thing we have to a pirate in this town, would tell me the scariest stories you ever heard. A lot of folks don't care for Mort because he's a drunkard, but I've always been fond of him," Alexandra mused.

Once inside, Fontaine led Alexandra up the stairs into one of the bedrooms and closed the door. After seating her on the bed, he said, "I'm not sure you fully understand the peril befalling you: the presumed murder of a general's son by a deranged Southern woman who breaks God's laws by clothing herself in men's attire. Such a turn of events might convince even the most reluctant Yankee to take up arms against you. Some might argue that any culture capable of producing such a spectacle of humanity ought to be brought down. I'm not inclined to make that argument, but there are some."

"I haven't done any of those things. I didn't murder Red. I don't know where he is. I can't prove that he's even alive, but Barrymore has no proof that he's dead."

"Martial law has been declared. He won't need proof. Besides, there is enough circumstantial evidence to hang you for treason."

"I haven't committed treason. I'm not a spy. I acted within the rules of engagement."

"Rules established for men. As a woman, you are not an authorized combatant, so what other category is there for you but traitor to your country and your kind?"

"I haven't done anything wrong, and I'm not a 'spectacle of humanity.' "

"It won't matter whether or not you actually committed any sins. The newspapers will say you did, and even your own family will believe the press before they will believe you."

At first, Alexandra didn't want to admit Fontaine was right, but then she remembered how many times during her childhood that her own mother had taken Meredith Kilroy's word over her own. "So, unless Red shows up to testify, Barrymore is going to hang me."

"Yes."

Alexandra reached into her pocket and pulled out her Bible. "Well then, if it wouldn't be too much of an imposition, would you give this to Cana?" Her voice broke. "In case I don't see him again."

When Fontaine opened the Bible and saw the record of marriage, he paused before he turned the page to the record of births and the record of deaths. He glanced through the list of the dead.

Not wanting Fontaine to think her callous, she confessed, "I'm sorry I didn't know the names of your men that Quinn killed or the one I killed in battle."

"I didn't know their names either," Fontaine admitted with a hint of shame in his expression. He sat next to her on the bed. "The day of the battle when I stopped Cana from killing Barrymore, I tried to convince him to turn Drake Corbin in and be done with it. At the time, I didn't understand why he was being so irrational about it, but I see now."

"He was really going to kill Barrymore?"

"It sure looked that way."

"Why did you stop him?"

Fontaine studied her closely. "I stopped him because when Cana's in that state of mind, I'm afraid he can't distinguish between a rabid dog and a wounded one."

Alexandra pressed her fingertips to her eyelids, trying not to picture the man she loved standing over the body of the man she had known as her father. She wasn't there when Ramsey shot Jonas Corbin, but she was there when Barrymore hanged her brother. Even if Fontaine was right about Ramsey not being able to tell the difference between a rabid dog and a wounded one, she could. "Well, this time I think it was you who made the mistake, Major."

"Maybe so, but until you've witnessed for yourself what Cana Ramsey is capable of, you have no right to judge me."

When Fontaine left the room, Alexandra listened as he gave orders to the guard at her door and tromped down the stairs. She lay back on the bed wishing she was back in Cade's Mill or at least, back at camp surrounded by her fellow soldiers—and Cana. She fought down the lump of regret that was rapidly expanding in her throat. What would she say to him the next time she saw him, if she ever saw him again?

Her heart jumped at the knock on the door even though she knew it couldn't be Ramsey. If it was, that meant he had been captured, too. She was both relieved and disappointed when Garrett entered the room with a large box in his arms.

"I brought you something," Garrett awkwardly announced as he set the box on the bed and pulled out a beautiful, green day dress. When Alexandra took a hesitant step toward the dress, Garrett walked to the door and stood aside for Lellen to enter.

Lellen smiled and cried when she saw Alexandra. When Garrett remained in the room, Lellen scowled at him. "You want me to dress her up or not? Can't do it with you standin' there gawkin' at her."

With a hesitant hand, Garrett patted Alexandra's shoulder and looked as if he was about to speak, but he kept silent and hurried out the door.

Tossing aside the societal rules that separated the two women, Alexandra hugged Lellen as the older woman stroked her hair, "Oh, child."

When Lellen released her, Alexandra sat on the bed. "Did you know the truth, about Elias being my father?"

Lellen sighed, "Yes, Miss Alexandra, I know the truth about a lot of things."

"Why didn't you tell me?"

"Because it wasn't my place. Besides, it wouldn't have changed what really mattered: that Master Jonas loved you, raised you, and though I can't say he would've approved of how you been goin' about things lately, he would have been here standin' by you to the end."

"Did you know that my—" she caught herself, "that Jonas was going to kill Elias when he found out, but Cana Ramsey stopped him, and that's how he died?"

Lellen gasped, "No, I didn't know that."

"I feel like I ought to hate Cana for it, but I don't, and I don't know why."

After a long pause, Lellen said, "It's because deep down you know if Cana Ramsey hadn't been there, the man you loved as your father would have lost something worth far more than his life. He'd have lost his name. All the good he'd done would've been forgotten. Folks would've only remembered him as the sheriff who murdered Elias Kelson. Ain't no cause to hate Cana Ramsey. I never liked that boy, but if he stopped Master Jonas from doin' evil, he saved you from livin' with the shame he's had to live with on account of his own father."

Lellen drew a handkerchief from her pocket and dabbed Alexandra's cheeks. "I haven't seen you cry since you were seven or eight and Cass told you the story about Colonel Travis and Davy Crockett and all those men dyin' at the Alamo, and you cried and cried. Next mornin', I found you packin' your bags. You were gonna go down to Pop Brady's and get yourself a Bowie knife so you could go down to Texas and get those Mexicans for somethin' that happened 'fore you even came into this world."

Alexandra smiled.

"You done with all this?" Lellen asked, waving her hand at Alexandra's uniform. Alexandra nodded and unbuttoned her gray coat. She shook it off and let it fall to the floor.

Chapter 42

Aftermath

Ramsey wiped blood out of his eyes as he surveyed the damage to Storm Chase. He was grieved at the sight of dead bodies laid out under his mother's pecan trees and scattered across the pasture next to the house where he learned to ride his first pony. The house had taken a few hits but was still standing.

During one of the artillery barrages, Ramsey had sustained a minor head wound and injured his hip when he fell, but for the most part, the day had gone better than he had expected. Fortunately, Fontaine had only brought a third of his force. Combined with Barrymore's men, they had numbered less than six hundred, outnumbering the Confederates two-to-one which would have meant certain defeat if the Confederates hadn't dug in on the high ground. Unlike the battle of Cade's Mill, which had amounted to a series of mad dashes with unnecessary bloodshed, the battle of Storm Chase had been a small-scale pitched battle: both sides were dismounted and engaged in proper volleys, albeit, no textbook contained the proper counter-maneuver for when a crazy woman ran out onto the field in the middle of an artillery barrage. It would be a while before Ramsey got over that harrowing experience, if he ever did.

Leaning on McCabe for support, Ramsey cursed when the Scot set him down roughly on the porch steps. "Sorry, Cap'n. I'm no nursemaid, but we'll have to make do, aye?"

"I have to find Alexandra."

"How do ye plan to do that when ye canna walk and ye canna see for the blood in your eyes. Besides, I dinna think the Yanks will harm a lass." McCabe rummaged in his knapsack and retrieved a round, slightly rusted tin about three inches in diameter. When he opened it, several of the men who were sitting on the porch gagged.

"Gosh-dog, McCabe! What is that stuff?" one of them yelped.

"I canna tell clan secrets," McCabe replied. "Now, hold still, Cap'n. 'Tis a wee cut right above your eye. This'll cure it."

He slathered the foul-smelling concoction onto a clean cloth and was about to press it to Ramsey's head when the captain caught his arm and growled, "You touch me with that stuff and I'll cut your hand off."

"Watch yourself, laddie," McCabe growled back.

"You watch yourself, McCabe."

The big Scot grinned wickedly at the four men sitting closest to Ramsey. "Lads, hold him down."

Ramsey fought the men who held him down while McCabe doctored the wound. When McCabe finished, he secured the lid on the tin and stuffed it in his knapsack before he gave the order. "Turn him loose, lads."

Ramsey sprang to his feet, nearly passing out from the pain shooting through his hip.

St. Clair rode up. "What in tarnation?"

"Cap'n Ramsey had a wee scrape," McCabe grumbled. "I'd rather tend a wounded bear."

St. Clair huffed, "Is that all? Why, with all that ruckus, I thought y'all were tryin' ta shoe Red Sticks."

Ignoring the laughter, Ramsey waved at Bradford to bring Solomon over.

"Where do you think you're goin'?" St. Clair asked as he maneuvered Vindicator to block Ramsey's path.

"To get Alexandra back. If you aren't gonna help me, get out of the way."

St. Clair dismounted and laid his hat on the pommel of Vindicator's saddle. "Well, I was hopin' it wouldn't come ta this, but, Gawd help me, you have driven me to it."

Before Ramsey knew what was happening, St. Clair's fist smashed into his jaw. He stumbled backwards and fell on his injured hip. He must have blacked out for a moment—when he opened his eyes, St.

Clair was sitting on the porch alone, and the rest of the men were tending to their horses.

Ramsey sat up and motioned for St. Clair to help him stand.

"You owe me an apology," the lieutenant declared, clearly miffed.

"I owe you an apology? You almost broke my jaw."

St. Clair narrowed his eyes.

"Fine. Thaddeus, I apologize for whatever it is you think I ought to apologize for. Now, will you help me up?"

"That hardly qualifies for an apology, but as that is tha best I'm likely ta get, I accept." St. Clair hopped off the porch and pulled Ramsey to his feet. "Now, you care ta tell me what you did ta cause your wife ta run out onto tha battlefield and surrender ta tha enemy?"

Ramsey limped over to the porch and sat down. "My father didn't kill Jonas Corbin. I did."

St. Clair didn't react at first. Instead, he came over and sat next to Ramsey. "I assumed tha alternate course of action was worse than death?"

"I thought so at the time, and even now, I still believe I did the right thing."

"You shouldn't have kept that from me, Cana. It's not good for a man ta bear somethin' like that alone."

"I know."

"So you told her."

Ramsey nodded. "I thought if I broke her spirit, she'd give up and go to Chattanooga where she'd be safe, at least for the time being."

"You're a gol-dang fool, Cana Ramsey."

"I know."

"Well, what's tha plan ta get her back?"

Ramsey shifted his attention to the cannon sitting in his yard. The seeds of a plan began to take root in his mind when a horse and rider came galloping up the drive.

When Ramsey saw who it was, he handed St. Clair his knife and gun, intending to strangle the man with his bare hands. He limped over to the horse, yanked Garrett Rainier out of the saddle, and threw him on the ground. Garrett attempted to scramble away, but Ramsey jumped on top of him, fasteninng his hands around his throat. "I told you to kill him! You could have stopped him, and you didn't do it! Now she's going to die because of you!"

Consumed with rage, Ramsey didn't hear St. Clair yelling for him to stop. St. Clair tried to pull him off Garrett, but Ramsey wouldn't let go. Finally, as Garrett was about to pass out, St. Clair punched Ramsey in the hip. Ramsey hollered in pain and immediately turned Garrett loose. The pain was so intense that he didn't struggle when St. Clair dragged him away from Garrett.

"You will not become Cranston Ramsey!" St. Clair thundered as he aimed his revolver at Ramsey's chest. "You made me swear an oath that I would stop you if you ever got ta that point, and Gawd is my witness, I will keep my word!"

Ramsey drew a sharp breath through his clenched teeth. "I think you broke it."

"I have never broken my word in my life!"

"I was talking about my hip."

St. Clair turned to Garrett who was still lying on the ground, coughing and choking. "Help me get him in tha house."

Garrett sat up and glowered at St. Clair. "He just tried to kill me!"

With his hands on his hips, St. Clair loomed over Garrett. "And I could've let him, but I didn't, so you owe me your life. Now, do as I say or I will dispatch you ta tha hereafter myself."

Garrett obeyed. They carried Ramsey inside and laid him on the settee in the library.

"Not here. Not this room," Ramsey groaned.

"This is tha only piece of furniture left ta sit on, so it'll have ta do. Besides, it's not as if it's your death bed," St. Clair answered.

"If Red doesn't get here soon, it might as well be my death bed," Ramsey muttered.

"What do you mean?" Garrett asked, his voice shaking slightly. "I thought Belgrave was with you. Are you telling me he is not?"

"I let him go."

This time the panic in Garrett's tone was evident. "Why did you do that? Alexandra is going to stand trial this afternoon. Without Belgrave to testify," his voice trailed as he stumbled back. "They are going to hang her."

"I'm not gonna let that happen." Ramsey slung his arm over the back of the settee as he struggled to sit up. "My orders from Whisenhunt were to stop Barrymore and Fontaine from sending reinforcements to Bridgeport, and we did. So, all those Yankees who would have been in Bridgeport are now stuck in Marlbridge, which is why I told Elias to take Alexandra to Chattanooga before it was too late. Now, my only option is to wait for Belgrave."

"Even with Belgrave's testimony there is no guarantee Barrymore will not hang her anyway like he did Cass."

"That's why Belgrave isn't coming back alone."

"If he comes back at all," Garrett fumed. "I cannot believe you put Alexandra's life in the hands of the Council. You are aware that General Belgrave is the Head of the Council?"

"Yes, and according to Red, the general himself wants Barrymore removed for reasons that have nothing to do with Alexandra or Marlbridge."

Garrett chewed his lips as he investigated the room. He ran his hand across Cranston Ramsey's prized possession: the massive, mahogany partners desk for which he had commissioned one of the best craftsmen in England. While everything else of value had been carried off by thieves over the years, the desk had been left behind because it was too heavy to move and because no one had dared touch anything in the library at Storm Chase lest Sheriff Corbin's ghost still haunted the premises.

Garrett turned back to Ramsey. "I know the way things look to you, Alexandra is going to die because I did not kill Barrymore, but I confess that I never saw it that way. The truth is, Ramsey, you and I will never see eye to eye on anything because you despise your heritage, and I value mine above my life."

"Above Alexandra's life?"

As Ramsey expected, Garrett didn't answer the question directly. "If any of this is my fault, it is not because I refused to kill Barrymore. It goes back further than that. If I had married Alexandra when I had the chance, I could have stopped her. I could have made her stay home."

"Why didn't you?"

"Marry her? You know why." Garrett sighed. "I know it is not Alexandra's fault that she is illegitimate, but—" He threw his hands up. "It is just as well I did not marry her. I cannot imagine the shame a husband would endure if his wife left him to join the army. Of course, as it is, Alexandra will bear her shame alone, and that I do regret. Even if I were able to marry her, I doubt she would have me now."

When Ramsey didn't volunteer the truth, St. Clair chimed in, "It is too late for that course of action as she is already married."

Garrett's eyes went wide. "You mean, she actually did it? Because of what her mother said?"

"Because I convinced her it was the right thing to do," Ramsey answered.

"I assume it was you she married?"

Resenting Garrett's condescending tone, Ramsey slowly got to his feet, placing most of his weight on his good leg as he limped over to the desk where Garrett was standing. One eye narrowed slightly. "Yes."

"Has the marriage been...consummated?" Garrett stammered. Before Ramsey responded, he quickly added, "Do not answer that. Under the circumstances, it would be better for everyone to assume that it has been. A married woman fighting alongside her husband can be forgiven her indiscretion, and the shame would fall on her husband instead of her." He groaned in frustration. "What was she thinking?"

Ramsey leaned against the desk next to Garrett. "She's just trying to save her town, Rainier."

"It is not her responsibility."

"I know. It's ours, and it's not fair to blame her for trying to do what we should've done. Maybe that's the problem. There is no *we*." Ramsey shifted his weight to relieve the stress on his hip. "We may all agree that Barrymore must be dealt with and Alexandra must be saved, but you have your way of doing things, Alexandra has hers, Elias has his, and I have mine."

Garrett took a deep breath. "I will stall as long as I can, but if Belgrave does not arrive in time to testify in court, Alexandra will hang. So, if you have not already made secondary arrangements, I suggest you do so."

Ramsey waited until Garrett reached the doorway before he said,

"I was wrong to ask you to violate your conscience, Rainier, about Barrymore. I apologize. I thought you would see things the same way I see them because of the dog."

"The dog? Lucy? You still hold that against me? I was ten."

Ramsey raised his hand. "I don't hold it against you, but everybody in Marlbridge loved that dog, and you stabbed her with a pitchfork."

"She had rabies. If she had bitten you, you would have died. I did what anyone else would have done."

"I couldn't do it. When I asked you later how you were able to do it, you said, 'I didn't kill Lucy. Rabies killed Lucy. All I did was put a pitiful beast out of its misery before it killed somebody.' "

"Are you blaming me for how you have chosen to live your life, because of something I said?"

"No, that's not what I meant." Ramsey retrieved his gun from St. Clair's custody and weighed it in his hands. "This is what I use to protect the people I care about, and I've gotten really good at it over the years."

He holstered his gun. "I can't be there when Alexandra faces her enemies. The reason I brought up the dog was to remind you of who you are, Rainier, because right now, Alexandra's life is in your hands, not mine. You say whatever you have to say to protect her."

Garrett stuck his chin out and snarled, "I am offended that you thought for an instant I would do otherwise."

Chapter 43

The Trial

THE interior of the courthouse in Marlbridge was only half-finished when the war broke out, and no one had voted to spend town resources to complete it. When word spread that Alexandra was to stand trial at the courthouse, Mrs. Kilroy covered the unfinished wall at the front of the courtroom with the only piece of material left in town that was large enough to conceal it: the massive Union flag that Heppinstahl had erected at the Commodore mansion. Most of the citizens complained that she had created an even greater eyesore, but to Mrs. Kilroy, her secessionist leanings notwithstanding, no Cause was worth sacrificing one of the pillars of Southern society: the right to hide one's imperfections.

The flag was the first thing Alexandra saw as Sergeant Minford, a stout Yankee with droopy eyes, led her down the aisle to the front of the room where Garrett was waiting for her. She kept her back straight and her head high as her mother had taught her since she was old enough to walk. The shawl Lellen had given her partially concealed the shackles on her wrists. Only when her escort handed her over to Garrett did Alexandra glance back at the crowded pews to see who all was in attendance. Wilson was there with Laura Catherine whose veil was more opaque than what was deemed fashionable in the spring of 1862. Mrs. Porter was jabbering away to a man Alexandra had never seen before. By the way he was devouring every word, he must have been a newspaperman of some kind.

All was as Alexandra had expected except for the presence of a few people she had not dared hoped to see. Mama and Pop Brady were there, in the crowd, not the defendant's chair. So was Reverend Land and Brandon McKinney.

"Barrymore released the prisoners?" Alexandra asked Garrett.

"Only the civilians," he answered. "Elias convinced Heppinstahl to release them. I do not know how he convinced him, but you can see for yourself they are free."

Alexandra did not see Elias until the door at the front of the room opened and her accusers, led by Heppinstahl, filed into the room and took their places at the table in front of the flag. Elias slid into the room after them and closed the door. Without looking in Alexandra's direction, he sat next to Luke on the front row.

Heppinstahl peered down at Alexandra. "So, you are the woman who has caused so much trouble. What do you have to say for yourself?"

Alexandra bit her lips. Garrett had instructed her not to speak. A week ago, she wouldn't have listened to him.

Garrett cleared his throat. "Your Honor?"

With an impatient sigh, Heppinstahl replied, "What is it, Mr. Rainier?"

"Your Honor, I submit that Miss Corbin has nothing to say for herself because no formal charges have been brought against her, and if there are no formal charges, what is the purpose of this trial?"

Heppinstahl glared at Garrett. "I was getting to that," he snipped as he yanked a piece of paper out of his pocket and unfolded it. "There are indeed formal charges, a lengthy list, in fact. Let us review them, shall we?" He paused to scan the paper before he read, "kidnapping, fraud, accomplice to murder, murder, espionage, and numerous acts of treason, up to and including the impersonation of an enemy combatant. How do you plead?"

Garrett answered for her. "The defendant pleads 'not guilty,' Your Honor."

Heppinstahl grumbled, "You deny these charges?"

"Yes, Your Honor, she does."

"So, you deny these charges, yet in the face of overwhelming evidence, you have nothing to say for yourself, Miss Corbin? What is this court to do with you? Must I hold you in contempt?"

Garrett replied, "Your Honor, the prosecution is supposed to present their case first, and opening statements are in order. If it pleases Your Honor, the prosecuting attorney may begin." He made a big show of glancing around the room. "You do have a prosecuting attorney, do you not?"

"Mr. Rainier, I already know what the prosecution has to say. Besides, this is not a convening of the Supreme Court. We may dispense with formalities for such a small, municipal affair."

Garrett instructed Alexandra to sit. "Your Honor, proper procedure goes well beyond mere formality. It is the very essence of our judicial system, particularly when a young woman's life is at stake. Surely, Your Honor does not consider it a small matter to put a young woman to death without due process of the law, if indeed she has done anything worthy of death, a question the prosecution has yet to even ask let alone answer. According to the late and venerable Supreme Court Justice Joseph Story:

> Not to dwell farther on these important inducements "to form a more perfect union," let us pass to the next object, which is to "establish justice." This must for ever be one of the great ends of every wise government; and even in arbitrary governments it must, to a great extent, be practiced at least in respect to private persons, as the only security against rebellion, private vengeance, and popular cruelty. But in a free government it lies at the very basis of all its institutions. Without justice being freely, fully, and impartially administered, neither our persons, nor our rights, nor our property, can be protected. And if these, or either of them, are regulated by no certain laws, and are subject to no certain principles, and are held by no certain tenure, and are redressed, when violated, by no certain remedies, society fails of all its value; and men may as well return to a state of savage and barbarous independence. No one can doubt, therefore, that the establishment of justice must be one main object of all our state governments.

"Chief Justice John Marshall—" Garrett continued.

Evidently unimpressed by Garrett's discourse, Heppinstahl smacked his hand on the table. "Mr. Rainier, I understand your concern for procedure and precedent, but to what procedure and precedent are you referring? I have before me a young female who has been parading about dressed as a man and then she proceeds to take up arms against the national government. Has anyone ever witnessed such rebellion on the part of the fairer sex since the Garden of Eden? I say not. It is the opinion of this court, convened by me, a representative of the national government, that such rebellion is an affront to decent society and must be dealt with harshly. Therefore, unless you have any evidence to present, Mr. Rainier, I've a good mind to declare the defendant guilty on all charges without one word from either side."

When the crowd began to murmur, Heppinstahl pounded the gavel and bellowed, "Quiet!!" He eyed the crowd with suspicion. "Nevertheless, who am I to overturn the great Justice Story? You may call your first witness, Mr. Rainier."

"Your Honor, my witness is Corporal Edwin Belgrave."

Heppinstahl's eyes bulged. "You can't call Corporal Belgrave. He is the victim."

"Presumed victim, Your Honor."

"Belgrave was kidnapped by this woman," Heppinstahl declared. "Do you dispute the fact?"

"The only indisputable fact is Belgrave's absence, Your Honor. The cause and circumstances of his absence are a matter of speculation considering all those who might have confirmed such details are dead. For all we know, the man deserted. In which case, he is the one who should be on trial here, not Miss Corbin."

By that point, Heppinstahl was beside himself. "You dare to tarnish the name of a fine, upstanding officer of the United States Army to protect the interests of this...this libertine? I will not stand for it, Mr. Rainier."

Garrett raised his hands in acquiescence. "Your Honor, I meant no disrespect to Corporal Belgrave. Indeed, I would never condemn anyone for seeking to escape the strain of combat. I meant only to acknowledge the lack of evidence that Miss Corbin was involved in any wrongdoing, unless you consider wearing trousers a heinous crime.

Even if it was a crime, who can blame Miss Corbin for experimenting with other garb? Have you ever tried to go about in a hoop skirt, Your Honor?"

At the thought of such a ridiculous sight, laughter broke out amongst the people, Mrs. Porter's cackle the loudest of them all.

Heppinstahl glowered at Garrett. "The peddler, Virgil Doggett, saw Corporal Belgrave taken away by Drake Corbin, who has proven to be none other than this woman."

"So, the prosecution does have a witness? Why did you not say so, Your Honor? By all means, let us make time for the prosecution to present the government's case." Garrett sat down.

Heppinstahl shot a nervous glance at Barrymore. "Have you no other witnesses than Corporal Belgrave, Mr. Rainier?"

Garrett stood. "No, Your Honor, and as you are aware, the man is not present. If the prosecution rests, justice demands a recess until Belgrave can be located." He sat down.

Barrymore compelled Heppinstahl with no more than a raised eyebrow. "There will be no recess," Heppinstahl declared. "We will resolve this matter as quickly as possible." He gulped and cleared his throat as he returned his attention to Alexandra. "Miss Corbin, were it not for the lie you told concerning the whereabouts of Corporal Belgrave, I might have opted for leniency. However, rather than send you to an institution for females who...have problems, this tribunal finds you guilty of treason and espionage and sentences you to hang by the neck until you are dead."

The room erupted.

Alexandra looked at Elias. He remained expressionless and silent. She didn't know what she had expected from him, but she hadn't anticipated that he would sit by and let Barrymore and that fat colonel have their way in his town.

Garrett sprang to his feet, "You can't do that!"

Heppinstahl leaned forward, the table almost buckling under the pressure. "Mr. Rainier, you will restrain yourself, or I shall hold you in contempt of court."

Garrett seethed. "This is not a legitimate court! I move to have all charges dismissed."

"On what grounds?" Barrymore asked.

Garrett continued, "Primarily upon the grounds that the prosecution has no evidence. Secondly, if Miss Corbin has done anything unseemly it is almost certainly the manifestation of temporary insanity brought on no doubt by the untimely death of her brother, an act for which this man is responsible." He pointed to Barrymore. "In light of this, I submit that if Miss Corbin is speedily returned to a healthy environment, she will soon recover her good senses."

Alexandra stared at Garrett. Either he was lying or he really believed that what she had tried to do for her town was insane.

Heppinstahl was about to speak when Barrymore stood and came around to the front of the table, his cold eyes shifting between Alexandra and the crowd. "What is to be determined here is not the sanity of this woman. It is her willful and reckless disregard for the customs passed down to her from her forebears. Since my arrival, I have heard from the lips of many citizens the grandiose praises of Jonas Corbin. We would expect the offspring of so great a man to honor her father and mother, to conduct herself in a manner befitting a lady, and to keep to her own domestic affairs. Yet, she appears before you shorn of her glory," he continued as he touched her hair, "unrepentant of abandoning her rightful abode and consorting with enemies of our holy and perfect Union. These are the sins for which atonement must be made. These known facts far outweigh the allegations of kidnapping and murder for which four others have already paid the price. Thus, I ask the defendant, do you repent?"

Alexandra stood and answered the charges. "Of dishonoring my father and mother, yes, I repent. Of deceiving others by pretending to be something that I'm not, yes. Of falling short in every way befitting a God-fearing woman, yes. Of trying to do what I believed was the right thing, namely resisting a foreign oppressor, I only regret that I didn't go about it the right way."

Tate got to his feet and eyed the crowd with a menacing gleam. "Y'all just gonna sit there and let 'em hang Sheriff Corbin's girl? Well, us old folks ain't gonna stand for it." He raised his cane and swung it at the nearest Yankee, but the soldier caught the weapon and jerked it out of Tate's hand. He was about to use the cane on Tate, but Mama and Pop Brady got between them.

The action emboldened the crowd, and they began to protest against the Yankees. Fontaine tried to quiet them down, but they persisted, even when the guards stationed at the front and back of the room raised their weapons. The people were just beginning to work themselves into an angry mob when Elias abandoned his seat, marched to the back of the room, and took hold of Barrymore's son who was sitting on the last row with his caregiver. The onlookers gasped when Elias held a gun to the boy's head.

Heppinstahl cried out and tried to stand, but he got stuck in his chair. He looked to Fontaine, but Fontaine did nothing except to order his men to hold their fire.

Elias ignored them all as he faced Barrymore. "I tried to avoid this, Colonel, because I know what it feels like to lose a son. You don't have to be a good father to feel that. I tried to warn you. Fontaine tried to warn you. Even Heppinstahl tried, but you just wouldn't listen. So now, either you let the girl go, or I'm going to put a bullet in this boy's head."

Raulston Porter leaned toward Elias and said in a strained whisper, "Elias, for heaven's sake, man, what are you doing? Stop this madness!"

When Barrymore made no move to release Alexandra, Elias cocked the pistol.

"No!" Alexandra screamed. "No matter what this boy's father has done, he is innocent. If you kill him, even to save my life, I will never forgive you."

Alexandra and Elias stared at each other for a long time. Neither Garrett nor the townspeople nor the Yankees interfered as she left her place at the front of the room and came and stood before Elias. When she reached for the gun, he let her take it out of his hand. She gave the gun to Fontaine.

As Yankee soldiers descended on Elias and bound him with shackles, Alexandra was taken away to await her judgment.

Chapter 44

Time Cut Short

Luke sulked as Sergeant Minford locked Elias in the cell next to Alexandra's. "You gave up your kingdom for her. I didn't think you had it in you. You wouldn't have given it up for me."

Alexandra sat up on her cot and leaned back against the bars.

"You got five minutes," the sergeant grumbled to Luke as he left the cell block.

"Funny how things turn out." Luke pulled a gold piece out of his pocket and flipped it. "Did anybody ever find out what happened to Johnsey Carroll? They caught him in Huntsville, then the next thing I hear, a riverboat captain says he saw his body floating down the Tennessee. What a disappointment for Lawrence, his son ending up like that. You think he would've disowned him?"

Instead of acknowledging Luke's foolish babble, Elias checked his watch and sat on his cot with his back to Alexandra.

"That's what happens to people who try to do good in this world. Try to help people and they turn on you," Luke glowered as he returned the gold piece to his pocket. "By the way, *Father*, I got assurances from Hanson Rainier that your attorney won't change the will to include her when you're gone." He cut his eyes at Alexandra.

After checking his watch once more, Elias stood and walked over to the cell door. Reaching through the bars, he placed his hands on Luke's shoulders. "While you were consorting with my enemies, did you also think to get assurances that you were ever in the will?" When Luke gave him a surprised expression, Elias grabbed the boy's cravat with his left hand and choked him.

Alexandra sprang to her feet, but she kept silent as Luke sank to his knees, struggling to free himself from Elias' grasp. Luke looked to her, his eyes bulging and begging her to save him. Keeping his hold on Luke, Elias turned his head toward Alexandra. "You're not going to stop me?"

"He's your son. Do what you want with him," she replied.

Elias let him go. "He's not my son."

Luke coughed and rubbed his throat. If he had more to say, he kept it to himself when Sergeant Minford appeared in the doorway and announced, "Your time's been cut short. Colonel Barrymore says no visitors."

Elias waited for Luke to leave before he opened his right hand to reveal the gold piece he had filched from Luke's pocket. He glanced at Alexandra, "You seem inappropriately calm given your sentence."

Alexandra set her jaw. "I had a duty to fulfill, and I fulfilled it the best I could. I've repented of my sins, at least all the ones I could think of, so if this is my Alamo, no sense fussing about it."

"Well, you can stay here and play Davy Crockett all you want, but I'm not playing Travis." Elias hollered for the guard. When Sergeant Minford came, Elias said, "Major Fontaine. Go fetch him. Now."

"But Colonel Barrymore said—"

"Colonel Barrymore's not the law around here." Elias held up the gold piece.

Minford did as he was told.

As Elias waited for Fontaine to arrive, he sat on his cot and pulled a deck of playing cards from his coat pocket. "Poker?" he asked, waving the deck at Alexandra.

She turned her nose up and looked away.

"You don't know how to play poker?"

"Of course not," she snipped.

"Cassino?"

She ignored him.

He sighed and removed a queen from the deck. "Old Maid it is." He dealt the remaining cards and began sorting through his own hand, discarding all the pairs.

He smiled as he held up a pair of queens. "That leaves one unmatchable queen. Since she's obviously not in my hand, she must be in yours."

Alexandra glared at him out of the corner of her eye.

"I know you know how to play Old Maid."

She huffed, "If I play, will you leave me alone?"

Elias paused to consider the odds. "I will leave you alone *if* you win, and it's best out of three. Those are my terms."

"Fine." She reached through the bars and snatched her cards.

They each took a few turns before Elias asked, "How did you make it in the army not knowing any card games?"

"I was only there for a week."

"A week is a long time in camp life."

"Well, I spent half of it fighting with Cana Ramsey and the other half in bed with a fever."

Elias hesitated before he drew a card from her hand. "I didn't know you were ill."

"Would you have cared?" she snorted.

He rearranged his cards and held them out for her to take one. "Me and your mother—it wasn't…It wasn't intended as a betrayal of Jonas."

"How could you think of it as anything else?"

"Listen, everything you've done over the past week you did for Marlbridge, didn't you?"

"Yes."

"Did you intend for those Yankees to die?"

"No."

"Did you intend for Cass to die?"

"No!" She threw the cards at him. "He was my brother! How could you even say that?"

Elias gathered her cards and handed them back to her then proceeded with his confession. "I've never met a man who wanted to be a father more than Jonas did. When you and your brother were born, he thought it was God answering his prayers, but it wasn't God; it was just Laura Catherine doing what Laura Catherine always does when she's determined to get her way. I refused her the first time she told me what she wanted me to do 'for Jonas.' The second time, it was after the

Founders' Ball, and I'd had too much to drink and she…" Elias closed his eyes for a second. "She looked so much like Charlotte that night. Which, of course, is exactly what she intended." He reached through the bars and picked a card when Alexandra extended her hand.

She sat quietly for a moment before she reached to take a card from Elias. "How could she? How could she do that to my—to her husband?"

"Well, if she hadn't, you wouldn't be here."

"But Jonas Corbin would."

Elias shrugged. "Maybe, but who's to say he wouldn't have died the next week from some other cause."

"Is that how you live with the guilt? Thinking they might have died anyway from some other cause?"

Elias looked at her. Her questions weren't accusations—she really needed to know. So, he gave her the best advice he had at the moment. "Don't spend the future trying to bury the past."

She didn't respond right away. Instead, she pulled her knees to her chest and rested her chin on her kneecaps. "Still, it would have been better for everyone if Cass and I had never been born, wouldn't it?" She turned her head to look at him.

He rearranged the last two cards in his hand. "Jonas wouldn't see it that way."

She drew a card. "But you see it that way."

Elias held Alexandra's wrist for a moment before he reached for a card. "I didn't say that."

He ran his finger along the top of Alexandra's two cards. The faint crease in the corner of one of the cards was invisible to most people, but Elias could feel it. He took the queen out of her hand and let go of her wrist.

Alexandra narrowed her eyes. "You knew the whole time which card was the Old Maid."

"And now, so do you." He held out the two cards. "Take the jack because if you don't, this game will never end."

Just as Alexandra was about to choose, the door to the cell block opened and Major Fontaine entered, alone. "What do you want, Elias?" the major groaned impatiently.

"My apologies for the theatrics in the courtroom earlier, but I needed to deliver a message."

"And you thought getting yourself thrown in jail would be the best way to achieve that purpose?"

"If that were my only purpose, no, I admit it was a terrible idea, but, all things considered, getting myself thrown in jail was my best play." Laying the queen and the jack face-up on his cot, Elias stood and retrieved a blood-stained letter from the pocket of his waistcoat. He sauntered to the cell door and held the letter out to Fontaine.

Fontaine reached for the letter, but when he saw the design of the broken seal he jerked his hand back. "I wasn't aware that you worked for the Council."

"I don't. Well, not all the time, but I find it's in my best interests to keep apprised of their operations. Let me guess. You and Ramsey were hoping young Belgrave would go to his father and the general would send his army to force Barrymore out of Marlbridge, except there's one major flaw in that plan." Elias tapped the corner of the letter against the cell bars. "Apparently there was a coup within the Council. General Belgrave is dead."

The blood drained from Fontaine's face as he snatched the letter and scanned it. "I had nothing to do with this."

"You and I both know who did."

Fontaine closed his eyes and dropped his head. "I should have seen it coming." After a short bout of profanity, he settled his gaze on Elias. "Did Ramsey know?"

"It doesn't matter if he knew or not. If the Council suspects that he knew, he's as good as dead."

Alexandra jumped up and came over to the bars that separated her from Fontaine. "Not if he stays away. Major Fontaine, please, if Cana is still alive, please find him and tell him he has to stay away. I don't know anything about whatever Council y'all are talking about, but you know that Cana is my husband, and I don't want anything to happen to him."

"Husband!" Elias exclaimed. "Since when?"

"Yesterday, evidently," Fontaine answered for her as he showed Elias the Bible Alexandra had given him.

Alexandra took it from him. "I asked you to give it to Cana."

"I couldn't. He's…" Fontaine bit his lips and took a deep breath to fortify his nerves. "I don't know where he is."

Elias stiffened in alarm. "What do you mean you don't know where he is? Is he not at Storm Chase?"

"The Rebels left Storm Chase." Fontaine directed his report at Elias. "At first, I assumed they had gone to Bridgeport to reinforce Danville Leadbetter, but Virgil Doggett showed up at headquarters right after the trial and said that a group of Confederates about the size of Ramsey's force attacked the rail bridge at Paint Rock River." Fontaine glanced at Alexandra then quickly looked away. "According to Virgil, Ramsey was killed during the assault."

"No," Alexandra declared. "Virgil is wrong just like he was wrong before about Cass. Or he's lying. Cana is not dead. That's not how this is going to end. I know I'll probably die in the morning, but not Cana Ramsey. He can't."

"I'm sorry," Fontaine said quietly. "Truly, I'm sorry. I considered him my friend."

Elias picked up the jack of spades and flipped it over in his hand. "Well, Alexandra, I guess you're on your own, then."

Alexandra reached through the bars and clutched Elias' forearm. "I know he isn't coming for me, but I also know he isn't dead. Promise me you'll find him and tell him…" Tears began to pool in her eyes. "I never told Jonas that I loved him, but he knew that I did. I don't think Cana knows that I love him. Please, will you tell him?"

Elias stared at her for a moment. "He killed Jonas."

"I know."

"And you forgive him?"

"Elias, I'm going to die tomorrow. I don't have a say in that, but I do have a say in how I spend the time I've got left. I have loved Cana Ramsey since I was eight years old, and I'll be damned if I'm going to sit here and let anger over something that can't be undone take that love away from me. That's mine. The enemy can take my town, my life, and everything else, but *that* he will never take from me. So, no more lies, no more games, all I want from you is one promise. I've spent all this time trying to set right what other people did wrong, and in do-ing all that, I didn't tell Cana that I love him. Now, I have no hope of setting that right, so I need you to do it for me. Promise me you'll tell him. If I've ever meant anything to you, promise me. Father, please."

Stunned, Elias was powerless to stop the single tear that escaped. Nor did he dare move his hand to brush it away for fear she would let go of his arm. He had loved like that once, and no one had taken it from him—he had buried it. The way Alexandra was looking up at him, with that face that favored Laura Catherine but reminded him of Charlotte, he knew he couldn't part with her, but neither could he allow the love he had buried to resurrect now when all his plans were so close to fruition.

He pulled away from Alexandra. Reaching into his coat pocket, he retrieved the land deal documents and handed them to Fontaine. "Get me out of here. I don't care what you have to do—use these to force Heppinstahl's hand—but get me out of here."

Chapter 45

The Gallows

April 29

ALEXANDRA had tried not to let herself hope that someone would rescue her, but her heart still sank when dawn broke, and no one had come for her. Hanson Rainier would have forbidden Garrett to do more than he had already done. Her mother would be too ashamed to show her face. Elias had abandoned her. And Ramsey.... If he wasn't dead, he had a war to fight, and she could no longer fight beside him. It would be foolish for him to give up fighting the enemy to get himself killed trying to save her when it was probably too late for that anyway.

When the door to the cell block opened, it was Barrymore himself who came to escort her to her death. He even offered her his arm, and she almost took it out of habit, but she jerked her hand away.

"I have never executed a woman before," he explained, "so I do not know the proper procedure for escorting a murderess to the gallows."

"I'm not a murderess."

"Whether or not you killed Belgrave or anyone else is irrelevant, for I know that you are a murderess. You would murder me if you were given the chance, would you not?"

Alexandra honestly didn't know whether she would or not, but then she remembered that she had been sorely tempted to murder Prichard Benefield in his sleep. Maybe Barrymore had been right all along. Maybe she was a murderess, in her heart at least, but she would not give in to the man who murdered her brother. "Cass was no murderer."

"Perhaps not, but every so often the shedding of innocent blood is required to purge the people of their sins. 'Almost all things are by the law purged with blood; and without the shedding of blood there is no remission of sins.'"

"You accuse me of violating God's law while you yourself are in violation of it. God's law requires two witnesses, and you have none against me."

Barrymore turned and looked at her as if he was shocked that she had even a shred of Bible knowledge. "The blood of the slain cries out against you."

"Then I will rest in the knowledge that my blood and my brother's blood will cry out against you."

As Alexandra walked to the gallows, she refused to look at the crowd. If any of them were willing and able to help her, they would have done so by now. She wouldn't let herself blame them—most of them were either too old, too fat, or too genteel to present any serious opposition to the enemy.

Old Joe, a deranged veteran of the War of 1812, met her at the foot of the gallows. He didn't say anything, just smiled at her with that lopsided smile that reminded her of Quinn. Joe nodded and patted her arm as if she was going to the creek to be baptized.

Alexandra mounted the steps. Reverend Land was at the top, waiting for her. When she reached him, he bowed his head and said a prayer before he spoke directly to Alexandra. "Forgive me, child. I fear I did not prepare you for this."

"It's all right, Reverend. You didn't know any better than I did."

With a heavy spirit, Alexandra stepped past Reverend Land and stood where Mort Grimshaw, the county hangman directed her. When she looked into the hangman's haggard face, she tried to put on a smile. "It's all right, Mort. I know you have to do your job."

Mort patted her shoulder. "I remember how you used to come in the sheriff's office and you'd come over to my cell and listen to me tell stories." He shook his head. "Sheriff Corbin woulda never let it come to this. He woulda—"

"Proceed!" Barrymore yelled at Mort.

As Mort tied her hands behind her back and slipped the noose around her neck, Alexandra kept her eyes on the boards beneath her feet until several Yankee soldiers started hollering and running toward the opposite end of town. Alexandra looked up to see a white horse with black mane and tail standing at the end of the street. It was evident by the way Ramsey sat his horse that he was wounded.

Fontaine got to him first. Otherwise, Ramsey would have been forced to dismount by the gaggle of Yankees who were running toward him. Fontaine and Ramsey spoke for a moment, then Fontaine reluctantly waved his arm and his men parted the way, making room for Ramsey to ride up to the gallows. No one made a sound.

It wasn't until Ramsey dismounted that Alexandra saw that he was unarmed except for his Colt. The blood from the wound above his right eye had dried, leaving a dark red streak down the side of his face. He handed the gun to Fontaine then limped to the steps. Alexandra winced at the pain on his face as he climbed to the top of the gallows where Reverend Land was waiting. After the reverend helped Ramsey with the last two steps, he moved to the back of the platform.

Mort turned to Barrymore for instructions. When Barrymore ordered him to carry on, he tossed a second rope over the beam and tied the loose end on the rail at the back of the platform as he had done with Alexandra's rope.

"Cana, what are you doing? No, you can't do this," Alexandra protested as Ramsey took his place beside her.

He whispered in her ear, "We aren't gonna die today."

Her eyes went wide. "How do you figure that?" she whispered back.

"Because I have a plan."

"Red isn't coming."

"I know. That's why I have another plan."

"Well, it doesn't look like your plan is working," she remarked as Mort bound Ramsey's wrists and secured a noose around his neck. With an exasperated sigh, she asked, "What do you want me to do?"

"What do you mean?"

"You said you have a plan, so what do you want me to do?"

With Mort standing by the lever and Reverend Land standing

along the back rail, Ramsey leaned toward Alexandra as far as the rope would allow and rested his forehead against hers. "All you have to do, Alexandra Ramsey, is trust me."

Mort sniffed as he dabbed at his eyes with a dirty handkerchief. "Say your last words if you got 'em."

Alexandra looked into Ramsey's eyes. There was so much she wanted to say, but she had no words for any of it except: "I trust you" and "Does Jane marry Rochester?"

Ramsey chuckled and looked up to heaven. "After a long and painful separation, Rochester marries Jane." Then, with no regard for the rope cutting into his neck, he kissed her.

Seconds later, a trumpet blast reached Alexandra's ears. Ramsey's lips pulled away from hers. With her eyes still closed, Alexandra heard Mort pull the trap door. She began to fall, and she kept falling for what seemed like a long time until she landed on her back and hit her head on the ground.

At first, she thought she must be dead. She kept her eyes closed, struggling to recall everything that Reverend Land had said about heaven. He hadn't said anything about a trumpet. She began to panic when she heard a loud explosion and screaming. None of it sounded like heaven. Then, she smelled smoke.

"No!" she yelped. Someone was grabbing at her. She tried to roll away, but her attacker pinned her down and reached for her neck.

"Alexandra! Stop! Woman, are you gonna fight me to the very end?"

Alexandra opened her eyes when she heard Ramsey's voice. They were lying on the ground underneath the gallows. He was on top of her trying to free her from the noose. She stopped fighting him. "We're not dead?"

A familiar voice called down to her from the hole in the gallows floor, "Are you all right, Miss Alexandra?"

"Mort! What did y'all do?" Alexandra gasped as Mort and Reverend Land peered down at her.

Mort grinned and tossed the loose ends of both ropes down the hole. "Looks like I didn't tie y'all off so well. Reckon I'll lose my job after this."

"I told you I had a plan," Ramsey said as he dragged her out from under the gallows. People were running in all directions as Confederate soldiers poured into Marlbridge driving a herd of horses in front of them. One of the horses veered into the courtyard, close enough for Alexandra to spot the U.S. brand on its rump. The stampede tore through the town while artillery shells blasted the Union camp that was at the far end of town, the direction from which the Confederates had come. Alexandra caught her breath when she saw Captain Stark. She was about to ask Ramsey how he had freed the Confederate prisoners when he jerked away from all the chaos and led her to the back of the courthouse where Fontaine was waiting for them with Ramsey's gun and two horses.

Fontaine handed the gun to Ramsey and turned to help Alexandra mount. She grabbed his hand. "What about Barrymore? He'll kill you if he finds out you helped us."

Fontaine secured her foot in the stirrup. "Not if someone else gets to him first. Now, go."

Ramsey slipped the Colt into its holster, but before he mounted, Fontaine extended his hand. "Godspeed, Cana."

Instead of taking Fontaine's hand, Ramsey embraced him. "I don't want to see you until the war's over."

Fontaine returned Ramsey's embrace. "Agreed." With a curt nod, the two friends parted.

Ramsey mounted his horse, and Alexandra followed him to Storm Chase.

Chapter 46

Devil Take the House

Ramsey and Alexandra didn't slow their horses until they reached the gate to Storm Chase. As they walked the horses up the drive, neither of them spoke. About halfway up the drive, Ramsey reined in his horse and waited for Alexandra to come up beside him. "I was so intent on getting away, I forgot to ask if you were all right. You didn't act like you broke anything when you fell from the gallows, but I still should've asked."

Alexandra looked away. "I'm fine."

"What about your head? You hit the ground pretty hard."

She kept silent.

He leaned over to touch the back of her head. "Alexandra, I know it hurts."

Her head was aching terribly, but she wasn't about to admit it to Ramsey. She pushed his hand away. "When I said 'I'm fine,' I meant 'I'm fine,' " she snapped.

Ramsey didn't say another word as they continued the rest of the way.

When they reached the house, Alexandra dismounted and ran over to the porch where Lellen and Clarence were waiting for her. Tears filled her eyes when Clarence handed her a sack containing her uniform and her boots. "Clarence, I'm sorry for the way I acted when I left."

"Ain't no need to speak of it, Miss Alexandra. I'm jest glad you safe." He glanced at Ramsey, but didn't voice the uncertainty in his expression.

Lellen handed her a small sack of treats. "Matthew sent these for the horse. And this," she announced as she reached into her basket and pulled out a book, "is from Mr. Wilson. He and your mama gonna join you in Chattanooga soon, but he thought you might be wantin' to finish it."

Alexandra put the sacks on the porch then took the book from Lellen and held it against her chest. *Jane Eyre.* "Thank you, Lellen."

With a curt nod, Lellen pursed her lips and brushed away a tear. "You be good, and don't you be givin' Mr. Ramsey any trouble, now. I raised you to be a lady no matter what you're wearin'."

Alexandra put the book in the sack with her uniform and turned back to Lellen. "How's Mama?"

"You'll have to forgive Miss Laura Catherine, child. She's all tore up about Cass and you and everything that's happened. Been so out of her mind, Mr. Wilson was scared to leave her, so me and Clarence came instead."

Alexandra bit her lips. "I know I've been a great disappointment, and I didn't expect her to show her face today."

Before Lellen responded, a buggy drove up to the house. Lellen and Alexandra looked at each other in surprise as Wilson waved from the back seat. "Alexandra! Wait! Don't run off with Captain Ramsey just yet. There is more that needs to be said."

Lellen eyed Alexandra. "You be kind to your mama." Alexandra nodded, and the two women clasped hands.

When Lellen and Clarence began the long walk back to the Corbin farm, Alexandra approached the buggy and peeked in to see her mother sitting next to Wilson.

Laura Catherine didn't raise her dark veil, and despite a little hoarseness, her voice was prim as ever. "Alexandra, your stepfather and I decided it wouldn't be proper to send you away without at least some kind of farewell."

"Laura Catherine," Wilson warned, "we discussed this. We agreed there is more to be said."

When her mother didn't say more, Alexandra spoke up. "Mama, I'm sorry. I didn't mean for any of this to happen."

"Of course, you didn't. No one ever does." Laura Catherine tightened her grip on the handkerchief in her lap. "I spoke with Elias. He informed me that you know the truth."

"Yes."

"Well, it is some consolation that I won't have very far to fall since you never thought very highly of me to begin with."

Alexandra reached into the buggy and put her calloused hand on top of Laura Catherine's black-gloved hand. "That's not true. I've always thought you were the finest lady in the world. The reason I never tried to live up to your image is because I knew I would have failed. I've learned my lesson about living up to an image of myself instead of just *being* myself. I wish you could do the same."

Laura Catherine cleared her throat and sniffed softly as she lifted her veil and examined her daughter's face. "Anyone can see that your willfulness comes from me—I can't deny it—and your eyes are your father's, but you are also surprisingly gracious. I hadn't noticed that before, and I have no idea where it comes from."

Neither did Alexandra, but she was shocked to discover that it took so little to have the beginnings of the first civil conversation she'd had with her mother in years, perhaps ever. She showed her mother the record of marriage. "I did what you said. I married Cana Ramsey."

Laura Catherine let out a tired sigh. "Oh, Alexandra, out of all the times I told you to do something and hoped against hope that you would do it, you pick the one time I wish you hadn't done what I said." She handed the Bible back to her daughter. "Do you love him?"

"Yes."

Laura Catherine folded her handkerchief in her lap and smoothed out the wrinkles. "In that case, I will not do to you what my mother did to me when I married Jonas. You will always be my daughter, and whether you believe me or not, I will always love you. In my own way, yes, but it is love nonetheless. I hope one day you will understand."

Alexandra reached up and pulled the veil down to cover Laura Catherine's face. "I love you, too, Mama."

"Yes, well," Laura Catherine stammered as she looked out across the yard. "Where is that Ramsey boy, anyway?"

Alexandra scanned the yard, but Ramsey wasn't in sight. "I don't know. He was just here." She started to panic. He had saved her life, and she hadn't been very kind about it. She had been so angry that he hadn't told her his rescue plan ahead of time, that she hadn't even thanked him for carrying it out. He had every right not to want anything to do with an ungrateful brat.

Evidently noticing Alexandra's distress, Laura Catherine chirped, "Don't worry, Alexandra. He hasn't left the premises. Isn't that his horse?" She pointed to the horse Fontaine had supplied.

"No, but Major Fontaine said he would have Shadow and Solomon brought here."

"Then you have nothing to worry about. One thing you need to learn: a Ramsey might leave his wife, but a Ramsey will never leave his horse." She turned to Wilson. "Time to go, dear. We have said enough."

Wilson gave Alexandra an encouraging smile and slapped the reins. The buggy lurched forward, and the moment Wilson and Laura Catherine were out of sight, Alexandra darted into the house. She searched every room on the main floor, whispering Ramsey's name as if she was afraid to disturb any spirits that might be lurking. Finally, she crept upstairs and found Ramsey in one of the bedrooms. He was retrieving a leather pouch from a hole in the floor. "Is that the gold from the train?" Alexandra asked as Ramsey replaced the loose floorboard and slipped the pouch in his pocket.

"No."

"What is it?"

Ramsey tilted his head back to look at the ceiling. "Alexandra, my head hurts, my neck hurts, my whole body hurts. Please, no more questions."

After several moments of silence, Ramsey gave Alexandra a suspicious look. "Aren't you going to ask me a question?"

"You said no more questions," she replied, using her small voice.

"I know what I said, but I'm shocked you actually heard me say it."

Alexandra frowned. "I always hear you. How could I not hear you? You bark at me all the time when it's something you want me to do, but then, when I really need you to speak to me, you say nothing. You let me sit alone in a jail cell believing that no one was going to come for me, that no one was even going to try. At first, I thought Elias had tried, but that scene in the courtroom was just another one of his ploys. Truthfully, I didn't expect anyone to come, not even you. I wouldn't let myself be so selfish as to wish you would risk your life to save mine when your country needed you. Saving me wouldn't help the Cause at all, but how could you plan to come all along, and then let me believe that you weren't coming?"

Ramsey's eyes never left her face. "When we were up there on that gallows, you said you trusted me. Is that true?"

"Yes."

"You weren't just saying it because you thought that's what I wanted you to say?"

"Why would I do that? That would be assuming I know what you want, and I never know what you want because you never tell me anything. You just scowl and bark at me all the time."

A flicker of amusement touched his eyes. "You said that part already."

Alexandra stared at the floor.

"Why did you think I was going to let you hang?"

She jerked her head up, astounded that he evidently didn't realize what he had done. "Because you sent me away."

Startled by the revelation, Ramsey took a half-step back. "When did I do that?"

Incredulous that he evidently didn't know the answer to that either, Alexandra stormed, "Yesterday, at Storm Chase! You think I don't know how Elias just happened to be there before the battle? You arranged it. You were going to send me to Chattanooga with Elias—the last place I wanted to go and the last person I wanted to go with."

This time it was Ramsey who stared at the floor. "I arranged for you to go to Chattanooga with your father because I thought I was going to die."

"What?" She caught her breath. "Because of the bear dream?"

"No, because of the whirlwind."

Ramsey kept his head down, so Alexandra tilted her head to look into his eyes. *Ashamed and haunted.* "Does the whirlwind ever actually hurt you?"

He looked up at her. "No, it destroys the house then goes away. I guess I've just always thought one of these days it's all gonna finally catch up to me."

Alexandra took Ramsey's hand and ordered him to follow her. She led him downstairs and made him stand in front of the fragments of wood and plaster that was once the parlor. It made no difference whether it was a whirlwind or an artillery barrage—the damage was the same. While Ramsey stood there, Alexandra picked up the portrait of Cranston that had been lying on the floor since she had taken it down from the wall the night Cass died. She offered the portrait and its broken frame to her husband. "Cana Ramsey, I don't think the whirlwind was coming for you."

Ramsey searched his wife's face, hoping that what she said was true. Seeing no doubt in her eyes, he took the portrait, carried it across the demolished parlor, and placed it on the mantel of the fireplace that was still standing.

Leaving Cranston's image to oversee the ruin, Ramsey followed Alexandra to the front door. When she opened it, she screamed and jumped back, crashing into Ramsey's chest.

Joab Barrymore was standing in the doorway, armed with a Colt Navy, his face ashen and his gray eyes clouded with pain. The blood dripping from his side had already begun to pool on the floor.

Ramsey grabbed Alexandra and pulled her behind him. They backed away as Barrymore stumbled into the foyer. "What can I do for you, Professor?" Ramsey asked, struggling to keep his voice calm.

"So, this is the house that Cranston Ramsey built." Gripping the banister to steady himself, Barrymore surveyed the foyer and what was left of the parlor. "I've never met the man, only heard the stories. What sort of man is he really?"

"Dead," Ramsey replied.

"Is he? My research into the Council left me with more questions than answers, so if you say Cranston is dead, I shall have to take your word for it. I shall include this new information in my notes nevertheless."

Barrymore glanced at Cranston's portrait and turned to Alexandra. "I know how you survived your own hanging, but how did you survive the death of your brother?"

Alexandra looked to Ramsey. When he gave her a slight nod and squeezed her hand, she answered, "I survived because I had to. I had a job to do."

"And now that you have fulfilled your purpose?" Barrymore asked.

"As long as I'm still living, won't I always have a purpose?"

Barrymore cocked his head as he considered her question. "Yes, I suppose that is true." He turned to Ramsey. "Have you a library?"

Ramsey nodded his head toward the library door.

"Excellent. Every home should have a library regardless of class or taste."

When Barrymore waved his gun at them, Ramsey gripped Alexandra's hand and led her into the library.

"Has blood been spilled in this room?" Barrymore asked as he sniffed the air then looked down at the floor.

"My father died here," Alexandra replied, glancing at Ramsey. "Both of our fathers died here."

"Jonas Corbin and Miles Ramsey, yes, I remember reading about that." He looked around the room. "It's a good place to die."

"Not today," a voice answered from the doorway.

Alexandra and Ramsey turned to see Garrett Rainier standing there with a pocket revolver.

Barrymore shuffled through the books on the bookshelf. "If you intend to finish me off, Mr. Rainier, I advise that you do not hesitate. I heard about the dog. It's quite a popular story around Marlbridge, which is overrun with gossips, I might add—an absolute infestation. Under other circumstances, I would be happy to assist you should you wish to rectify the situation at some point in the future, Mr. Rainier." He pulled a cigar from his pocket. "Might I trouble you for a light, Mr. Ramsey?"

Ramsey stepped to the fireplace and struck a match from the tinderbox and held it for Barrymore to light the cigar.

"You tried to have me killed, Mr. Ramsey. Do you deny it?"

"No, sir."

"A rabid dog, you said."

Ramsey shifted his gaze to Garrett who shrugged and shook his head.

"Is that what I've become in your eyes?" Barrymore looked as if he was genuinely surprised.

"Professor, I was wrong to ask Mr. Rainier to put you down, but the way I see it, Joab Barrymore, the kind-hearted man I knew as my history professor, died in that fire with his family."

Barrymore studied Ramsey for a moment, then looked up at the crown molding. "Does this house mean anything to you, Mr. Ramsey?"

"Only as a memorial to the dead."

"Yes, there's too much blood, I think, for it to continue in its purpose as a dwelling place for the living." Barrymore took the desk lamp and poured the oil out onto the desk. "Shall I burn it for you?"

Garrett raised his revolver, but Ramsey held out his hand for Garrett to wait. "Professor Barrymore, you are wounded, sir. Do you not want me to send for a doctor?"

"No, that won't be necessary. Perhaps you and your wife and Mr. Rainier should go now. I have work to do."

"Yes, sir." Ramsey slowly pulled Alexandra into the foyer, leaving Barrymore alone in the library.

Garrett was close on their heels. "Ramsey, what are you doing? The man is crazy. Are you really going to let him burn your house?"

Ramsey seized Garrett by his shirtfront. "Devil take the house. If that's the price I have to pay to get us out of here alive, it's a bargain."

Garrett made no more objections as he followed Ramsey and Alexandra out into the yard.

After securing Alexandra's belongings and leading the horses away from the house, Ramsey turned to his wife and clasped her face. "Are you all right?" When she nodded, he pulled her to him and held on to her as Storm Chase burned.

Alexandra buried her face in Ramsey's chest. His shirt smelled of blood, sweat, and smoke, but she had never felt more at peace in her life. Through no design on her part or Ramsey's, the Father had set things right. She rested there for a while until she heard the sound of horses. She raised her head to see Elias riding into the yard at a fast gallop, bringing Shadow and Solomon with him. He jerked his horse to a stop in front of the burning house. He stayed in the saddle to watch the smoke and flames shooting through the broken windows.

After a moment of stunned silence, he began to laugh. "Whose idea was that?"

"Barrymore," Garrett growled.

The amusement vanished from Elias' face. "I thought you killed him. Where is he?"

Garrett waved his arm toward the house. "I imagine he is dead by now."

"Who set the house on fire?"

"I already told you!" Garrett exploded. "Barrymore did it. When I got here he was in the library holding Alexandra and Ramsey at gunpoint. I was going to kill him, but Ramsey would not let me."

Elias looked at Ramsey and Alexandra before he directed his attention back to Garrett. "Rainier, do you mean to tell me that you chased Barrymore all the way out here for the express purpose of killing him, but *Ramsey* stopped you, and the man I sent you to kill ended up killing himself by burning Cranston Ramsey's house to the ground?"

Garrett scowled at him. "That is exactly what happened."

Elias chortled, "Well, this day just keeps getting better and better. I don't think even I could have planned a more perfect day." He dismounted and sauntered over to where Alexandra and Ramsey were standing. "Are you all right, girl?"

Alexandra slapped him. "You left me."

Elias stared at her in disbelief. "If you're upset because I didn't attend your hanging, I want you to know the reason I wasn't there was because somebody had to get your horse back from the Yankees after you ran out onto the battlefield and threw your life away for no good reason! On top of that, it just so happened to be the very same horse that you stole from me!" He reached into his pocket, yanked out a bill of sale, and slapped it into her hand.

"I wouldn't have had to steal him if you hadn't stolen him first!" Alexandra thundered back.

She lunged at Elias, but Ramsey caught the back of her dress collar and held her back. "That's enough," he ordered them both.

Elias took a deep breath. "Alexandra, I didn't steal your horse. I bought the horse and kept him in my stable so the Yankees wouldn't commandeer him. And, I hoped it would keep you out of trouble.

What I hadn't planned for was *him*." Elias glowered at Ramsey. After taking another moment to compose himself, he put his hands on Alexandra's shoulders. "You have made my life hell for the past week. But Jonas would have been proud of you. You're my daughter, but you're his likeness." He cleared his throat and stepped back. "Now, go get on your horse."

Alexandra chewed her lips. She knew the words were gonna leave a bad taste in her mouth, but she said them anyway. "Yes, sir."

When she marched off, Elias addressed Ramsey. "Have you noticed that when she says 'yes, sir' it sounds more like 'go to hell?'"

Ramsey grinned. "I have noticed."

Elias faced Ramsey. No poker face, just truth. "If you hurt her, I'll kill you."

"It's what Jonas would expect you to do." Ramsey extended his hand.

Elias shook Ramsey's hand then gave him the same letter he had shown Fontaine. "I thought you should know."

After he saw the broken seal, he tucked the letter in his pocket without opening it.

"You're not going to read it?"

"I don't have to. I know what's coming."

As Alexandra and Ramsey rode away, Elias felt a surprising twinge of sadness. The girl Jonas Corbin raised was leaving him, the house where his best friend drew his last breath was burning, and the man who saved his life and his daughter's life was about to lose his own at the hands of the Council, but there was nothing he could do to stop any of it.

All of the plans he had made over the past decade had been for the purpose of making good on his promise to Jonas and to himself that he would do his best to keep the girl out of harm's way. Her brother, too, but he had failed on both counts. His one hope was that maybe Cana Ramsey would have a better go of it, and if he didn't, at least he wouldn't let the girl die alone. The man had proven that much.

When Garrett mounted his horse and turned to leave, Elias drawled, "I underestimated you, Rainier."

"Not as badly as you underestimated Ramsey."

"True," Elias acknowledged as he took the reins of his own steed. "But who knows, Rainier, you might end up with the girl, yet. If my informant is right, Alexandra will be a widow before the end of the summer."

Garrett groaned. "Will the bloodshed never end?"

"Not in our lifetime."

Garrett shook his head. "After all I have seen, I am beginning to think I backed the wrong horse. The Union might turn out to be more wicked than the Confederacy."

Elias mounted his horse and gave his last cigar to Garrett. "Union, Confederacy, Patriot, Loyalist, it doesn't matter. At some point, it's all gonna go to the Devil anyway, at least for a time. Until then, we might as well hang on to our little piece of it for as long as we can."

THE END

AUTHOR'S NOTES AND ACKNOWLEDGMENTS

To be American is not…a matter of blood;
it is a matter of an idea—and history is the image of that idea.
—Robert Penn Warren

Dear Reader,

Thank you for taking a chance on this book. Whatever your reasons for doing so, I hope you were not disappointed.

The making of a book is too big a job for one person. Even if I had somehow managed the formatting, cover design, editing, etc. all by myself, I still cannot take credit as the sole creative intelligence that brought this book into existence.

First of all, I am fortunate that YHWH[1] has provided me with parents who believe in me and have been my benefactors for the six years that it took to get this story into its current form. To write down all of the ways in which Phil and Charlene Bain have helped me would fill another book, so, putting aside all self-interest, I feel at liberty to shamelessly implore you, the reader, that if you liked this book, go tell everyone you know to buy it so that Phil and Charlene will get a good return on their investment.

I want to thank my sister, Emily, and her husband, Rob, for all the free meals, for tolerating my diatribes on sundry subjects, and for bringing my little nephew, Levi, into the world. I would also like to thank my sister in Christ, Adrith, a true prayer warrior, armor bearer, and mother to my nephew in Christ, Charles.

There are hosts of friends and family members who have participated in the making of this book, everything from offering prayers and encouragement especially Uncle Crandall and Aunt Holley; Uncle David and Aunt Debbie, to listening to me blame everything on writer's block, to providing me a free place to stay and a change of scenery (especially Aunt Karen and Uncle Billy; Aunt Tammy and Uncle Vic). A special thank you goes to my grandparents—Jerrone and Catherine

---

1   the Latin letters of God's name in the Hebrew Bible, replaced with LORD in most English translations.

Kennedy and L.W. and Jean Bain—for all the support they have given me over the years, the piano recitals, the graduations, the ballgames, so many events.

As for those individuals who directly participated in the publishing process, I want to thank my publisher, Randy Young of Sleepy Town Press for his devotion to quality and craftsmanship; Mark Mijares for his excellent cover design; Jon Hout, for his assistance with the website; Sue Lester, for her thorough notes and words of encouragement; Joe Megill, for his sharp eye and in-depth critique; Gillette Elvgren and Dennis Bounds, for pushing me to keep writing and rewriting; and my beta readers for their valuable input and time: Tammy McCarn, Paula Austin, Lauren Davis, Christy Sharp, James E. Albright, and the members of the Jacksonville Alabama Writers Group.

Like the people who came together to participate in the making of this book, *The Girl I Left Behind* is a melting pot of sorts—a patchwork comprised of snippets from some of my favorite films, television shows, books, and moments and stories shared with friends and family. I have relied upon YHWH, the Creator of all things, to help me decide which pieces to include and which to set aside for later, how the pieces should be arranged, and to what end.

Regarding the purpose of the book, *The Girl I Left Behind* is not history. While I consider myself a student of history and have taught history at the collegiate level, I do not consider myself an expert on any particular topic or time period. In conducting research for this book, I benefited from the works of many historians and storytellers whose scholarly and literary achievements extend far beyond my own, so I have included a bibliography at the end of the book for anyone interested in further research.[2] One resource that I highly recommend as a scholarly work on Union occupation of North Alabama during the Civil War is Joseph W. Danielson's book, *War's Desolating Scourge: The Union's Occupation of North Alabama*. Another academic source that I found to be an excellent study on female soldiers during the Civil War is *They Fought Like Demons* by DeAnne Blanton and Lauren M. Cook. In addition to these written resources, I have been fortunate to learn from

---

2   Any errors found in *The Girl I Left Behind* should be attributed to the author alone, not to the author's sources of information.

the armies of reenactors, sutlers, historical interpreters, and park rangers who have devoted countless hours and resources to "keeping history alive" at battlefields, forts, state and national parks, and museums.

Furthermore, this story is not a scholarly analysis of the South or of the character of its people—white or black, free or slave, male or female, rich or poor, Unionist or secessionist, or any other dichotomies into which we tend to rope people off and separate them from each other. Nor do I feel it necessary to represent every side of the story, or rather, every attitude that human beings living in the South at the outbreak of the Civil War had about secession, slavery, God, and guns. Suffice it to say that we Southerners are not, and never have been, monolithic in our opinions on a vast number of issues. And not everyone who wore Yankee blue was actually a Yankee (i.e. a Northerner). Thousands of Southerners fought for the Union, and in Winston County, Alabama, Union sentiment was so strong that the citizens of that county proposed the idea that if states had the right to secede from the Union then Winston County had the right to secede from the State of Alabama.

However, one thing that all Southerners generally have in common whether we are of English, African, Native, Scottish, Jewish or any other ancestry is that we do not like to be told what to do—not by George III, not by the federal government in Washington, and not by God. The difference between our struggle with God and our struggle with the federal government is that while we have wrestled with God, we also know, whether we admit it or not, that in the end YHWH will set things right. The federal government's success is less certain as the federal government is not the Almighty, and there is nothing that the rulers of this world can do to make it so.

Putting aside my abbreviated rant against human monarchs and institutions who overstep their boundaries, I do want to clarify that the attitudes and opinions of the characters in this fictional story are not necessarily my own. I am not of the opinion that the Confederacy was any more or less wicked than the Federal Republic housed in Washington, D.C.; therefore, I cannot say that I wish the South had won the war. I am, however, of the opinion that human beings are fallible, inconsistent, and often downright selfish regardless of the nature of the political body into which they organize themselves. For this reason, I feel it necessary to point out that while the institution of slavery as it was practiced in the South was wrong on multiple levels, the debt slavery perpetrated by elites on both sides of the Mason-Dixon is wrong on just as many levels, then and now.[3]

Which brings me to "the Council." While there were real secret societies in operation before and after the war, organizations such as the Knights of the Golden Circle, the Council referenced in *The Girl I Left Behind* is a purely fictional secret society. Intended as a plot device that will play a larger role in the second book of the series, the Council should not be taken as a scholarly representation of any particular society that may exist in the real world.[4]

Thank you for taking the time to read these last few pages. "The conclusion, when all has been heard, is: Fear God and keep His commandments, because this applies to every person. For God will bring every act to judgment, everything which is hidden, whether it is good or evil."[5]

---

3   For a scholarly examination of monetary policy gone awry, see Timothy James Barnett's *America's False Recovery*.

4   For further investigation into secret societies and other "fringe" topics, please go to my website where I have compiled a list of helpful resources. www.StephanieBain.com

5   Ecclesiastes 12:13-14

Bibliography

Bain, Stephanie. "To Be One of the Boys: Women Soldiers in the Civil War." M.A. Historiographical essay. University of Alabama, 2003. Print.

Barrett, Jenny. *Shooting the Civil War: Cinema, History and American National Identity.* New York: I. B. Tauris, 2009.

Blanton, Deanne and Lauren M. Cook. *They Fought Like Demons: Women Soldiers in the Civil War.* New York: Vintage Books, 2002.

Danielson, Joseph W. *War's Desolating Scourge: The Union's Occupation of North Alabama.* Lawrence, Kansas: University Press of Kansas, 2012.

Elley, Derek. *The Epic Film: Myth and History.* Boston: Routledge & Kegan Paul, 1984.

Faust, Drew Gilpin. *The Creation of Confederate Nationalism: Ideology and Identity in the Civil War South.* Baton Rouge: Louisiana State University Press, 1988.

---. *Mothers of Invention: Women of the Slaveholding South in the American Civil War.* New York: Vintage Books, 1996.

---. "Ours as Well as That of the Men." *Writing the Civil War: The Quest to Understand.* Ed. James M. McPherson, and William J. Copper, Jr. Columbia: University of South Carolina Press, 1998.

Griffith, Paddy. *Battle Tactics of the Civil War.* 1987. New Haven: Yale Nota Bene, 2001.

Hirsch, Foster. *The Hollywood Epic.* South Brunswick, N.J.: Barnes, 1978.

Horwitz, Tony. *Confederates in the Attic: Dispatches from the Unfinished Civil War*. New York: Vintage Books, 1999.

Landy, Marcia. "Introduction." *The Historical Film: History and Memory in Media*. Ed. Marcia Landy. New Brunswick, N.J.: Rutgers University Press, 2001. 3-12.

Leonard, Elizabeth D. *All the Daring of the Soldier: Women of the Civil War Armies*. New York: W. W. Norton & Company, 1999.

Linderman, Gerald F. *Embattled Courage: The Experience of Combat in the American Civil War*. New York: The Free Press, 1987.

McPherson, James M. *What They Fought For: 1861-1865*. New York: Anchor Books, 1995.

Rable, George C. *Civil Wars: Women and the Crisis of Southern Nationalism*. Chicago: University of Illinois Press, 1989.

Rogers, William Warren, Robert David Ward, Leah Rawls Atkins, Wayne Flynt. *Alabama: The History of a Deep South State*. Tuscaloosa: University of Alabama Press, 1994. 186-222.

Rosenstone, Robert A. "The Historical Film: Looking at the Past in a Post-literate Age." *The Historical Film: History and Memory in Media*. Ed. Marcia Landy. New Brunswick, N.J.: Rutgers University Press, 2001. 50-66.

Russell, James. *The Historical Epic and Contemporary Hollywood: From Dances with Wolves to Gladiator*. New York: Continuum, 2007.

Warren, Robert Penn. *The Legacy of the Civil War*. 1961. Lincoln: University of Nebraska Press, 1998.

Watkins, Sam R. Watkins. *Co. Aytch: A Confederate Memoir of the Civil War*. New York: Touchstone, 1997.

Wheelwright, Julie. *Amazons and Military Maids: Women Who Dressed as Men in the Pursuit of Life, Liberty, and Happiness*. London: Pandora Press, 1989.

Filmography[1]

Beulah Land. Dir. Harry Falk and Virgil W. Vogel. Perf. Lesley Ann Warren, Michael Sarrazin, and Eddie Albert. Columbia Pictures Television, 1980. TV mini-series.

Birth of a Nation. Dir. D. W. Griffith. Perf. Lillian Gish, Mae Marsh, and Henry B. Walthall. David W. Griffith Corp., 1915. Film.

The Blue and the Gray. Dir. Andrew V. McLaglen. Perf. Steve Nevil, Stacy Keach, and John Hammond. Columbia Pictures Television, 1982. TV mini-series.

The Civil War. Dir. Ken Burns. Perf. David McCullough, Sam Waterston, and Jason Robards. American Documentaries Inc. and PBS, 1990. TV mini-series. Documentary.

Cold Mountain. Dir. Anthony Minghella. Perf. Jude Law, Nicole Kidman, and Renée Zellweger. Miramax Films, 2003. Film.

Friendly Persuasion. Dir. William Wyler. Perf. Gary Cooper, Dorothy McGuire, and Anthony Perkins. Allied Artists Pictures, 1956. Film.

Gettysburg. Dir. Ronald F. Maxwell. Perf. Tom Berenger, Martin Sheen, and Stephen Lang. TriStar Television, 1993. TV movie.

---

1   This is not an exhaustive list, and it is not intended to be a blanket recommendation as the quality of each film/series varies according to budget and craftsmanship.

Glory. Dir. Edward Zwick. Perf. Matthew Broderick, Denzel Washington, Cary Elwes, and Morgan Freeman. TriStar Pictures, 1989. Film.

Gods and Generals. Dir. Ronald F. Maxwell. Perf. Stephen Lang, Robert Duvall, and Jeff Daniels. Turner Pictures, 2003. Film.

Gone with the Wind. Dir. Victor Fleming. Perf. Clark Gable, Vivien Leigh, Olivia De Havilland, and Thomas Mitchell. Selznick International Pictures, 1939. Film.

Hell on Wheels. Creators Joe Gayton and Tony Gayton. Perf. Anson Mount, Colm Meaney, and Robin McLeavy. Entertainment One Television, Nomadic Pictures, 2011-1016. TV Series.

The Horse Soldiers. Dir. John Ford. Perf. John Wayne, William Holden, and Constance Towers. The Mirisch Corporation, 1959. Film.

Jezebel. Dir. William Wyler. Perf. Bette Davis, Henry Fonda, and George Brent. Warner Bros. Pictures, 1938. Film.

The Last Confederate: The Story of Robert Adams. Dir. A. Blaine Miller and Julian Adams. Perf. Julian Adams, Gwendolyn Edwards, and Eric Holloway. Strongbow Pictures, 2005. Film.

My Brother's War. Dir. Whitney Hamilton. Perf. Whitney Hamilton, Dana Bennison, Rebecca Damon, and Gerry Green. Bjornquist Films, 2005. Film.

North and South. Dir. Richard T. Heffron. Perf. Kirstie Alley, David Carradine, Patrick Swayze, and James Read. David L. Wolper Productions, 1985. TV mini-series.

The Outlaw Josey Wales. Dir. Clint Eastwood. Perf. Clint Eastwood, Sondra Locke, and Chief Dan George. Warner Bros., 1976. Film.

Pharaoh's Army. Dir. Robby Henson. Chris Cooper, Patricia Clarkson, and Kris Kristofferson. Cicada Films, 1995. Film.

The Red Badge of Courage. Dir. John Huston. Perf. Audie Murphy, Bill Mauldin, and Douglas Dick. Metro-Goldwyn-Mayer (MGM), 1951. Film.

Ride with the Devil. Dir. Ang Lee. Perf. Tobey Maguire, Skeet Ulrich, and Jewel Kilcher. Good Machine, 1999. Film.

Rio Lobo. Dir. Howard Hawk. Perf. John Wayne, Jorge Rivero, and Jennifer O'Neill. Cinema Center Films, Batjac Productions, 1970. Film.

Shenandoah. Dir. Andrew V. McLaglen. Perf. James Stewart, Doug Mc-Clure, and Glenn Corbett. Universal Pictures, 1965. Film.

The Undefeated. Dir. Andrew V. McLaglen. Perf. John Wayne, Rock Hudson, and Antonio Aguilar. Twentieth Century Fox Film Corporation, 1969. Film.

Wicked Spring. Dir. Kevin Hershberger. Perf. Brian Merrick, DJ Perry, and Terry Jernigan. Lion Heart Film Works, 2002. Film.

About the Author

Stephanie Bain grew up in Oxford, Alabama, home of the Oxford High School Yellow Jackets of whom she has been a fan since she was old enough to walk in her saddle oxfords and her homemade, black-and-gold cheerleader outfit. Today, her wardrobe has expanded to include business casual when she is teaching History and Political Science; jeans, T-shirt, and closed-toed shoes when she's on a film shoot; and writer garb that can double as pajamas and still be okay to wear to the grocery store. She has an MA in History from the University of Alabama, graduate work in Political Science from Jacksonville State University, and an MFA in Screenwriting from Regent University. What she has learned is that no matter what she's wearing or what she's doing, what is required of her is to do justly, love mercy, and walk humbly with God.

www.StephanieBain.com
www.VindicatorArtists.com
Facebook.com/AuthorStephanieBain

CPSIA information can be obtained
at www.ICGtesting.com
Printed in the USA
FSHW04n0439160318
45551FS